W9-CGQ-508

Founder's Praise

Also by Joanne Greenberg:

The King's Persons
I Never Promised You a Rose Garden
(as Hannah Green)
The Monday Voices
Summering: A Book of Short Stories
In This Sign
Rites of Passage

Joanne Greenberg

Founder's Praise

HOLT, RINEHART
and WINSTON
New York

HOUSTON PUBLIC LIBRARY

76-040270-1

R01 0219 0291

Copyright © 1976 by Joanne Greenberg
All rights reserved, including the right to reproduce
this book or portions thereof in any form.
Published simultaneously in Canada by Holt, Rinehart
and Winston of Canada, Limited.

Library of Congress Cataloging in Publication Data

Greenberg, Joanne.
Founder's praise.

I. Title.
PZ4.G7985Fo   [PS3557.R3784]   813'.5'4   76-3968
ISBN 0-03-015391-3

First Edition

Designer: Kathy Peck

Printed in the United States of America
10 9 8 7 6 5 4 3 2 1

To Rabbi Gershon Hadas and Ann

סב טוב; ידידה טובה

Edgar

1

"Edgar!" His father was calling again.

He came around the corner of the house toward his father, wondering at the look of annoyance on the man's weathered face.

"Go check the fences like I told you!"

Without answering, Edgar turned and walked back toward the barn behind which the three strands of barbed wire separated Ralph Bisset's planted fields from the persevering scrubland. On the other side of the wire the high dry plains took up again after the momentary interruption of their farm. Edgar was eleven years old, a silent boy who, his parents said, treasured grudges. He was thickset and big for his age, not thin like his sister or his parents. His mother said he idled away his time in school and skipped work at home. His father scolded him for neglecting his work, but added, not without pride, that the boy was so stubborn he would be beaten unconscious rather than promise to change his ways. If denied food he would take that punishment too with the same grave stolidity, the anger banked far away from his eyes where it might burn or die away in secret.

The thing they said most was that he was ungrateful. This year, the year of the house, he heard his father say to his mother, "That boy ain't fit for simple gratitude!" But he was grateful, deeply so. Now in the winter they wouldn't have to live like moles, but could pass back and forth before many glass windows in a house that had two floors and a room for cooking, rooms for sleeping upstairs, a parlor, and a separate pantry where the household things were kept. Edgar's mother was a changed woman since they had left that soddy. She and Tempe had mooned around, mad over choices of floursacks for matching curtains; they had argued and whispered and planned and sewn. Edgar had only gone into his new room under the roof, without a word.

"I didn't expect him to kiss my hands," his father told his mother bitterly, "but ain't it worth a word, a smile, a nod of his head? You give that to a dog or a horse you care somethin' about!"

She had not answered. It was one more cross.

Cora Bisset was a hill woman from Tennessee. The horizon-to-horizon flatness of this country seemed to have sucked her soul away. More than once she had risen after a night of dreams to go out into the morning and look about in despair, whispering, "They've taken everything—they've taken it all away." But for her flintlike piety, she would have died of the loss of mountains years ago. When a rare visitor remarked at the length of the prayers before meals and after, Cora only said, "Prayer makes strong people. Jesus watches. Jesus is watching all the time. That is why he was made Man, to know the dark places in every soul. And for them that need the rod . . ." And she would turn away, her lip quivering, her eyes stung with tears.

Edgar loved his sister, Tempe. The thought of her made him want to smile. She was a plains girl, as accepting as the plains and as patient, but more joyful and more generous. She could laugh and read the clouds and the land with honest eyes, and because rain, sun, wind, and frost were not dependable in her country, she lived without expectations. The changing of seasons gave her pleasure because her eyes were plains eyes—set for subtle differences. Asked what the seasons were, Ralph Bisset would have said heavily, "Slaughtering, planting, haying, and harvest." Cora would have answered gratingly, "Mud, drought, grasshoppers, and tornado." Temperance would have smiled and said: "Root herbs, leaf herbs, berries, and hips, and then the winter when there's

4

Christmas." Edgar would have said nothing, or if pressed might have sighed, "It don't matter, it can't none of it be changed."

Edgar seemed asleep. His body moved and worked, carried wood in and ashes out, fed the stock and himself, watered the two fruit trees, and drank, all in silence. When asked his opinion he looked betrayed.

In himself, he wondered why he was a mystery to his family. What stopped him from speaking was not that he had nothing to say but that he had everything to say and could give none of it weight of place over all the rest. Things swarmed in him like flashes of snow before the wind; thoughts driven by other thoughts, dreams passing from darkness to darkness, caught in his mind only a second. As for his opinions, *yes* came so weighted with conditions and exceptions that *no* soon overtook it. His moment of pleasure, because it was rare, was so deep and important to him that before he could speak of it lightly and with joy, it died of its own weight. He did not know why he could not seem to show his love for Tempe. The small ways he found were usually overlooked: letting her sit closer to the fire, or taking up the haircomb she had left on the table before Cora noticed it and scolded her. It was never possible for him to speak of the love or the favors. For his father, he had simple fear, and for his mother, a vague love so clouded with wretchedness that even at special times, Christmas or Thanksgiving or after the harvest of a good year, he couldn't feel the warmth he knew he should have for her. Day after day at every meal and before bed, his head bowed under the flail of her words, he felt nothing but loss for himself and shame for her. It confused him to be dying of sins he had never chosen, and all because Jesus had been sent by God or his mother to spy upon him. Jesus found Original Sins, so many that they had to be taken up to The Father who judged them in all their timebound dustiness. His father was too hard-working to sin; Cora and Tempe had no sins. He knew this because he had often stolen looks at them from under the protecting fringe of his hair or behind the prayer-hands held up defensively before him. Tempe's face was still and untroubled; sometimes she even smiled, happy for the brief rest that prayer gave her before she had to jump up to serve food or clear the plates. He had always been able to know if his sister was sad or angry and usually the reason for it; she was so clear and direct. As he watched first Cora and then Temperance take up the prayer, demanding blessings without a quiver or a tear, he knew it was because they were already among the saved and that all these prayers were meant for him.

Once or twice in town he had heard some talk about his parents. Townspeople took little account of children, and often when someone left the feed store or the dry-goods emporium a word or two was said without care for the young ones hanging back to look at the penknives. Once when Edgar had stayed for a moment's extra warmth by the stove he heard a woman say of his mother, "That Cora Bisset's so pious it's a wonder the Lord don't beg *her* pardon."

"Pious as all that, you'd think she'd come to church more."

"Too pious for that." And there was some scattered laughter.

It surprised Edgar that he had never thought about this before. Why didn't they belong to a church? Tempe would know—if it wasn't a shameful thing, perhaps she would tell him.

"Tempe, why don't we go to church?"

"It's too far; besides, the only churches in town are Total Immersion and Ma and Pa don't believe in Total Immersion."

"Were you ever in a church?"

"Once, when Powell was buried."

"What was it like?"

"You've passed it a hundred times."

"I mean inside."

"It's big of course—lots of room. There's a big table or bench in front facing the people and a place for the minister to stand. On the table are big candlesticks and a big cross. When we went there everybody sang and sang. I don't remember much—except how they had songs, a whole bookful, and they sang and sang."

It became Edgar's plan to get inside a church. He had never heard people singing together except once when a wagon of harvesters went by between the farms. As they had passed on the road and he heard them from far away, he had run out toward the sound. He had thought they were the angels his mother spoke of. Could men sing with so much power? Could men produce so much strong, rich sound so effortlessly? His sister hummed sometimes at her work and in school there had been singing before the new teacher came, but this singing of the harvest men was nothing like that. The men's voices lifted and danced, jumping from sound to sound. It made him happy just remembering it and he had carefully saved what he could of the way the song went. (In heaven there must be carts of harvest men going by every day—twice a day, singing that song, and others. In a church they might sing about Jesus, but if they sang all together like the harvest men it wouldn't matter.) He began to lay plans. He thought about running away on a Saturday, getting into town somehow in time for church, and coming back on Sunday, but there would be whippings and questions and more sin. (Is there any singing in hell? No, that's what makes it hell. Is it a sin to pity the Devil?) Maybe Tempe would help because it might mean she could see Joe Kornarens. Joe was sweet on her and he lived close to town. It would have to be done in a special way, though, explained just right to Ma and Pa. Nothing about singing or church. Only a way to get to town on Sunday morning and have the free time there. Edgar was wrestling with plans, stewing and scheming, when the chance fell ripe, warm, and perfect into his open hand.

Charlie Dace got out of jail and came back to the place where he had once worked to see if there was work for him now. At suppertime one day in early summer, Edgar came in from the barn and saw his father already at the table. Sitting with him was a stranger, very small, gray-faced, almost grown-up. This stranger had hair cut short and a new shave—the lower part of his face was white and his forehead was white to the line where he wore his cap. Edgar stopped and his father said:

"Don't you remember Charlie, here?" The stranger's eyes were blue and they turned toward Edgar starkly, from the weathered part of his face.

7

"Oh, Edgar was too young," Cora said.

"Anyway," his father continued, "Charlie here has come to stay with us and help." Edgar could not conceive of anyone coming to stay with his family unless he had to. At supper when his mother began the long and involved bill of grievances against the Lord, which she took for prayer, Edgar turned his head slightly and raised his eyes. Charlie's head was also lowered and he had not gone for his fork at the end of the first prayer, as their other infrequent guests did. Now and then a barely perceptible smile came and went on his face. He's really been here before, Edgar thought. Yes, he's been here.

After the meal the men remained at the table and later went out together to chores. When they came back, Ralph said, "Edgar, are you using the shuck mattress?"

"Yes, sir."

"All right then, I'll get some hay and sack it and that'll do till tomorrow. Charlie is goin' to stay with you up there and see how you both get on. In the morning he's got to go back to town and get his things. Cora'll hate to break the Sabbath, but Monday's work can't wait."

The thing ran by itself. Temperance asked to go with Charlie so that she could see her young man and Edgar found himself begged to go along "for company." He nodded yes in his silent, expressionless way. It had come by magic, but magic things, he knew, usually evaporated before the wishers got any good out of them. He had read stories in school about this problem. He bade his eagerness lie down and be silent.

They left before ten, and Edgar didn't have to say a word. He thought that Charlie might want, besides his few things, to make some provision for the life he would have to lead in a home of people so coldly pious. Beautiful things, maybe; warming things. Temperance asked him to pull in for just a minute at Kornarenses' and with only a small sigh he did as he was told. Joe's people were Germans with the accent still heavy in their mouths. They were a hearty, friendly family with a farm barely a mile from town, and when Temperance and Edgar jumped off the wagon they were greeted with waving hands and shouts of welcome.

"Say," Joe cried, "we was just leavin' for church. Why don't you folks come with us!" "Sure!" the parents cried, and the children cried "Sure!" in echo. Tempe shot Edgar a look across the space between her virtue and his sinfulness, indicating that he should not mention Tollamersion and hurt Joe's family. Edgar stared back, his face mute. The knowledge that they would be lying to their parents did not seem to bother Tempe at all. Tempe's lies were not sins. Later, as he mounted the steps to the church, with the Kornarenses, Edgar had a moment of fear, but looking about he saw no one singling them out as not belonging; no lightning was being readied in heaven. Charlie had slipped away. He had muttered something about churches and gone. Joe's little sister had taken his hand and was telling him something and then there was the music. He could hear it from the steps, strings of sounds crossing and recrossing one another. He was almost smiling as he made his way inside.

Tempe had been correct. They sang. And there were books, just as she had said, full of their songs. At the front of the church, behind the preacher, seventeen people were sitting. Townspeople. And when the hymns began, these people sang also, but with their voices broken apart from one another in a way that made Edgar shiver with delight. Elfrieda Kornarens, whose seat he was sharing, showed Edgar the board on the wall where the numbers of the hymns were shown. In the book were marks that instructed each voice where to sing to make so wonderful a sound. As the choir sang the four verses of the hymn, Edgar followed with great care, listening for each of the voices as it rose and fell, apart and then together with the others. And this was done, he perceived, by laws that he could feel in his own mind. In heaven, he thought, there must be hours dividing the day, and each hour is brought past the people of heaven in a cart in which are harvest men and choirs, first one then the other, voices together, voices spread. In heaven the people must sing welcomes to the carts and the voices must blend.

When it was over, Charlie was waiting for them with the wagon, and after quick good-byes to Joe and the family, they took the back way out of town and set off at a good pace for home. Charlie had a moist-eyed, removed look about him. He also smelled strange, a smell like the sweat in a sickness. He drove steadily but absentmindedly, as though he didn't care where he went or how soon he got there. Temperance and Edgar sat in the back of the wagon, facing toward town, their legs hanging over the end. Temperance looked out at the dwindling farms set in the hugeness of the land.

"Joe asked me to marry him," she said, more to herself than to Edgar beside her. He heard her, and the bolt that had not been sent against him when he entered the church broke full on him now. Women leave home when they marry. They go away. They leave houses airless, sunless, and hopeless behind them. Tempe was still talking.

"I will marry him, too. Joe is eighteen, but I'm almost sixteen. I think his family likes me all right." Then she turned to Edgar. "If I marry Joe you'll be part of that family, too. How would you like that, to have Joe's folks for kin?"

Edgar couldn't answer. If he wasn't happy at home, where he was at least familiar, how would his silences be taken in the laughter and closeness of Joe's people? They were wonderful people—everyone said so. Their family was as happy as all families should be, but to Edgar they seemed as strange as city people or Chinese, as unreal as his own future, as terrifying as God's hunger for human love. He couldn't tell her these things. She had been looking at him but after a time when he still didn't answer she looked away again and they rode on in silence.

Charlie Dace fitted into the life of the family. He was almost as silent as Edgar, and when he did speak it was only about the ordinary work of the day. He slept in the loft with Edgar. He had marks on his back where he had been whipped while he was in prison. Edgar never mentioned this to anyone, nor did he mention that Charlie never rose of a morning without drinking a quarter bottle of the whiskey he kept by his bed. Charlie in his turn said nothing about the stolen hymn book that was under Edgar's pillow. After Charlie had had his whiskey, he would swallow something out of another bottle to cover the bad smell on his breath. Edgar's fascination with those hymn tunes and the beautiful mathematics of the partings of the voices was less easily hidden. The sounds of the music haunted him and he found himself humming in his steely-thin child's voice the tracings of the bass lines, alto lines, and a reedy, chilly treble where the tune went tinnily along in miniature.

> *Oh, hap-py day*
> *Oh, hap-py day*
> *When Je-sus waaaaaaashed*
> *My sins a-way.*

Once or twice his father came upon him staring into the distance, his hand on the pump handle, the bucket misplaced beneath the spigot. He could see his father wondering if he might not be touched.

And one day the song would not be contained. It was a day in high summer. It had rained during the night, a wonder in itself, and Edgar and Tempe were out pulling the weeds from the rain-softened earth of the vegetable patch. Tempe worked well, talking softly to the plants or the sky, her hands never slowing. As they came around the long last row of tomatoes and headed into the late peas, she began to hum. It was the "Crusaders' Hymn." Edgar had looked up the song in his book because it was one of the few he knew, and as they hummed, he found himself singing the alto part, harmonizing sweetly with her voice so that he opened out to full voice and so did she, in delight and amazement, to the end of the verse.

"Sing it again," he said, "I'll sing the other part." And they did:

"Fair are the meadows, fairer still the woodlands . . ." He sang tenor part above her like a descant because his voice was still much higher than his sister's. Still singing, they worked away from each other down the row and he was singing louder so that she might hear him. As her voice faded, he strained to catch the notes of the blending and was dumbstruck when his mother came up behind him and caught him by the shoulder. He hadn't heard her, though she walked heavily and her skirts had brushed the leaves of plants on either side.

"What are you doing?" she said loudly, staring down at

him. The singing down the row stopped and Tempe hurried back. "What are you doing?" his mother demanded again. He stared up at her. Tempe's face was red with the heat under her bonnet.

"It's a wonder, Ma, it's a wonder! He sings part-singing, just like church, all the parts—he knows them!"

Edgar felt the earth disappearing from under him. The sky and the women and the plants at his feet were suddenly swollen and unhealthy-looking.

"I don't feel good," he said.

He lay in the sweltering attic waiting for the day to die. His mother had whipped him until she was tired, prayed over him, made him pray. Was it for singing? For idleness? For idleness and singing together? She had drawn blood and the sight of it later had shocked him more than the fact of the punishment or the pain. Tempe had run alongside as his mother was pulling him into the house. His sister's lips were going with words he couldn't hear through his terror. During the prayer when he was on his knees, he saw her standing pale at the kitchen door. He remembered her look and the hysterical eyes of his mother with a sick breathlessness. Shame is watering heat, hot like the air warping over the turned earth, like the heat of whipping. At last he fell asleep.

The sun was low when he woke up but the attic room was still stifling. Slowly, he crept downstairs and silently stood behind the kitchen door, unsure whether or not he was wanted. There was a long silence—the women were at their dinner preparations. Temperance was stringing beans as his mother came from the pantry with a jar of venison.

"Do you think Edgar will be down?" Tempe asked. Edgar couldn't see his mother through the crack in the kitchen door, but he heard her voice and the knife cutting the cornbread into squares.

"I don't know, but I don't think you got a call to judge me like you been doin'."

"I'm not judging, Ma," Temperance said. "Edgar wasn't working when you came up on him, and that was wrong. But it was my fault as much as it was his. I told him to sing. It's really a blessing, Edgar knowing how to sing like that. He's got a gift, Ma." She said it gravely, in an unknowing echo of Cora's own voice saying, "I've got a cross, Jesus."

"I know he's got a gift! Don't you think I don't know God has touched him! It was 'cause of that I whipped him. I done it to make God answer for Edgar. It is to make the Devil stop haunting my boy the way he has haunted me!"

Edgar heard the bean bowl rattle a little as it was put down, then he heard the sound of the tableware being moved.

"I don't understand you, Ma."

Cora's weeping stopped. There was the sound of her clearing her nose. A plate scraped another.

"If Edgar's gifts ain't God's, a whipping will drive 'em off soon enough, and then he'll have some peace, and if the gifts are God's, God won't let a harness strap stop Him from His desire, no, nor the begging prayer, nor the wind, nor the dust, nor the prairie fire—" There was a sound at the back of the room and Cora stopped abruptly. Charlie Dace had come up the back steps and was standing at the open door.

2

When Temperance married Joe Kornarens, there was talk of their staying on in Bissets' old soddy and eventually taking over the land on the other side of the new house. Edgar prayed nightly for this to happen, knowing that it was too wonderful to happen. Then, at the wedding, old man Kornarens, having eaten double portions of everything, having danced and sang until everyone else was exhausted, sat down on one of Ralph Bisset's porch chairs and died. Joe was the oldest boy. He and Temperance found themselves master and mistress of a big house and a huge farm.

Edgar ached for her. The house ached for her. The land went gray pale, the underside of the sky went livid and smelled of clay. With Tempe gone there was only Charlie Dace left, and Charlie was as poor and sinful as he. Charlie could have been as young as Joe, but he had a tiredness about him. Because of squinting from the sun so often, he had the look of someone who was just about to laugh, but he never did. His small, tanned arm worked quickly, his gestures were nimble, but there were nights, many nights, when Charlie woke weeping from bad dreams and his morning's awakening was with a groan of despair. Edgar knew well how the outward body lied. The most extreme case of this, he thought, was his own. His outer self was that of a sleepy child.

His voice was high and sometimes whiny. He did not feel like a child at all, but like a very old man stooped beneath the weight of what he knew, powerless against the greed of his senses, the sight, smell, hearing that leaped out ahead of him, and like his mother at prayer, begged, demanded, Oh, give me, make me, grant me, bestow on me, with the greed of the miser who would eat the world.

He kept himself from failing in school by a hairbreadth, feeling safe because his teachers thought him dull. He would furrow his brow, sweat, lick his lips, working the problem as though he were reaping it. He did not play in school, smile, clown, or swap stories with the other boys. When the changes came, a sudden, awkward growth, hair at his groin, a breaking voice, and sodden, sin-filled dreams, his silence closed even harder upon him. He would not stay in school although his father, to his surprise, urged him to keep on ("I didn't have enough to do no good"). At fifteen he loomed in doorways or felt himself looming, a huge, hulking ox of a boy-man who rattled the dishes in his mother's cupboard when he passed. Sitting between Charlie and his father, he found himself double their size. The single advantage of his bulk, he found, was a certain freedom. He was able, when he wished, to finish his chores early and go off to visit Tempe and Joe without begging permission.

He loved those visits, the loud welcome, the chair pulled up, the talk all around him. Even as he rode into Kornarenses' yard, he felt smaller, neater, less hulking.

"Hi, Ed!" they would cry, and, "What's new down at your place?" not torturing him for his answer, but sailing out on their own good spirits with words enough for anyone. There were moments when he felt loved. Once he was helping to clean out Joe's chicken coop, and, feeling faint in the ammonia-fumy heat of the place, had gone outside to sit under Joe's cottonwood and rest for a minute. He heard Joe and Tempe talking on the back porch. Joe was bringing up Tempe's canning jars from the dugout under the house.

"I'm going to get a cool drink for Edgar," Tempe said, in the comfortable rattle of the glasses being set down. "He's been out there all afternoon."

"He's good family," Joe said, and there was the sound of

scraping. "I sure wish he'd say somethin' now and then or just *look* some way, happy or sad or somethin'."

"He does things," Tempe said. "You see what he does to know how he feels. Look how he lets Elfrieda devil him this way and that, changing her mind a dozen times about them flowers she wants to plant, and how he went and did what she said last week, so willing every time. And how he is teaching Martin how to fish that sometime creek near Ma and Pa's. He don't talk much, it's true, but I never seen him portion things either, 'I done this, so you do that,' or, 'This part's mine and that part's yours.' I never seen him come to the end of giving." Her voice had been full of warmth and sweetness. Edgar sat back against the tree, stunned with an emotion he could not name and surprised by the tears that welled in his eyes.

There was also, in this freer time, even a moment from Cora.

It happened a year later, when Temperance had her baby in the dry time of summer. Cora sat in the Kornarenses' kitchen with her Bible in her lap. Edgar had been shooed away with Joe's brothers while the women shared their mysteries. The four of them went to the barn and sat smoking and swapping lies while Edgar looked on in shock. He was angry at the indifference Joe's brothers seemed to feel at his sister's suffering.

"What's the matter?" they asked him. "You sick or something?"

"No," and he sat back with no heart for work or talk until sundown, when Joe came and told them that it was a boy. They went to the house together, Joe with his arm around Edgar in the spendthrift camaraderie of relief. Old Ma Kornarens came over to him, beaming, "Tempe done fine. You see her later. Meanwhile, you got a good nephew." A woman came up to him with a small bundle. Edgar could not look. He tried desperately to say something in politeness, but he found no voice, no words, not even a single clear feeling.

Mama Kornarens looked up at him. "Edgar, ain't you gonna say nothin' about your nephew?"

Hadn't she known all this time about his silences? Didn't

they all know how hard it was for him to bring up feeling, all the contending things, into some limiting word? Everyone had now turned toward him, faces expectant. He stood and stared back at them, bereft of all words, all comfort, his shoulders inadvertently beginning the hunch he was used to giving instead of speech.

Then, through the crowd of women came a high, nasal sound: "Man that is born of woman is of few days and full of trouble." It was Cora, busy with the Book. Some of the women jumped. In the blanket, the tiny thing was startled. There was a fuss of old ladies and young ladies and then a voice from upstairs said that Tempe was wanting to see the baby. Everyone trooped up to congratulate the new mother. Edgar, not knowing what to do, was about to seek the barn again. He turned for a moment and caught his mother's eye. She was sitting stiff-backed in the hard chair she had brought from the kitchen. Her hands were in her lap, smoothing the page of Scripture she was about to read. But she was not looking at the Book. She was looking at Edgar, and when their eyes met, her mouth moved quickly in a guileful, triumphant, phantom smile.

They named the baby Andrew. If Joe seemed a little harried and hard-pressed, it was natural enough. A young man, not yet twenty, could hardly feel easy as family head and master of a large farm in an eyeblink. Sometimes he would ride over to Bissets' with the excuse of borrowing some wire or returning something he had borrowed, and while he looked in the barn with Charlie or oiled tools with Ralph, he would ask them what they thought of his plans for his acreage on the south or his pasture on the west.

"How the hell should I know what's right for him to do?" Ralph said querulously to no one in particular. "His place lies low and catches more water than mine, and it's out of the wind. He's got three times my acreage. What's he askin' *me* for!"

Charlie shrugged. "He's been askin' everybody in town, but I don't think he even hears the answers."

Ralph nodded. "Well, it ain't lack of help that's makin' him worry." Ralph looked over the table hard at Edgar, who was too often at Joe's doing farm chores while work remained at home. Edgar looked down at his plate. It was March, and the favored canned and smoked foods had long since been eaten, the fresh not yet ready. March is the dry rind of the year. Edgar could not conceive of his life being anything other than what it was. He wondered if Joe felt like a stranger in his own life. There was a silence.

Charlie said, "Kurt Bayless down at the store, he says we're gonna be goin' to fight over in Europe."

"That man's a fool," Ralph said, without real irritation. "There'd be no purpose in it. What would be the purpose to fight over there? Win land from 'em? Farm it?"

"Be a hell of a walk home at night," Charlie said and sat back.

Ralph turned to him. "Charlie, sometimes you don't make good sense. Walkin' home ain't the subject we was talkin' about."

"Why can't you think of us in a war?" Cora interjected. "America ain't no different from any other worldly nation. Has the mountain of the Lord's house been established as the head of the mountains? Not till then will men study war no more. That don't come to pass till the end of days. It . . ." She had lost the point somewhere. Her voice trailed away. With Tempe gone, Cora was beginning to feel herself cast off and alone. Sometimes the men came upon her arguing all by herself, going at her proofs of God's omnipotence and the sinfulness of man with more vigor than she ever had when talking to them. Her arguments were scriptural mostly, fierce duels, verse against verse, and after them she often wore a look of complacent satisfaction. The men laughed gently at it. Women get lonely away from town. Cooped up in the house so much of the time, they suffer more. Many farm women talked to themselves, their dead children, their dead parents. Some drank or had fits when they would let the work go, appearing with bleared faces, their dresses closed with pins where the buttons had gone, their hair unbrushed. Then springtime would come or some inner shift, and they would get up, stiffly, take the little china pieces down from the what-not shelf and dust them, and if one of the pieces fell and broke, they might burst into sobs as heavy as though a child had died.

Edgar knew that his mother walked in two worlds and that each was beyond the horizon of the other. Cora's reality was the world of prophets and kings, good and evil—God and the Devil. Most of all, a world of mountains. From that world, she received intrusions from a place of shadows and clouds, flatness, towns, neighbors, weather science, and reasons. Sometimes it amused him to think that the battle between the rancher and the farmer was still alive in his mother. If there was a war, he would go to it. He might die a hero's death, the death of someone who belongs to his event.

They saw him off, Tempe, Joe, and his father, on one of the springlike days of April, the days that deceive miles of budding grasses before the battering by later snows. He felt that the war had come to free him, and while he was surprised at how few of his friends were joining up, he knew that were he truly patriotic he would be staying home to work at the fields that fed the armies. Joe, seeing Edgar off at the depot, stood with his legs apart, his gestures large, his voice booming. The government wanted him to stay behind, yet he was ashamed. In his embarrassment he played a part—bull-male, hiding his gentleness. Edgar saw the pose as one player sees the false gesture, the planned move, of another. It made him want to disappear into his seat. What a world it was, when good honest Joe had to act the part of a man a tenth as good as himself. Even his father was acting, saying the things that were required—that Edgar should be a credit to his family and his upbringing and to send his money home for afterward. The only person not acting in the drama was Charlie Dace. Charlie had been awake when Edgar climbed up to the loft on his last night home. He had taken a pull from his whiskey bottle and handed it to Edgar, saying slowly, "Go on, have a drink your last night."

"Thanks, Charlie. I'll bring you some back from Europe. I hear they make good stuff there."

"Edgar—"

"Yeah—" That was his play act then, swigging the whiskey, imitating the ruthless, fearless fighter he had shimmering in his mind.

"Edgar, it may be worse out there than you figure—I don't mean the fightin'—"

"What do you mean, then, Charlie?" He saw that the talk wasn't going to be a simple one. He worked at the carelessness in his voice. Charlie was sitting up on his mattress, his back against the wall. Edgar could almost see Charlie's mind forming approaches and discarding them, one after the other. But when Charlie finally spoke, the words were unexpected.

"How old do you think I am?"

A shrug.

"How old?"

"I dunno—thirty-five, maybe, forty. Old." The tone was as flat as he could make it.

"I'm twenty-six," Charlie said slowly. "I'm a year younger than Joe Kornarens." Without knowing why, Edgar began to feel anxious. "I only want to tell you one thing," Charlie said quietly. "The way you get hurt is by what happens inside you when you find out the things—all the things you *think*." He grappled with the words, "I mean bein' afraid includes the way you hate yourself because of it—some of the fear is in waitin' for . . ."

"You're talkin' about the jail, ain't you?" It came out sneeringly, so as to make Charlie remember his shame and stop bringing the damned reality of things too close, but Charlie drew past his defenses as though he hadn't even noticed them.

"When you go to jail, they tell you how much time you have to stay, but your mind starts workin'. You think: They'll forget—they'll lose my number and they won't bother lookin' for it and I'll stay here forever. They'll forget I'm in here in this cell—they'll forget to take my bucket and I'll drown in my own shit. When you break the rule and they go to whip you, you know how many hits it is—twenty-five, like they give everybody else, but when you stand up and the thing starts, your *mind* whips you faster, harder, without once drawin' back. I thought—What if them guys lose count, forget, keep goin' on and on until the flesh tears off and then the bones break? What if they tear through everything and hit my lungs and then my heart?" Charlie's voice had remained at its slow level; he could have been talking about digging a fence post. "The punishment is—"

"It's just crazy talk," Edgar said loudly. "You're talkin' crazy." His voice was high; it sounded like his mother's. The patriot in his mind went hunchbacked.

"Sure, it's crazy," Charlie said gently. "That's just what I been tryin' to tell you, and what's not real has got to be paid for. It wasn't my body that got hurt so much, see. Because of what I *thought* in the jail, I stopped trustin' people. No one can do to you what your mind does—when people have that power over your life."

"Oh, shut up, Charlie, because I ain't goin' to jail."

"I'm glad you're takin' my advice," Charlie said quietly. He moved down on the bed and turned away to sleep.

Still angry the next day, Edgar did not say good-bye to him, but as he turned in the cart to wave to his mother and sister, he saw Charlie's figure at the attic window. Charlie was still in his winter underwear, a gray blur in the uncurtained space. He raised his arm and waved once only before Edgar turned his head.

He had gone to war to be set free in the wide world. Coming home from it, it amazed him that he ever could have thought so. How can a man be free when there is no reality, no continuity in which the freedom is held? He had been in this camp and that, grouping and separating, marching and waiting, drilling and waiting, and then going across the ocean to do the same thing in a less ordered way. Men surged over unnamed ground, took the same trenches, waited, retreated, waited; men gathered at other ground for the same running and waiting, the same random kind of death. Only the seasons (he had been surprised to find seasons in France, just like home) remained to remind him of a life where there might be purpose and choice. He had no friendships to remember from his war days. Three times the companionship of fear and waiting had given him hope in someone, and three times the hope had ended; once by transfer, once by machine gun, and once by suicide. Because of his silence and the closed look of his face, there were men in his platoon who had been with him since training and did not remember his name. Now, riding back on the train, he couldn't even imagine himself having run up shell-pocked hills, their features worn away by the feet of men in everlasting advance and retreat, to aim his gun into a row of imagined foreign faces. If anything troubled him it was that he had gone through all of it with neither rage nor injury. In the hailstorms of bullets, the washes of fire, he had stood untouched. Men had died all around him; circled by the dead, he had wondered if he had escaped killing because it is only possible to kill what lives.

His father and Joe were waiting. He saw them stretching and craning to see him first, to know the changes so that they would not be shocked to his face. He walked toward them with his usual set face, waiting for recognition. Joe had changed the most—but how, Edgar could not define. His father reached forward as though to hug him, wavered, and dropped his arms, then decided on a handshake and wavered in that, too, so that they ended standing with an empty space between them, eyes down.

"Hello, son."

"Hello, Dad."

"Hello, Ed."

"Hello, Joe."

And then his father's sigh, "Well, let's get on."

They drove through town, Edgar watching for changes, marking them as they went. Joe's face and his father's face were set; the lines of dryness made them look angry. Instead of turning the rig east, Joe kept on straight through town and out the narrow road that disappeared into the railroad right-of-way. Joe reined in the horse and slowly, like an old man, set the brake and tied the reins in their holder. Then he reached into his pocket and took out what looked like a small black cloth.

"Son—" Edgar looked away from Joe and into his father's face. The flat blue eyes were watering. He found himself thinking, The old man isn't feeling so good—look how his eyes are. I should get him to the doctor. Then, foolishly, There's a party home and they're tryin' to keep me till it's time. His father was murmuring something that he couldn't make out, and, from its edges, the sun was beginning to freeze.

"Edgar—" It was Joe.

Edgar waved him away in absentminded impatience and whispered, "I don't want to hear—I'm not ready."

"Ed—look at me!"

Again, "I'm not ready!" Then Joe turned him so that Edgar had to see what the cloth was, a black armband. Joe had put it on the way people do who have dead to mourn. Edgar's mind stopped, still, for a long moment, and then feelings rose in him, a slow, overwhelming anger. Why was Joe dressing up like them, like the foreigners? He had worked so hard to keep death away from here. Was this all the thanks he got, that they brought death here by another way, in spite of all his efforts?

"In France," he said with quiet rage, "it ain't like here. I didn't see no gully-washers over there, nor no duststorms, nor no dry-wash creek beds. France is *no ways* like here. I seen that with my own eyes." But even as he spoke, he knew that defense was hopeless for him. He began to bargain for the victim.

"Who is it died?"

"It was the Spanish influenza," Ralph said. "Tempe was sick with it when she was five, six months along of another baby. Ma went over and got her away from Joe's, where there were so many people, and brung her back home, and then your ma sickened up. We thought they would both get over it, it seemed like they was goin' to, both of them, and then, well, they just suddenly died; first Tempe and then your ma, both."

As though to convince Edgar of his innocence in this, the old man said, "There's been many folks died, many. Rich folks in town with doctors, gauze masks to wear and all. Men, women. Newspaper says even the Army got it."

Edgar nodded, yes; it was all he could do and be silent again.

"Charlie," Ralph Bisset said, and then cleared his throat, "Charlie, he said for us to write to you, Joe and me both, and tell you before you came home, but I didn't have the heart to do it. Charlie's a good man, dependable. I won't hear nothin' against him, but he's kinda hard. He don't have no gentleness to him."

Edgar saw that his father was trying with all his might to bring back the normal world, unfold it, and drape it over the three of them like a quilt through which no cold is felt, and the sharp edge is blunted. He went on talking about crops and prices. Edgar sat and did not answer. After a while, he turned to Joe with a gentle half-smile, embarrassed. The eyes that met his were full of tears. He looked away. Ralph caught the motion of it and stopped in the middle of a thought.

"We was goin' to bury 'em out at the place, but there was talk about infection, and Joe's ma wanted Tempe up there with them, so we took 'em up to the cemetery . . . if you want to see 'em. . . ."

Edgar shook his head, and so they rode home.

On the morning after his return, Edgar went to town to buy work clothes that would fit the grown man he had become. By mid-morning he was back at the farm, busy. He did not speak of the deaths in the family or remark at any of the changes, great or small, in the barn, or the house, or on the land. When Joe stopped by the next evening to say hello and hear about the battles and the victories of the strange-named, distant places, Edgar sat silently while Joe asked questions that echoed back to him unanswered. Joe was worn out when he left and did not come back again in the same friendly way after that. It wasn't long before everyone forgot that Edgar had ever been away from the farm—had gone to a coast, crossed an ocean, and been two years in a land of strangers, doing strange and terrible labor. His days were the same as they had been. Only the seasons changed his work. If he wasn't plowing, or harrowing, or planting, or cultivating, or weeding, or spraying, or irrigating, or harvesting, or binding, or threshing, or sacking, or haying, or mulching, or fertilizing, or covering, he was grazing the stock, or milking, or dosing, or cleaning, or calving, or slaughtering, or dressing the animals out.

He would see Ralph and Charlie after early chores and tell them what he planned to do for the day. At lunch they would ask him how the work was coming and he would nod or shrug. At dinner he would say if he had done the work or if it would go over into the next day. On Sunday he went to church, the largest one in town. There he sat, bolt upright in his place, listening with great intensity, so that his face was forbidding. After services, he greeted all the Kornarenses with slow deliberateness and the concentration of a stutterer, never smiling, but giving his big hand to them all, one after the other and to Joe. When Tempe's little boy, Andy, was big enough to come, Edgar would hunker down to be at eye level with the boy and would gravely shake his hand, saying, "Hello, boy, I'm your Uncle Edgar," with the same deliberate care.

The seasons came, wore away their welcome in work, and went away. Clothes got old and were mended, got threadbare and were replaced. Stock was born and the old were killed off or sold away. They got rid of the mules and got a tractor and equipment that hitched on to it for many kinds of work. When Joe saw Edgar the Sunday after he had disked his first field, he made a great point of asking Edgar what he thought of it. Edgar had simply said, "It works." Joe told that around awhile to show his brother-in-law "at his chattiest."

One Wednesday evening in August, Edgar appeared in town, parked the car in front of the church, and went in to where the choir was meeting for practice. Without a word he stationed himself in the bass section, where he sang in a strong but somewhat toneless way. Thereafter, he was to be found Sundays and Wednesdays in the back row at the far left of the choir, tapping the time against his hymn book or score. There was no expression in his singing but he kept the tune.

When Andy was eight, Edgar appeared at the house at dawn one morning in late spring with two fishing rods, and thereafter he would come and get the boy and they would go, in silence, to a stream five miles away. Later, when Andy was ten, they fished under the bank of a creek bordering Edgar's land. On Christmas of that year, a fine fishknife came in the mail addressed to Andy. There was no card with it and no return address.

3

In matters of the earth, the dead know more than the living. The living gamble for their futures; they hope and they plan. The dead endure. If the year is dry, the loam and clay dry below their surfaces, and the roots that hold the earth and the dead shrivel away and are pulled free. The earth freezes and thaws, and on the high plains, it cracks and yawns and makes a sound like thunder day and night. Six feet down, and deeper, there is a drawing-in, a terrible thirst that reverses upon the tough roots of scrub oak and ground-lying willow and pulls their hoard of moisture from them. Overhead, far overhead, upon the surface of the ground, the seasons turn; the prairie and the farm wear the colors of each season. The concerns of the living are so many that a man notices only that this year will be dry again. Talking with his friends, he may remark that the years have been getting drier without letup, five, six, seven years now.

"Our creek never was high like it was the year we started in to farming."

Another man will say, "Seven's the charm out here; the dry and the wet go in cycles."

And when the snows come and then the water from the runoff of the mountains to the north and west, people are comforted, even though the channeling creek seems lower than it was last year. The dead lie with their hands at their

27

sides, empty of work. There is time enough for bones to experience what living flesh has yet to learn.

Edgar never mentioned Tempe or the grief he felt at her loss, grief that sometimes reduced him to stifling a groan of anguish where he stood. Sometimes Joe would speak of the old days, the laughter, reminding Edgar of his many trips to the friendly, loud house where he had been made welcome. Joe would go on about missing Tempe and would remind Edgar of her tactful provision for his ways. Sometimes Ralph, too, would mention the loss of his womenfolk, and Edgar would sit silent, his mouth dry and his face reddening while Ralph counted Cora's virtues and remembered Tempe's laughter. Joe had tried to get him and the old man to come for visits and for holiday meals. Tempe's kin was still their kin, Joe said, but Edgar stayed away. He was afraid that if he visited at Joe's, the sorrow he felt would go sullen and raw, turn to anger, and burst forth to bury them all.

A man doesn't see his wife begin to sicken. He looks for his supper on the table, and his clean shirt, and if his wife is slow or mentions that she's tired, it's all he can do to stay his impatience. It must have been that way with Joe, who was bluff and busy, anyway. "Hurry up, Tempe, why ain't you ready now!" And while she was pregnant, he surely kept on demanding, like a big bull goat. Edgar knew these sour fantasies of his were only inventions—Joe had loved Tempe, surely he had treated her well. . . . But Edgar could not face Joe easily. The years of his silence layered themselves like falls of snow, one covering the other. A powerful worker, Edgar Bisset, but more than quiet—missing something, grim like a man who'd never been a boy.

Things had long since hardened into a decade of habit. The work, the Wednesday night at choir, the Saturday in town for shopping, Sunday for church. Each Sunday a word to the boy and a moment to listen to some adventure or other of his, a fall, a hunt for rabbits, a penknife. Then Joe would talk weather and land that wasn't coming back as it should, even though last year's crops had been good. After church, down the street and across the tracks to the coalyard. There

Edgar would have a slug of the terrible popskull that Charlie had been drinking for an hour. Charlie would get his week's supply and they would head back over the long land to a Sunday dinner, raw or burnt, which Ralph prepared, reminding them all, bitterly, every Sunday, that he had been doing women's work. This was why on Sunday afternoons, after the dishes had been washed and put away, Ralph would sit (porch in summer, parlor in winter), light his pipe, and begin to hold a monologue with his son.

"You seen that Plunket girl, the older one, up there at the store Saturday? Solid girl. No ways. She'd do good around here. . . ."

Edgar would deepen in his silence until it closed over him leagues deep, and his father would growl, "Don't you never want a good meal or a mended shirt? There's things a woman's got to bring to a place!"

And Edgar would nod and be silent.

At last they got a widow in from town two days a week.

"Better than nothin'," Edgar said to Charlie.

Charlie shook his head. "Her ways ain't ways of pleasantness."

Edgar looked across at Charlie, who was keeping his eyes straight ahead. Years ago, when he was no more than a boy, Edgar remembered, Charlie had complimented Cora on some cooking of hers. She had given him fifteen minutes of Scripture to show him that it was only her duty. The biblical reference made Edgar smile. He wanted to say, "Ma would have been pleased you remembered," but he was not able to say anything.

The widow didn't stay long.

Drayton, at the hardware store, and the newspapers said that it was people back East doing something to the prices. Everyone's production was up—the papers said that grains and broom, and hay and cane and corn were doubling, yet the prices had fallen so low that people were losing their land. The low of the early 1920s was a war thing, people said, something that happened to prices and markets after every war. But '25 was no better, '30 and '35 no better than that. In spite of the dryness, there was bounty, and by planting more and more, people had money for ground dressing and fertilizers to make the land richer. They planted and dressed over the planting with mulches to hold the water. The new irrigation plans were brilliantly successful. The farms gave and gave.

It wasn't until late spring that Edgar got time to do any fishing. He had asked Andy to come over early, and the boy was standing, ready, in the kitchen before sunup. At sixteen years, Andy was still skinny and break-voiced, and he reminded Edgar, in his movements, of Tempe. He smiled at Edgar's nod and picked up his equipment, carrying the creel and the net, always one more thing than Edgar, to show his strength and independence. They slipped out together into the not-yet-day. It would take an hour to get to the place. The birds began as they cut across the back field to a footpath that led over the treeless scrub. In a few hours the heat would start to dry-bake the ground, but even now the scrub was harsh and made a papery sound beneath their feet. Cowboy's delight, early for the year, glowed in iridescent patches against the grayness of the foredawn. They walked on in single file for a mile or two until they hit the dry bed of a tiny stream. It was almost imperceptible in the flatness of the land—only their feet felt the difference. In Edgar's boyhood memory it had carried water sometimes, earlier in the spring. They followed its dimplings for another mile. The irrigation dam, to the north, must have closed this one up, as it had done so many of the seasonal streams and creeks.

It was now full light and the warmth of the sun pushed them on. Andy began to whistle. Edgar looked ahead. They were coming to it. Up the dry wash would be a little grove of cottonwood and willow. There was a banked place there where the water had once changed its course and left the ground cut away. They came to the place and Edgar stopped in the middle of a step, so Andy nearly bumped into him and lost his balance. The cottonwoods were standing in their places, but they were skeletons, gray and leafless. The largest of the plants seemed to have pulled up its roots, or else the earth had shrunk away from them, as gums shrink from the teeth in a dead man's mouth. Edgar walked on curiously, Andy following him toward the trees. Edgar thought of a time in France, a time just after dawn on a path up a hill when he had tried to silence his steps, when he had walked on something that crackled like this. Above him had been the ruin of a line of trees. . . .

Six magpies were resting on the bones of a cottonwood. Alerted, they began to chatter. Edgar and Andy walked crouched, primed for some obscure ambush.

"What happened to 'em?" the boy asked.

Edgar shook his head. It wasn't disease, mites, insects, wind, or winter kill. At the base of each tree were its powdered, dried leaves, and two feet from it a new sprout, a tap from its root. In drought country, all trees made such bargains with death. Edgar had seen the signs before.

"Starved," he said. "Water."

Andy went on ahead to see into the creek but Edgar knew it would be dry. The soft alluvial sand shone with pinpoints of flaked metals, base and rare. The black matrix of gold values showed in one tongue where the last wash of water had left it. Andy looked over to Edgar for some instruction. Were they to go or stay? Edgar put down his fishing rod.

"Dig, boy," he said.

"Dig? What for?"

"Dig!" Edgar cried, and jumped down into the sand beside the boy. For a moment Andy almost cowered from him and then dropped to his knees and began to paw away at the dry sand. Beside him, Edgar knelt and scooped up the loose material from the side of the hole. They were down six inches when they reached the bottom of the new alluvial wash and hit pebbles and hard ground. Edgar took out his knife and pried at the caked earth. He knew his single-mindedness must be frightening to the boy. They scraped and scrabbled until they were more than two feet down, and Edgar looked into the hole between his bruised hands.

"Jesus God!" he said in a whisper.

Andy peered down to the bottom, then turned querulously to his uncle. "There ain't nothin' there. It ain't even cooler!"

Edgar nodded, but his eyes were not on the boy. He was

acknowledging the hugeness and the power of the thing that was coming toward them. The bottom of the hole was dry. Powder-dry. Dust-dry. As dry as death. On the way back he bent down and touched the infant sprout at the base of a willow. Its gray-green leaf, with a sound like cellophane tearing, came off in his hand.

4

The winds started in February and March, just as the ground began to thaw. Evaporating instead of melting, the moisture rose and blew away, leaching the land dry-white and pulling the loosened topsoil up to blow off uselessly. The winter wheat that had been planted in that earth blew, dead, to Oklahoma.

In April the winds died down. There was some light rain, and they planted again. The heavy downpours that should have set the seed did not come and they harvested a late and scanty crop. With all the land that was under the plow there was barely a fourth of the expected wheat, although the broom did not seem to suffer.

"Broom never fails," Ralph said.

"Pity you can't eat it," Charlie answered.

"Sell it all to them poor saps in Oklahoma so's they can sweep our good topsoil out of their privies."

Edgar only worked harder. That year, he mulched extra deep and sowed the ground with special cover to hold it. Then there were more winds drawing the snow off early, and in March again not rain but wind. The blow was from the south this time, the air the color of dried blood. It scoured the newly turned earth, tore the holding scrub up by the roots, and bore it away. Edgar and Charlie tried to go out between the squalls, hoping that each was the last and that if they planted again, rain would come. They came in from their fruitless work with set faces like captives under torture, pitting their will to endure pain against the captors' power to inflict it. May dragged in without water.

"It's got to break!" Ralph said. "We'll put in spring wheat or maybe beets or beans this year. The stuff blown out here from Kansas is black. Looks fertile. With good rain—" But the days were hot and the nights warm. The dust settled but did not hold. June came waterless.

Whenever the winds went down, Edgar would work. He swept away the miniature hills of sand on the bedroom floor, washed the gritty black sheets the three of them lay in, the gritty black clothes they wore, the gritty gray food they ate. He took apart all the machines when the earth drove into them through any protective covering—barn wall, shed wall, tarpaulin—they could put up against the wind. He never spoke about the farm losing hold on an earth and air gone mad. He kept to the plan of the days' chores and when there was no ground to farm—when all the ground was in the air, beating the boards bare of paint, scouring the tractor to its naked metal—he fixed old harness, oiled old machinery, remade the porch steps, and rehung the barn door.

They weren't regular at church on Sundays now. The car had never worked right since the last storm and people said there was sand in the gas and it ruined engines. On the Sundays when they didn't go, Edgar would pace the house in a kind of stoked anger and do whatever work there was in a mood like fury. Once Charlie came on him on a Sunday patching a ripped place in his work pants. He was drawing the needle in and out so fast that the thread broke and he swore, damning the threads and the patches and the pants they were in, in his dry, toneless voice.

"I never knew you missed the psalm singin' so much," Charlie said quietly. "Course, I ain't had no booze either in three weeks. It takes a saint to stay up here with you two buzzards and work this place without a bottle or two."

Edgar looked up at him bleakly. Then he shrugged and went back to the sewing.

The winter came full of false promises of snow. The weather reports they heard on the radio spoke of the deep packs on all the mountains so that Edgar dreamed of being buried on the side of a banked-in cliff, or standing up in a column of blue-green ice and looking down the illimitable distance to the plains below him. He dreamed of water again, the ocean on which he had sailed to France. He had wanted many times to tell Ralph and Charlie about the strange sights of the sea—rainstorms, the overplenty of water on water, with its sound of hissing like a steam locomotive; sprays, sheets, hills, mountains of water, moving, pouring, flooding over the rim of the world. He woke to the drawn-out line of the horizon separating the gray-white snow from the gray-blue sky where nothing moved.

Edgar hunted more that winter than he ever had before and came back with less. He and Andy would search for the little prairie hens and the small rabbits whose holes dotted the unplanted scrub places on the far side of the dry watercourse. It had been a good place once, watered except in high summer. Now there was too little growth for the animals to eat and no cover from their enemies. Sometimes Edgar and Andy shot birds and brought them home to make stew of plucked carcasses no bigger than Andy's fist.

That year they planted early, in February. There was less to plant because seed was scarce and so was fuel for the tractors, parts for the tractors, and money for all of it. Ledyards, Mattoxes, and Crails were off their farms—people who had lived in the county all their lives. Ledyards had come through only last week and given Ralph the things they couldn't take with them to Idaho where they said there was no dust and farms were making money. Edgar stood mutely on the porch, his hands hanging at his sides. He did not want to seem overeager for the washtubs and the canning things and the rolls of barbed wire and the wooden barrels they brought. At last Ralph called him off the porch and ordered him to help, and he saw Simon Ledyard, who was Ralph's age, give him a look of mingled pity and contempt as he came down, sifting the new-blown sand through his worn-out shoes.

It seemed to Edgar that this time the ground was moister and might hold. Sometimes, in a low place, there would even be a wet spot where the moisture stayed, a little darker patch where he could see in his mind the wheat coming sooner and thicker, holding the ground. Then, over the tractor's noise, he heard the vast whispering of a mile of green wheat under a gentle wind. It was a sound so palpable and real to him that once or twice he had to stop the tractor to see if what he knew could not be true was true. There was only a terrifying silence. The fields around him, which had once been busy with millions of barely heard calls of mating, danger, and combat, the gibbers of tiny mice, the dry scrapings of grasshoppers, and the clackings of the skeleton armies of beetles, was stilled. All the living things were gone. In the mild day, Edgar shivered in his lined working jacket and started the tractor motor again.

He saw a fine dust line moving forward on the road and he sighed. Somebody to see him and make him late with this field. Somebody from the government, federal, state, or county, seed inspector, expert, planner, or a Grange man, or salesman, all the experts with desperation on their faces. When the dust-up passed the house, he breathed easier only to see the car pull over to his side of the road and stop at the edge of the field he was working. He cursed silently. It was Joe. He could see it was Joe as the man got out of the sand-pitted car and stood up. Joe walked slowly over the newly turned soil of the field. Edgar got down from the tractor and went toward him.

"I didn't aim to take you from your work—" Joe shouted ahead of himself.

(What else could he be doing on an afternoon in planting time?)

"I saw you out here when I was passing and thought I'd stop—" He stood wavering in the mild light, one hand slightly raised as though to explain or apologize. Edgar felt more strongly what he had felt before in Joe: an uncertainty of expression, a feeling that Joe no longer filled his own clothes or his own thoughts.

"Uh . . . I was goin' out to talk to Linthicum," Joe said, "about that new seed they got in at Rimple's."

Edgar felt a sour rage, like bile, rising in him. "Linthicum know much about seed?" he said cruelly.

Joe looked at him with a kind of fascinated horror. "No— I guess he don't. But he's an old man and lives alone and he don't gossip or tell tales or run his mouth in town about me losin' hold."

Edgar was horrified. He was about to frame some words like, "No one is talking," or, "Everyone is suffering," but the proper phrase died in his mouth, overwhelmed by what rose in his mind: Ledyard is twice the man you are and he's off his farm and gone! Instead, Edgar said nothing, standing with his hands at his sides and a betrayed look on his face while the features of the brother-in-law who faced him destroyed themselves, pulling away to a wincing tic. Joe had begun to cry.

In all the field there was no tree, or bush, or place to hide, while Joe stood with his face in his hands, sobbing like a dying animal. There was nothing for Edgar to do but stand by, hot with embarrassment, while some dry, unengaged part of his mind ground away against Joe. What kind of a fool comes to his enemy for comfort? Don't he know I hate him, for Tempe? Don't he know I can't see him in his weakness without hating him worse? Don't he know there's fine men off their land—men that didn't let their wives die because they couldn't think of what to do to save them.

"It's been too much for me—all too much!" Joe was sobbing. "Pa dyin' like he done and leavin' me with all of it. Then Tempe. The bottom fallin' out of all the prices and then the dust—the awful damned dust!"

Edgar did not move. He knew he should say something, do something, put a hand on Joe's arm or an arm around his shoulder, but he could not. He could only stand riveted in the middle of his half-done wheat field on the afternoon of a planting day, while the sun westered, degree by degree.

"And it's all on me!" Joe was moaning. "All of it. What

to plant and what to leave. What acres to broom and what to wheat. Join the cooperatives or stay on my own. Break new ground or give up, and all the time I'm supposed to be sure, Christian Kornarens's son, whose house is always open and who never has any doubts!"

Edgar's face got hot. That house had always been open to him. He hadn't forgotten all the greetings at the door, the chair pulled up, and Tempe's smiling face, the cookies, cakes, cider, coffee poured out and pressed on him as though it would hurt her if he did not eat. There had been Joe, too, in all of that, his greeting as loud, his generosity as open. Now was the testing time for that love and for Tempe, too, who had loved and married Joe and given him a son. Edgar's mouth opened, his head came up, he even took a step forward. What should he say? What would not shame Joe or embarrass Edgar in the saying? No words—a gesture maybe, something that wouldn't look like pity—his hand was hanging in front of him ridiculously. He saw then that Joe had stopped trembling. Helplessly, Edgar saw him becoming aware of how he must look, crying in front of his brother-in-law. Edgar moved forward to touch Joe's arm, but it was too late. Joe's face hardened. He stepped back, then shook himself neatly like a dog, his eyes elsewhere. He was trying to pretend he had stopped by his neighbor's to tell him hello, on his way down the road.

"Well," he said, "day's passin'—" There was an absentminded disapproval in his voice. "I see you only got half this field done—you better get busy—" And he walked with elaborate casualness to his car, waved, and was gone.

Edgar got back on the tractor and started it up. He was glad for the noise it made, a noise that drowned his muttered swearing at what or whom he did not even know.

Later in the afternoon, clouds came and a soft snow began to fall. Edgar worked on in a stillness that made the sound of his own tractor seem comfortingly far away. There was no wind. Edgar sat half asleep in the veiling snow. He saw the large, white flakes touch ground, stand poised for an instant, and then melt to leave a darkening spot of moisture. When there was enough of them, they would stick. Then the snow would begin to cover the ground, first shawling it, then quilting, deeper and deeper. Held against the earth, the moisture would sink in the slowly warming days, deeper and deeper to the dried-up undersoil and the sand-choked catch-creeks, and under the mulch-layered levels where the green seeds waited.

He worked until he could not see to work. He knew it must be cold because of the snow, but he felt warm and comforted aboard his shuddering tractor. He could almost hear the green wheat moving out of his way as he went up and down on the great, flat field.

One month later, when the snow was gone and all the fields were planted, the wheat came up in long, pliant stalks. The wind remembered them and broke hell across all the fields, and all the farms, and dried the ground, and killed the seedlings, and blew them stiff and dry into the farmers' faces.

5

It got so that the old man would sit in his chair by the front window and conduct the storm. When it scoured up from the south, he would dare it to drown them. When the storm lay its gritty black winds about them, he would shake his fists at it. Sometimes the wind would change in mid-storm, layering the colors—gray and black and red, and their own pale earth flung back at them, after a ride to Texas or Oklahoma. It was a game the winds were playing, setting down red dunes with black edges in one storm and carrying them off in the next, and whipping three years of dry seeds through air suddenly gone solid.

Now the ground was so dry that it wouldn't even clump if it was wetted. Inside the houses, the dust that had forced its way through every crack blew the air dark. They wore it, ate it, breathed it, spat it out black from dry throats every morning. "Like livin' in a coal mine," Charlie cursed. "Dark as a mine, even in the daytime."

When the winds were at their worst, there was nothing to do but stay inside. They wore dampened rags over their faces to keep the dust from their lungs. Between the dry storms, they worked until they were exhausted. The old man had to dig the house out, Edgar the northeast side of the barn. The wind drove dry bushes and the roots of old trees against their fences and piled the rubbish of distant farms against their outbuildings. The well went foul and silted up. There was no water, and they had to haul emergency supplies from town. More and more families picked up and left. There came to be a place in the services on Sunday when one or two or three men would get up and announce that they were leaving. "Anyone who feels I got a debt to 'em, come on over and take what's fair. There's tools and things—the wife's got a tea set and a cherry-wood chest." And he might laugh a little, embarrassed, at the joke he had not meant, a laugh that had no humor in it.

The Bissets did not see them go. Their place was east of town and no one went east.

The road beside the farm was a minor one, used once and now forsaken for the larger one, a mile or so to the north, that led directly through the town. On this road, people said, the cars and carts and horses and wagons moved in a slow stream. Stopping in town, people would look around through shocked, road-dulled eyes. "We thought it would be better here—they told us it was better here—" and they would go on.

It moved Edgar to see his father's rage. The old man had more energy in his wiry body than Edgar did—enough to curse the dunes that danced and changed, east, southeast, south-southeast, back and forth, changing color, as the wind changed direction. He noticed that after every blow the old man would shoulder his shovel and go to the same banked place that buried the front porch, the same downed fence. Edgar wondered how long the old man's spirit would last. He wondered how long he and Charlie would be kept from insanity, how much less they could eat and not starve to death, how many weeks it was to ruin. He did not speak. He seldom spoke five words at all between sunup and dark.

At the end of March the winds stopped abruptly and on the third of April it rained. It was a black rain, full of the north-winding dust that had been held in the clouds, and it left black grit wherever it fell. After the rain, Edgar drove their remaining four cows to browse on whatever new grass might have come up. The cows looked skeletal, and they barely had the strength to move. Erosion had made a cleft through what had once been Mutcher's farm, and at the bottom of this cleft there was a protected place and the barest haze of new grass. Edgar left them there and went scouting in the arroyos and dry creek beds for whatever else there might be. By noon he had worked all the way around to the east of the farm without finding anything on which the cows could feed. At lunch, Ralph told Edgar to go on scouting to the south for new grass. He would bring the cows back before dark. It was a scanty meal, barely enough to keep Edgar from cramping as he walked in and out of the eroded places in the vast, flat land. Edgar kept looking up at the sun, which seemed suddenly cold. He walked quickly to keep warm. Here and there he found a web of grass, hair-thin and almost too delicate to see on the south-facing sides of the arroyos. Too little. Too fragile. He noted the places and started for home.

As he walked, he thought of the cows, once good stock. The dust had filtered into their fodder as it had into everything else, and their teeth had been ground down, almost by half. They were so thin—

He was crossing the broom field near home when he saw the old man coming toward him, running, his arms out as though to stop himself from falling. Edgar began to run. As they neared each other, Edgar heard his father yelling his name and he ran faster, until they met between barn and house and Charlie Dace came running up from where he was working.

"Edgar!" the old man gasped. "The cows!"

"What?"

"The cows has been took!"

"What, stolen?"

"Took, took!" The old man coughed, gasping for breath, while Edgar in an agony of frustration almost jumped from one foot to the other.

"The cows has been took!" the old man finally gasped.

"Not stole, took, took against nature!" And before he recovered, half staggering, he led them to the old Mutcher place and the draw.

Looking down the draw, they saw all four cows, wandering aimlessly, having eaten all the grass there was. "You—don't—see—!" The old man gasped. "But I seen. Growin'. Growin' grass. The cows—is growin' grass!"

Edgar caught Charlie's eye. They might have laughed, except that Ralph's voice had hysteria in it, and his face showed terror sharp as the marks of a slap.

"What do you think?" Charlie murmured under his breath. Edgar shook his head. Slowly, they walked toward the bony cows.

"They seem okay," Charlie whispered. "Still got their winter hair, and they are awful skinny, but they seem okay."

Looking back, they could see Ralph standing above them, motionless now. "You reckon he's lost his mind?" Charlie whispered. Edgar said nothing. They went closer.

At first it seemed like winter hair, a thicker coat against the winds, and then they saw that what the old man said was true. The cows were green. Patches of new-sprouted prairie grass were growing from the backs and down the flanks of Juliet, Surprise, and Independence. Movie Star, whose place was near the far wall of the barn, had the left side of her body evenly covered with prairie grass, young clover, and wild wheat. Neither of the men wanted to touch the cows—there was a whiff of the old man's horror in them—but Edgar made himself remember that he had been on battlefields, and seen grass growing between the fingers of a severed hand. After a moment, he pushed himself forward and grabbed at Movie Star, raking at the green on her flank. She lowed and pulled away from him. Charlie, beside him, was cursing in a self-absorbed monotone as he pulled at the green weeds caught among the rotting hair of Independence's back.

"You can't get under it!" Charlie cried. "The dust has been drove up right into the skin and it's all matted in there with roots. These cows must be carryin' twenty, thirty pounds of dirt on 'em."

"You ever hear of this before?" Edgar asked him.

"One time, a long time ago, I heard a fellow tell about a tornado come through one year and done like that, drove dirt into cows' hides so hard it couldn't be got out."

"What happened to the cows?" Edgar asked.

Charlie stood, embarrassed, fussing with Movie Star and then Independence. "Man didn't say," he muttered.

Edgar sighed. Charlie had kept to himself so long that he had lost the talent for telling a convincing lie.

The next week another sandstorm crested and broke on the fields. Ropes of dust were held upright like cobras swaying from a basket. And the old man shouted curses at the storm in his dried-out plains voice. It lasted for four days. The air in the house was gray. The drying, abrading dust found each hair-thin fault and secret way inward to the heart of the house and the men there. They coughed and spat gray. They burned their kerosene lamps all day and still had to grope for doorways.

When the night-pots were full, the old man went to dump them out the back door away from the wind, but it saw him and turned and blew his piss, turned black with its moment in the air, back in his face. At the sight of him crusted, black, and stinking, Charlie and Edgar had a fit of hysterical laughter, but they couldn't laugh long because they began to choke—the air had gone solid again.

When it was over, they went out to the barn and slaughtered the cows. The hides were useless, the green patches gone to mold, rotten under their knives. Although the meat was not good, they boiled, smoked, pickled, and oven-dried it. They used every jar that could hold a seal, and processed them in the sour black water that the well pumped. They were stupid with exhaustion and threw the saved parts out with the rotten; there was no time to boil and settle the water they needed. So much was wasted and useless that the old man cried in rage.

On the twentieth of June the wind stopped. In the evening rain fell, black rain, but by ten or so it had conquered the dust and was falling clean. Edgar woke in the dark. He didn't know what time it was or why he had wakened until many minutes had passed and he realized that he was not hearing wind. Not even the soft, ground breeze of early summer. It was absolutely still. He rose and put on his shirt and blood-stained work pants, thought about shoes, and then went without them. There was nothing out there anyway but the dust. It had covered the broken bucket and nail-pocked plank, the stubble of beaten fields, and the planting of the new places, all failure and all hope.

It was as perfect as new snow. He stood outside the front door and looked at the land on which he had been born and raised. The hills and draws of this desert stretched endlessly before him. The night was brittle clear, but there was dust in the north—there were few stars. Perhaps the others had been blown out or scratched dull in the sky.

He went down the porch steps, grinding the blown earth into the boards. The sound of it was loud in all the stillness. As he walked out of the shelter of the house he saw his foot-steps following him, small sunken pockets in two lines. The form of them delighted him suddenly. They were as logical, as clean, as laws. Something had passed from there to here, the earth declared, a moving thing, a living thing of a certain weight, moving by its own will, on neatly jointed feet. If it had been heavier, the laws of the universe declared, the marks would have been deeper; if lighter, more shallow.

"And therefore," said the Presence of the Master of the Laws of the Universe, "it must be you." Edgar stood trembling and received this greeting. It was not given in words, nor did he hear it through his ears. It did not travel through any other place to come to him. It was immediate.

"My Lord?" Edgar whispered. "My Lord?" His perception was of a laughter, the rumbling of a joy too great to contain. It poured to fill its space, the corridor between the dust and the stars. The air vibrated with it soundlessly.

"Why have you waited so long?" the Presence questioned.

"I don't know—I didn't never know—" Then Edgar spoke without words, because it was faster. "I guess You came to me here because this has broken us," and he looked around so that the Presence might see through his eyes the land dead as the moon.

"Perhaps the farm is dead," the Presence corrected gently. "*You* are living. You are most wonderfully alive."

"Lord, was it because of sins that You did this? Was it because of our sins?"

"Are you ready for such sins? Are you great enough to sin so much that this would be the punishment?"

"I didn't mean Pa, or Charlie, because their sins are not evil, only stupid, little and stupid. I meant my sins, like—" and his mind stuttered, "how I feel about m-my ma."

The Presence said, "My stars are so far and My sky is big—"

Edgar whispered, "From Everlasting to Everlasting."

"Your neighbors then, are they the sinners?"

"No; mankind, maybe."

"And who are you, in this six hundred miles, to stand before Me and accept a punishment for all mankind?"

"But why, then, when we worked so hard?" It seemed as though the Spirit moved deeper into Edgar.

"Look around." Edgar looked. "Not at the farm. Look at the land as it is. Only as it is. Is it not beautiful?"

"No, Lord," Edgar cried to the thrumming silence. "Don't ask me to love the knife that's cutting me to drain my blood."

"Open your eyes!" the Spirit commanded. Edgar wondered for a moment if it was within his power to disobey, but if he did, perhaps the Presence would withdraw from him and he would not be able to endure that withdrawal. Then he wondered how the Presence, so recently known, could be so important to him. He forced himself to turn his attention outward to the land.

It lay unformed, purposeless under the half-moon. The few trees which had once given frame and feature to the plain had dried up, died, and been blown down and covered. The hedges and fields, the roads, paths, fences, all were obliterated. Only the house and barn and outbuildings stood against the flowing contours of the blown earth. Soon they too would give way, fall in, and be covered by the tidal dust. He looked out at the land rising in slight swelling mounds to the west. The rhythm of the wind had placed the mounds that way. In each small twist and pocket of dust, a shadow lay. The shadows also had a rhythm. As he looked across the

46

reach of what had been his father's fields, he saw the play of these risings and fallings, a flow between shadow and shadow, light and light. It was beautiful, so beautiful that it made him draw in his breath. How could he have missed seeing it before?

"My Lord," he said aloud.

The silent Spirit answered, "I know it has made you suffer. Yet—yet isn't it beautiful!" In the great corridor, as far as the eye could see, the presence of the silent laughter rose, and a bond in Edgar was loosened and fell away. From deep inside him a small, clean spring of laughter opened outward and began to flow. It widened and deepened, and he laughed aloud, body shaking, arms shaking, chest heaving with it. He fell down laughing, wept with it, gasped with it, and resting a moment looked up at the stars and laughed again. When he was exhausted and aching, he stretched out upon the ground.

"How many stars are there?" he asked the Presence.

"One at a time."

"Are they necessary to our survival?"

"No."

"Then they are a gift, extra, to rejoice at."

"Yes, to learn the harmonies of life from and to enjoy."

"And so many—clouds of them, seas of them—from rim to rim."

"Yes, and forever."

"I'm afraid to sleep—afraid You will leave," he said very softly in his mind.

"How can that be? I have always been with you all your life. Don't be afraid. I will not leave you. Go to sleep."

"Do You know my name, Lord?"

"I've always known it. What do you suppose I would call you?"

"Knucklehead?"

"A word like that, if you need a word," the Presence said. It felt to Edgar like a word of great tenderness. He lay down in the rain-held dust and slept.

The sun woke him. For a moment he wondered why he was here, five hundred feet from the house, caught in the hard eye of the sun. Then he remembered and looked quickly back at the house. Charlie and Pa would still be sleeping. With the cows gone, they had stopped getting up before sunrise. There was no work, no purpose.

"Lord!" Edgar whispered. "Lord, are You still here?" The Presence filled the air like laughter. "It's me, it's Knucklehead."

"I know," the Presence answered.

"It was real, then, what happened?"

"Yes."

Stretching and smiling, Edgar walked toward the house and then stopped about twenty feet from the front steps. He didn't know how to greet them, how to face them since wonders had happened to him. Perhaps it would be wrong to tell them.

"What shall I do?" he asked.

"What is natural to you to do," the Presence answered.

The old man was at the door, opening it to see what the day was like. He was surprised to find Edgar coming toward him.

"What's the matter? Is something the matter?"

"No, sir," Edgar said. He shot a furtive look at the old man, the first person he had seen since the Presence had spoken to him. His father's face was drawn with discontent, sleep without rest, the inactivity of a hopeless man. Edgar wondered vaguely how long it had been this way, or if he had seen this in his father's face before. He turned his head for a moment back to the sand-drowned field in which he had spent the night. Now the sun was whitening the black plain, making radiant everything it touched. The air was warm and the color of honey. The ridges, wavelets, liftings, and lowerings of the blown blanket of earth glowed with all the colors of the earths from which they had come, red-brown, russet, black, and in the shadow-hollows, blue and blue-gray, flowing, still flowing like a running sea.

"If it could be given to me to see," Edgar said softly, "why couldn't others see it—"

"What are you mumbling about?" the old man asked querulously, coming down the steps toward him.

"I'm talkin' about the glory, about the glory all around!"

He took the old man's hand. "Come here, Pa, let me show you. Let me show you what I saw. Listen, Pa, even if the farm is bust, we ain't! The thing is, we ain't! We can let go here if we need to, let God do his will here, but we got the privilege of seein'—" He had pulled the old man down the steps and they stood side by side in the rilling dust.

"What's happened to you?" the old man asked. Edgar had said more to him in these two minutes than he had said in twenty years, and all of it madness. "You see God's glory in this?"

"Look at it!" Edgar cried. "How the sun does, how the light comes on it, all red—how it's like music, like voices singin', if we could hear it—see the little hills, the voices there goin' up and the others there goin' down—"

"You see God's glory?" the old man repeated, and then to Edgar's amazement faced him with a look of pain and rage. "Ain't it fine, *now!* Where was the glory and the gratitude in you when I needed it? All them years when you was little and I set you by me and you never smiled, or spoke a word, or showed thankfulness, though I went without to let you have some ease? Where was that look on your face then, when you was back from the war and we had to tell you about Tempe dyin' and your ma and you walked around here for ten long years with your lips closed tight, askin' nothin', sayin' nothin', not to me or Joe that was dyin' to show our sorrow and be healed of it and couldn't, because of that closed-up face of yours!"

"Pa—" he said helplessly, "I couldn't then. I wanted to say things, to tell you about how I missed Tempe and how sad I was about Ma, about the war and what happened to me in the war. It never came to me that I was stopping you or Joe—I just *couldn't* then. Now I can and now I want to tell you all the things, all of them, because it's all changed now, the Lord has freed me, Pa."

"Just like Him, ain't it, freed you now, when we're broke and ruined and the land's gone and there ain't nothin' to do but lay down and die—"

Charlie Dace had come out on the porch, attracted by the sound of the old man's voice. There had been no work for him since they had all tried to save the last of the slaughtered cows. At the sound of Charlie's step on the boards of the porch, the old man turned and shouted:

"Don't worry none, Charlie, Edgar has come through for us. He has seen God hisself, sailin' the dust like it was ocean, plowin' the stars! The moon's gonna grow grain and the sun run water!" Charlie stood dumbly, his hands at his sides. The old man couldn't stop. "What you got to say to that, Charlie? Can't you say nothin'? Here's Edgar been conversin' with God. He has been unloosed and now we are all saved, and ain't the dust a *glory!*"

If Charlie had heard he gave no sign of it. He stood at the top of the steps transfixed. Then slowly his hands began to rise. They were trembling. The muscles in his starved face began to work. His whole body became seized, as though taken with a chill. His face was pale. It seemed as though he might faint. He stepped toward Edgar with his hands raised. Then he came stumbling down the stairs weak-kneed, like a drunken man. At the bottom, he fell in the soft banked dust, but he scrambled up instantly, running toward them, half tripping, to where they stood in front of the house. His eyes were on Edgar, fixed as death.

"I knowed it!" he cried. "I knowed it would happen and it's here! It took so long I almost quit hopin', but it's come, it's come like I knowed it would, like I always knowed!"

6

Most strange was the joyousness. People seeing Edgar in town felt the difference in him. It was there before he spoke or raised a hand in greeting. When he did speak, his simplest words had a kind of gaiety in them. And there was laughter that made people turn to one another with amazement. Edgar was a silent man. He had been a silent boy. He was a deep man, everyone knew that, a man who kept things to himself and did not show his feelings. And suddenly, here he was in town, in church, in Metheny's blind pig with Charlie, smiling as though his two hundred acres were heavy under their wheat.

Charlie didn't seem changed, although he stayed closer to Edgar than he had before. Of course they were more often in town, now. All the farmers were, since the dust had taken their work. Edger stood around with the others, not silently now, but always speaking with that strange unexplained joyfulness. There was no mention of how the joyfulness had come.

He might have tried to tell people about the awful glory, the cry of pain that opened to laughter, the great love that ended in tears; but he had failed with his father, who now suspected his sanity, and he had no wish that his friends and neighbors think he was crazy. Now that he could speak, he found he had a need for it, an appetite to tell and remember a lifetime of incidents and events so long withheld—the war, Tempe, the counting rhymes of his childhood, the fishhook in his foot when he was twelve, Tempe when she was a mother, music, that Tempe was gone. He tried to suppress this new desire, but he could not. The joy of it crept outward. His hands, which had hung dead at his sides, now began to move with his speaking; his face became active as he listened, and there were times when coming home through the long dunes, the banked, unfenced, unmarked vistas of featureless earth, he could no longer give equal voice to his pain and his joy, and he had to jump down from the coughing Ford, fording the dust-tided highway, and dance, singing at the top of his voice, "Fair are the meadows, fairer still the woodlands, robed in the blooming garb of spring."

"Charlie, I tell you, it ain't harps and halos in heaven like the idea is. There's work, hard work, man's work in heaven."

"Plowin' and cuttin'?"

"I don't know, but I know it ain't just flyin' around. There's no work here and people are sufferin' so much from it. God, Charlie, I want to tell 'em to look around, study the stars now they can't sleep, watch the sunrise now they can't work, learn all they can out of books till the time comes."

"Edgar, people are starvin'."

"I know, but the land will come back, I know it will, and if they can't sit this out, there's other land, good land for men who want to farm it. It ain't our sin that's done this. That means—it means we're free of it, free to go in peace, or stay and try to wait out the time."

"Charlie, I seen you goin' out last night. Did the Lord call you?"

"No, I went out again to see if He would, if I could hear anything."

"Did you have it? Did He put his hand on you?"

"No."

"Not this time—"

"Never. I never have heard."

"It's bound to be shown to you. He done it with me, and God knows I ain't no better, no smarter than you."

"You're younger than I am. You got more hope. You sure are less tired."

"I don't know, Charlie, why it happened to me. I've set up some nights wondering who I am to be allowed to listen to that Voice, to have that happiness pourin' in me. I'm scared to ask Him. It would seem like I was askin' Him to part the glory into east and west, into why and why not. It would be like I was judgin' *Him*—!"

"Charlie, have you tried to get the glory?"

"I waited where you wait. I stood where you stand, but it ain't no good. I got too much guilt in me—I guess I done too much wrong."

"I've done more wrong than you—you never denied your own ma."

"Cora wasn't no blessing to live with. You done the best you could."

"I denied her after she was dead. She comes to me in dreams when I'm happiest and most peaceful and she cries out at me that I denied her and it's true. Oh, God, Charlie, I didn't even miss her when she died. I still remember what I thought when Pa told me she was gone along with Tempe. I was grievin' so for Tempe and all I thought about Ma was just, Well, at least we won't have to have all them prayers no more before we eat. Just that, after all the years. I'm whipped by that memory so bad—"

"I thought that Presence you been talkin' about was supposed to bring you peace."

"Who told you that? I didn't never say that. He gives life, but not peace—joy and suffering, but not *peace*."

"I guess that's what I wanted from Him—maybe I should go out and ask for sufferin'. He sure has been liberal with that in the past."

"Just ask for his Presence, just for that, and it will be all you will need. The yearning starts then, the yearning for more of Him...."

In later years Charlie Dace would sit on the back porch, drowsing under the benison of a winter sun, and he would think mostly about the people—about what brought the people, what suddenly attracted so many different people to Edgar. In his years of silence Edgar had been less respected than many other reticent men. There were others who spoke little, but were accounted wise and prudent. For all his size, Edgar had seemed nondescript. He tended to be forgotten when people sought back over some event.

"Fire at the feed store? You and I were there, Johnson, the Miller boys, and who else?"

"Lord, that was a rattler hunt! Red Nelson got him seven and the Linthicum boys was there and Joe Kornarens—who'd we leave out?"

Charlie would try to remember if it was the children who came first or the grown people, the young or the old, and how and why, when Edgar hadn't spoken of his gift, not then, anyway. What sudden change, more than the change from silence to downright gabbiness, drew people toward him? It was something that made Charlie think of natural laws or some chemical force.

In town, people walked along as far as they could with him. Children came to him, even strange children, without the usual hesitation. The old woman who kept the tobacco counter at Burkett's store thought up all kinds of pretexts for detaining him, and when he had turned away to leave, followed him with her eyes, a quiet smile of pleasure on her face. She was a bitter old woman with dragging pains in her lower stomach, and a smile from such a body in this hollow season, in a town beaten by sun, its farmlands blown to cropless, treeless deserts, was something of a miracle. In the hot days of July, the wasted days of a bad year, with starvation and failure and calamity and collapse moving through the hard shadows of the town, there were people smiling, people laughing, people drawn out to Bissets' place to sit on the porch and wait for Edgar to come toward them with his smile and his greeting and his hand held out to them.

Ralph Bisset was amazed. "What in hell do them people want day after day? Look over there—did you ever see Craddock out here before? I never liked that bird at all and he never cared for me, yet here he sits, talkin' with Linthicum, and them ain't never been close neither."

"It's the idle time," Edgar said after the visits. "They have no work to do; they're clustering together like calves in a thunderstorm."

"Men with no work." Ralph sniffed. "What about the women come for miles for the loan of a quarter pound of butter we don't have. Some don't even have the shame to bring a dish for it."

"I reckon they're only followin' after the men."

"They're only comin' to make me so mad I'll lose my temper!" And he walked away muttering. Charlie always waited until the old man left to go to the barn or the privy, and then he would get up and go to the kitchen and put on coffee for the visitors.

It wasn't long before people began to notice the absence of Joe Kornarens on these visits. Sometimes his boy, Andy, would come, head down and diffident, to stand outside the parlor window or sit on the bottom porch step, his arms around his knees, listening earnestly to the night talk at the open doors and windows. He was noticed, and his furtiveness.

August and September stood motionless and bone-dry in the heat. In church on Sundays the voices in the choir cracked with it. People sucked pebbles to get themselves through the hymns, and even the marching hymns came slow and flat. People didn't have the energy for more.

After services Edgar always went quickly out the choir's exit and then around the side of the church to the front to greet Joe and Andy, but since the months of heat he had gone up the steps and into the vestibule near where Parson Hummel stood to shake hands with the people of the congregation as they left. Lately it was harder to get to Joe and Andy in the press of other people who wanted to exchange a greeting or ask for a favor or simply to wait for his look, his smile, and the healing warmth of his joy. He was not surprised one morning to find his way blocked, but called over the heads of his neighbors:

"Hey, Joe! Andy! How've you two been? I ain't seen you

since last week—" He was about to remind Andy that they had planned to meet so that Edgar could teach him how to make a corncob pipe. Then he saw Joe coming toward him, Andy following as well as he could through the crowd. Joe's face had a set look, a look that hardened as he came closer. Involuntarily, Edgar stepped back a little, and saw to his horror that Joe's face had gone to rage, a pale rage, not a red one, and that he was pushing the last two or three people away until he was standing close to Edgar, too close, and talking into his face.

"Listen!" Joe's voice was tight and low with his fury. "Now you're a big somethin' hereabouts. People are talkin' about the change in you, the great change, but you don't fool me at all. You been talkin' to everybody. You been tellin' people things against me. You been low-ratin' me to my own son and it's got to stop!"

"Joe—"

"Don't try and soft-soap me. I want that promise from you."

"I was only goin' to say let's both of us come out of the church. We can talk outside." Eyes on each other, they went down the steps. People fell away from them and there was a sudden, humming silence.

The sight of Joe's face froze the onlookers in the black-and-white street.

"Why are them folks standin' there, Portress and Nailor, and old Linthicum, and Charlie there?"

"I ride home with Charlie," Edgar said, stunned, "you know that. Lately Mr. Linthicum has been ridin' with us. The others—I guess they're just socializin' a little after church." There was a removed quality about the time, as though the sun had stopped. It made Edgar remember the sick unreality of the war, the first fire in a trench, the dead men staring up at him from a trench.

Joe was shouting at them, "Go on home!" Whispering, turning to one another, they moved back, but did not go away. Old man Linthicum made as if to amble toward Edgar's Ford, halfway up the block. Charlie did not move a muscle. Joe turned on him:

"Get out. This is between Edgar and me. Get in the car."

"Go shit a brick," Charlie said.

Joe turned back to Edgar in wonder. "How did you do it? I could murder that little runt with one hand and you've got him answerin' back to me. People here are so stubborn, half of 'em'll say yes just 'cause the others say no. You got 'em comin' to me, talkin' to me: 'Why don't you go over to see Ed? How come you ain't been to Ed's?' Now Andy comes to me, too: 'Come on, Dad, let's go over to Bissets'.' I told him no, and that he wasn't to go neither, and later I seen him come in all draggle-tailed, with cat-burr on his pants."

"Cat-burr? Where is there cat-burr? It ain't rained for—"

"Are you laughin' at me, you son of a bitch? I'm gonna put your ass in a sling!" He began to move down on Edgar, who was frozen between impossibilities. Why was his brother-in-law so angry? What had he done that the hate and rage should be so bitter? He could not endure the war feeling of unreality, and putting his head back, cried, "You, Lord! You, Lord!"

The sound was not finished before Edgar ceased all hearing and then all sight. The next thing he knew, Charlie was kneeling over him and he was lying down somewhere, looking up into a black-green, sun-dappled space.

"Charlie—"

"You're okay, Edgar. You just passed out is all. Me and Linthicum dragged you over here."

"Am I in heaven—all the green—"

"It's only the cottonwood shrub the Methodists saved. No closer to heaven than that."

"Joe—where's Joe?"

"He got tired of waitin' for you to come to so he went on home. He did look kinda silly standin' there yellin' at you to get up and fight."

"I couldn't have fought him, Charlie. The Lord knew it and saved me."

"Pity He couldn't have did it with a little more style. Here, let me give you a hand up."

Edgar and Charlie walked back up the street to the car. It was one o'clock, the street Sunday-empty; even the town's new poor were gone, sitting in the coalyard or down in their makeshift places by the railroad siding, out of the sun. Charlie looked over at Edgar and then back up the street. He got into the car beside Edgar, who sat behind the wheel, not moving. Old man Linthicum had gone home. "Ed?" Charlie said. Then he saw that Edgar was busy with the Lord.

Edgar thought he might be too weak to drive. His mind was dulled with the shock of Joe's hatred and envy. He felt the pull to race home so that he could go to the dry wash and thank the Presence for sparing him having to beat or be beaten by his brother-in-law.

"I never knew," he murmured to Charlie beside him. "I never saw how Joe was sufferin' all this time. I was so busy with the new people and the new things that I didn't even see—"

"Hell," Charlie said, "that man's been sufferin' for years. It had nothin' to do with you at all."

"But all the strength in me—the Lord's words—and yet I couldn't help him—" He started the car, whose gears ground their teeth on dust. As they drove out of town they saw that the packing-box-and-tin-can settlement down by the railroad siding had grown and was spilling over toward the dry wash where the cattle had once been watered, waiting for the train to carry them east.

"What an awful thing," Edgar said, looking out at the cluster of shanties, "havin' to live like that."

Charlie had pulled his bottle of popskull from under the seat. "It sure is," he said, and took a long drink. "Stuff's been gettin' worse and worse. Got grit in it all the time. Tastes like kerosene." The smell of it was rank in the air. Edgar began to feel a little ill.

"It makes me scared, Charlie, all the things Joe said—about me turnin' the neighbors against him—turnin' Andy against him. Where did it all come from? How did he get those things in his mind? I swear, Charlie, since—what happened to me—I love Andy better and Joe better than ever, and the anger I had over Tempe's dyin' is gone—"

Charlie turned toward Edgar and in the closed car his breath smelled sharply of acetone. "You never really knew what it was like here the year that Tempe and your ma died. I know it was hard on you, comin' back and no warnin', but they tried to tell you how it was here—people was dyin' right and left. There was whole families cut in half—"

"I know, Charlie, but that hate I had for Joe wasn't anything to do with knowin' those things. I knew he loved Tempe—I only—well, it's over for me now, but not for Joe. If only the Presence of the Spirit would come to Joe—"

"Why won't it come to Joe, then, or to me?"

"How do I know? Don't you think I haven't asked Him, begged Him?"

They were nearing home when Edgar suddenly sat bolt upright, cried out, and jammed on the brakes. The car skidded to a stop at the side of the road. With no other word but a cry, Edgar was out the door before his foot was off the brake, leaving Charlie dumbstruck in the front seat. Through the window, Charlie could see Edgar running off the road and into the rilling landscape of gray-white dust. Charlie put up his hand, calling, "Hey—, Edgar—" but the sound of his voice, loud in his ears, alarmed him and he put down his hand. In the other hand, he still held the bottle with its gritty lees. The sand swirled up in it. Craziness? Maybe Edgar had been given God and then madness. Then a horrible certainty blew across the dust flats of Charlie's thoughts. It was Joe. Joe was angry; he had been shamed in town and he was stalking Edgar. He had lain in wait with a gun, and Edgar had seen some clue, the sun on it, maybe, and had known immediately and was running for his life or maybe to save Joe from murder. How vulnerable they were in the lone car, the only moving thing on the endless plain, their dust plume signaling them from miles away. Charlie dropped the bottle and hitched around in his seat, peering out through the pitted windows, straining for sight of the gun or the hunter or the signal that Edgar had seen. Nothing. But as Charlie turned again, he saw Edgar scrambling up from an eroded draw. Oh, God, shot, in absolute summer silence and scrabbling in his agony—without help.

"Oh, Jesus, God!" Charlie shouted and bolted from the door. Magically, Edgar rose and came running toward Charlie, clutching something. "What in the goddamn hell is goin' on!" Charlie shouted.

"Praise God!" Edgar yelled, at a dead run toward him. "Praise God, Charlie, it's over, it's over!" He came back out of breath, laughing, and then, to Charlie's shock, picked the small man up in his great arms and whirled him around, hugging him and beating his back with mad joy. "Joe was right, it's cat-burr, cat-burr, Charlie, it made the burr on Andy's pants! Cat-burr and buffalo-burr, knotweed, bindweed, speedwell, dayflower! They're comin' in the draws, in the water places. I bent down and felt there, and way down there was a kind of coolness, and the earth held in a clump where I dug. Oh, God, Charlie, we'll be able to farm again!" His joy was half weeping. "We'll be able to break our butts again, we'll be able to wear ourselves out and leach ourselves dry and get back-sore and dog-tired—we'll be able to go broke again, like men, thank God."

A sudden thought sent Charlie bolting back to the car. The bottle had fallen over. The last gulp had spilled out and lay greasily on the floorboards. The air smelled like dead, wet rats. They propped the bottle up in the sand at the side of the road and put the hair-thin green weeds in it like a bouquet, laughing until they were tired.

7

That night there were people at the house again. They no longer came with excuses. There were 650 men left in the county who called themselves farmers where there had once been ten times that number. Even these men did not farm; they built roads and set privies for the WPA. They carved bed spindles and built the jail at the county seat. They made brooms and tanned leather and panned for alluvial gold in places where there was no water and no gold. The potatoes in which they refined their ore were worth more than the gold they got.

Sometimes there would be a short, hot, fugitive excitement —gold panning or the making of adobe bricks or getting some millionaire interested in water drilling or oil drilling or silver mining. As the idle summer and autumn months went on, the plans got wilder and more involved. Charlie wanted to move truckloads of men into the mountains where there was real gold.

"Sweet Savior, Charlie," Ralph cried, "your damn gold couldn't pay for gas to get us there and back. Gold creeks so full of fools already, you have to reserve space to be a fool in. Ain't that man from the sidin' told you how it was up there?"

Edgar shot a look at Charlie and met his eyes and Charlie gave a bare hint of a smile. The old man had never before recognized "the sidin'" in his house. He had counted the arrival of people to the squatters' jungle near town as a sign of the end of days as surely as his green-grown cattle. When one of them had come to his door to see Edgar, he had fought back as best he knew—by not recognizing the man's existence.

Edgar had met the man going from door to door for work in town. Edgar had told him that there was to be some food delivered up at the county seat and that he would help the siding men to get it. They spoke briefly, and two evenings later the man had come by. He came walking up the road, afraid to cross another man's fields, even though they were deserts now. When he got to the door, Ralph refused to notice him, but Edgar saw him and called out:

"Dilys, is that you out there?" He brought Dilys with him into the front room. There was silence as "the sidin' " came in and was given a chair among the neighbors. Edgar pulled up his chair and began to tell a story about his days in the Army training camp, before he had been sent over to France. It was a funny story and though he had told it before, the men liked hearing it in the presence of someone new. When he got to the good part ("These two fellers, bein' city-born, they didn't know how to do. *Nothin'* came to 'em easy—"), Edgar saw the visitor's posture ease. He interrupted himself, leaning forward toward the man. "Was you in the Army, Dilys? I was in the middle of this story, thinkin' of these two big clods, and I realized I was a clod too, not askin' you your experiences." Dilys nodded his head. Edgar chuckled, "Then you know how them Army camps was." Dilys nodded again, and as the story went on he smiled occasionally. His teeth at the sides were missing. "I was in Texas first," Edgar said, "and there was mostly farmers there, men who knew which end of the shovel was for the shi——, beg pardon, Mrs. Tempeler—which end to use." He went on, elaborating on the miseries of his clumsy buddies. Dilys nodded now and then or laughed so that Charlie, standing in the corner, could not believe he was the same man who had come to the door like a grim shadow not half an hour before. Charlie told Edgar later that the kerosene lamp had caught a glint of tears, once or twice, in his eyes. Dilys, they found, had been at "Bellowwood" and been wounded twice, had owned land and farmed it in Oklahoma, had lost it to the dust, and had been to Arkansas and California looking for work. When he left, Tom Jaspers offered him a ride home. Ralph Bisset had left the room on a pretext, rather than shake hands with "the sidin'," but afterward he quoted Dilys about the gold panning.

Dilys came by regularly after that and soon others came from the siding with him. Women began coming regularly, too, and children with them. They came because their men were at Bissets', and because they were ashamed of coming empty-handed, they brought with them what they could. Sometimes there was canned fruit and popskull, sometimes dried-nettle soup and bark tea.

"Party every afternoon, every evenin'!" Ralph complained. "Man can't find his way to his own kitchen for a cup of coffee to sit quiet and think anymore. Women and kids fillin' up the kitchen, men and boys in the front room. I thought the Elks club was in town. You ought to call yourself a lodge hall and collect membership dues! Man's got to go to his barn to get a little quiet!"

Yet, it was Charlie who noticed and reported gleefully to Edgar that the old man never did go to the barn or even upstairs to his room when people came. As for noise, there wasn't too much of that. People came to sit quietly and draw their meager comfort from Edgar's presence alone. There wasn't enough food for the expense of energy. People didn't even argue politics anymore. Sometimes it was only a whispered recital of grief, testimony to be given.

One day Joe Kornarens came by. He stood in the dust at the bottom of the front-porch steps and looked up into the row of faces of the men sitting on the porch in the November sun. He had a posthole shovel that he said he was bringing back, borrowed so long ago old Edgar probably didn't even remember lending it. People sat up; the chairs back-tilted against the wall came straight. Edgar, who had been inside, came to the door and then went quickly down the steps, greeting Joe and smiling. On the porch, the row was poised for trouble. The two men shook hands shyly and then Edgar took Joe by the arm.

"Come on up and sit awhile. We don't have no coffee, but there is some pie or somethin' back in the kitchen and the women have tea up—"

"Oh, no, I didn't aim to stay—I—couldn't we walk somewhere—I got things to say."

"Sure," Edgar said, and, putting his hands in his pockets, began to stroll toward the barn. "Let's get that shovel put away."

"I been smellin' snow at night, lately," Joe said after a time. "I think we're goin' to have winter early this year." Edgar nodded. "Of course, like it's been," Joe went on, "it don't matter when the winter comes or the spring or anythin' else." He turned slightly and gestured to where their tracks followed them in the sand like little wells that sifted and filled slightly with a draining in of sand. "I come to tell you I been a fool," Joe said. "Lay it to whatever you want—drinkin' or the drought, or the tractor fumes, or whatever."

Edgar was embarrassed. "Hey, Joe," he said, "remember what the old men used to say—that farmers lost their good sense because they followed the mules and breathed mule farts all day? Now we have tractor fumes to breathe. We're comin' up in the world, Joe, there ain't no doubt of it."

"I'm not kiddin', Edgar," Joe said. "I feel bad about—well, about everything."

"We're kin, Joe, and all the rest is just—just fumes." He laughed.

Joe looked out over the place. "I ain't been here since— well, for a long time. It's worse here even than it is on my place. Like a desert." And he shook his head.

"I guess it must seem like that," Edgar said, "like there won't never be nothin' growin' on it, that it won't never be rich as it was before. Still—" and he smiled at Joe, "it's ours. We're still here, you and me, and we still have the land and we still have each other."

"Ed," Joe said slowly, "I never told you thanks for the way you been to Andy all these years—things you done since he was little—how you talked to him when he was eighteen and we wasn't gettin' on good, the work you give him last year— God knows where you got the money to pay him—"

"Joe, for God sakes, don't thank me. I done them things

because I liked doin' 'em. He's a good man and he's kin. I thank you for givin' me the chance."

"In all my troubles—the dust, and other things—I didn't take the time I should have. Andy's a grown man now and I don't think of him but as just a boy, still. Because of all this trouble he ain't never come forward like he should have done—he's always been quiet, standin' in the background, waitin'."

"It's been like that for all of us, one way or another," Edgar said quietly, "but it's over, Joe, the drought is over." Then Edgar told Joe about the Presence.

Joe sighed deeply. "Brother-in-law, you must be plumb out of your head." He looked at Edgar, half smiling and shaking his head. "God told him. God ain't told the preachers or the government yet, but He told my brother-in-law."

Edgar said quietly, "*You* seen the cat-burr. You told me about it. We don't notice the water, but it's there, far down, it's there."

Joe gestured hopelessly. It saddened Edgar to see Joe thinking he couldn't talk sense to someone so removed, so God-struck. Joe had turned and was walking away. Edgar followed him back to the house.

"My Lord?"

"Don't worry," came the wordless words in the ringing silence. "He will be all the more glad. You will know great joy. You will all know great joy."

April 1939 is the time given by most sources for the beginning of the dancing. Talk through the winter had been full of despair, and in March the winds had begun again, darkening to midnight the Colorado noons with Texas dust. Edgar watched and waited, with a slow smile. One April evening at the house, old man Linthicum had burst into sobs as his foot grated on the dust which had blown in since the last sweeping. Then Edgar told him about the message of the Presence. The old man said he would as soon believe God as Democrats, Mr. Roosevelt included. Edgar spoke quietly of what had happened to him, of his years of silence unlocked, ended, opened, of the flooding into his senses of the wonderful, terrible glory of the Presence and the proofs of the holiness of life. He didn't exhort or preach, only told them with quiet eloquence. Once he wept, telling them simply that he did not know why he should have been rained upon with this gift while others, greater in every way, had been left parched and starving to winter in the desert and the death of hope.

"I asked Him, 'Lord, why was it me? Dilys has suffered more, Joe has more to bear—' and all of you—my neighbors —He knows you all, He loves you all, He told me so. . . ."

"What did He say then? How did He answer?"

"He wasn't angry, but it was like He was sayin', 'Don't stand in My light, don't dare to stand *before* them.' I ain't to bring no messages from the Lord."

"Then what's the use of it?" Linthicum muttered.

"He's tellin' you to go to Him yourselves, to ask Him *yourselves*. When I said again, 'Why me, Lord?' it was like as if He said, 'Is every man the same? Don't I love your differences? Didn't I make you different, every one?' "

As they sat, weighing the words, there was a sound on the roof. It sounded as though many small birds had come down to rest there, signing their bird-foot names with small scratchings on the shingles. Linthicum's head went back, left side up, his better ear straining to catch something. Charlie Dace heard it too, and went for the door. Unable to see anything, he opened it and went out. There was a sudden stillness throughout the house. They heard his tread over the sandscoured porch and down the steps, one, two, three. A fresh breeze had blown in through the house. It smelled of soil and, as Edgar thought, of the sharpness of stars. He spoke quietly, but his voice carried. "He has said Amen. The Lord has said Amen to us."

A woman bolted in from the back of the house. "Thanks be to Jesus," she cried. "It's rainin'! Look here on my hair—it's the rain!" Charlie came back, his steps as slow coming as they had been going. There was no need to tell them by then. A hard, healthy rain was falling straight down. In a sure knowledge of his own, Charlie went to the kerosene lamp and turned it out. Sitting down silently in the dark, some of the men found themselves weeping. Many closed their eyes and gave themselves up to the sound, the comforting, lulling, easeful sound of the rain.

After a while Dilys said, "It's rained before. Last year about this time—"

"Hush, son," Linthicum said. "Them little rains was over in ten minutes."

"And maybe this one will be and by tomorrow like it never had rained at all. I seen that, too, out here."

"Ain't you got no faith?" a neighbor said.

There was a long silence and then Dilys's voice, broken-sounding and young as a boy, "You don't none of you understand what it's like, bein' throwed off land where your ma and pa is buried and your baby sister and every dog you ever had. There ain't nothin' to have faith *with*."

There was a noise outside, a rattling up the steps, and in the door, a big man with a lantern, looking grimly from under his hat. "What's everybody doin' sittin' up in the dark?" It was Joe Kornarens. "Where's my brother-in-law?"

"Just quiet here, listenin' to the rain, Joe." Edgar spoke from a corner, walled off by a settee.

"Edgar," Joe said, in something like anger, "I come to tell you how things are now. God told you, man, He must have! Forgive me for doubtin' your word and please, for God sake, come help me get the lake out of my yard!"

A great whoop went up and then laughter no one wanted to stop.

Accounts differ as to exactly how the dancing started. Some say it was a spontaneous, sudden surging down the steps and into what was by then a gumbo mud. The mud took their shoes and weighted their clothes, but still they danced. Others say that the group that started over to Joe's began it, leaping and capering on the eroding rises and hollows of the land, dancing for joy because water never had stayed as it was staying on Joe's place. It was a sign, something that had not happened in any rain or thaw for a decade.

Blown dust had fouled all of Joe's pumps, and people went back to older ways—neighbors and buckets. Some did not bail at all, but threw themselves into the mud and wept for joy in it. In whatever form it began, people remembered the dancing. Later, there would be more dances, bigger ones, with formal steps and prayers, but the first image, the ikon picture, would be a group of people gaunt with poverty, so thin with hunger and hard times that they all looked the same, so covered with mud that they had no other color. And how they danced! Hands uplifted, faces uplifted, mouths open to bless the Lord and receive the sacramental rain, their tattered clothes like banners, their spirits like fiery angels, one leg buried to the calf in mud, the other held high, freed of the earth and all despair. Later there would be pictures of that dancing, formal, hieratic, with churches in the background. The men would come to be great figures with long prophetic beards, wearing outlandish clothes such as must have been worn in those olden times.

8

That February and March, a hundred towns in Kansas, Oklahoma, and eastern Colorado were ill with drought, dust, wind, and erosion, but death had gone. In the spring, the purple season, the high-plains wild flowers, lying close, misted the blown sand. Then came the yellow, in its old order, and then the gray-greens of wild grasses and grains. Dilys and his family, at Edgar's suggestion, squatted in what was left of the Durgan place down the road. When they left the siding there was a little party for them at Bissets' and neighbors pledged support in case of trouble with the law. After that, Edgar saw Dilys in town now and then but not back at the house. There were few people coming to the house in the evenings since the heavy rain. People were busy. There was work to do. The people came instead on Sunday, after church, dressed in church clothes, like people on a formal visit, and because of their clothes they didn't want to sit on the floor. They came with questions which left Edgar gaping. The knowledge of his talks with God had gone out all over the county. It hadn't been Linthicum or Dilys or others of the Rain-Dance, Mud-Dance night. It was Joe Kornarens mostly whose ways had returned to their old openness and whose manner was hearty again, now that there were 680 acres against which he could pit himself, thank God. In town, Joe brought his goods and shook his head and said:

"Pointed at the boy's pants and said, 'There's cat-burr, Joe, the worst is over.' But it wasn't only the cat-burr, it was the hand of God and it was the voice of God he's been hearin' all along. Edgar talks to God, talks to him like you would to your own pa. I seen him walkin' along down by the draw, walkin' easy like you do with a friend, hands were in his pockets and sometimes he was smilin'. He wasn't so took up that he was in some kind of religious fit like you hear of. Nothin' like that, only walkin' easy, so easy and so happy, I knew he was talkin' with God."

And so people began to come on Sundays and to ask Edgar all kinds of things concerning the Lord.

"Edgar, you said it wasn't our sins done this to us, this Depression and the damn dust. What was it then?"

"I don't know."

"Edgar, in the Bible it says, 'Ye shall not suffer a witch to live,' but then don't that mean that witches are real?"

"I don't know, I never seen none."

"Edgar, since Melora lost that second baby of ours, there ain't no kind of life in the house. She sets up all night and I hear her cryin'—"

"How long is it, John, since the baby died?"

"It's been a month. She took the first one easier."

"Tell me, John, what would you rather have, Melora cryin' and grievin' or Melora goin' on pleasant and careless, actin' like it didn't matter?"

"Well, everybody grieves—"

"I'm askin' you, would you have it any other way?"

"No, well, I guess not."

"Go somewhere yourself then, and cry, go out and set down on a ball-cactus and let it hurt you till your eyes water, and then cry. Cry with Melora and ask the Lord to help you. He can make stones weep. He can ease us, when nothin' else can."

"Edgar, is there a heaven?"

"Yes."

"What's in it?"

"For me, I think, hard work, back-breakin', tearin' work, and then rest, pains that end, wrongs that are put right. It seems to me like there would be music. I think there must be music all the time, and Him. Never away, never separated one minute, rooted in every part of us, seen clear, seen whole. Heaven must be growin' up and up to see more of the whole thing, ourselves and each other and Him. And lots of part-singin', only the sopranos won't ever be shrieky or the tenors thin, like some choirs I could name. In heaven there's got to be lots of dancin' and singin' and runnin' for joy!"

"Edgar, how come you never mention Jesus?"

"I don't know, Ollie."

"But, Mr. Bisset, the Bible speaks of Jesus as the Son of God."

"Yes, that's so, but we are all that, and so are all men and all women and children."

"What about children, Mr. Bisset, are children specially blessed?"

"I don't know, but from what I see around here, I don't think so. Seems to me like old folks see the Lord more clearly than kids do."

"Then the Lord says—"

"No, I never talked with Him about that, Herb. I ask much less than I praise. I suppose it's a fault, but I can't help it."

"But He would want you to think right, He would tell you what to think."

"Oh, no, I don't believe the Lord is that—that arrogant."

"Then what is He tryin' to tell us?"

"I don't know, Harvey, but one of the things He shows me is that He thinks life is a hard force and He don't seem to want to use force outside of our own laws. In the old times He commanded, and maybe He knows that now we ain't good enough to be commanded, so He just talks to us. Now, for the love of mike, don't ask me any more. I ain't writin' no new Bible. I ain't settin' up no Word, I ain't no more apostle than anyone else, 'cause we are all apostles, everyone is an apostle of His Word!"

"But how do you explain—"

"Go ask Him; I told you, go ask Him yourself!"

All winter, Sunday after Sunday, neighbors and strangers, town and farm.

"How do you know it is God and not the Devil talkin' to you?"

"I never seen the Devil."

"Didn't you ask Him who He was?"

"Wasn't no need. We seemed to know each other's name without any trouble. A person ain't usually introduced to his own father, is he?"

"But what if it was really the Devil?"

"If it's the Devil—well, the Devil ain't as big as the Lord. He couldn't fill up all the space inside a man, could he?"

"But what if it is the Devil?"

"A devil couldn't inspire so much love. It would unman him." He had tried his best, but they were embarrassed for him, his crudity and that he did not talk like the Bible and that he had no message for them, except that the Presence existed in eastern Colorado as far as the eye could see and forever throughout the universe. Always, Charlie Dace stood by and listened and when people left more hungry than they had come for whatever wisdom Edgar had, Charlie would offer his clumsy comfort.

"Them people couldn't tell an honest man from wet manure·"

"Oh, Charlie, why ain't it in me to show them, to show them the glory?"

"You told 'em where it was. Ain't the glory God's to give?"

"And I sounded stupid trying to answer them questions."

"Which questions are you thinkin' about?"

"All of 'em. Dear God, when Showacre's son come in with that baby of his and asked me why God let it be born wrong, what could I tell him? What did he want from me?"

"Wasn't nothin' wrong with the answer you give him, that it wasn't no sin of his or his wife's and that meant he couldn't blame himself for it, nor her; that he had been gave that piece of land as a gift and to go back and farm it the best way he knew—"

"And he set there and took it like the Word of God. People keep askin' why is there evil in the world, but never why is there good, which is the real miracle, which is what they should be seein' now in everything, or the hell we all been through ain't for nothin' but to forget the minute it's over—"

"People have to forget their pain, Ed, or they couldn't stay alive."

"I forgot my ma, Charlie, and lived to regret it. Forgettin' must be some kind of sin because it kills the gratitude along with the pain."

"Remember, you don't owe 'em holy wisdom or even your own. I give 'em coffee and they can set dozin' in the sun or in the shade, whichever they want, and that's all they can expect."

"Your coffee ain't that good," Edgar said, and they laughed and then sat looking out over the healing land.

They were used to seeing Andy come up the steps with a basket in his hand. Joe's sister Frieda was running the house, and since Joe's change of heart, hardly a week went by that Ralph's womanless house didn't get a basket of tea rolls, or a pan of cabbage stuffed with sausage, a chunk of venison, or a jar of relish.

"It's like a poor-folks' Christmas!" Ralph complained, and then he would overcook the venison. This time Andy came in from the chilly night and put the jar of pickled tomatoes down on the table in a way that showed he had come with other business on his mind.

He was a handsome man now, compact, with electric blue eyes and Tempe's thick black hair. Except for his eyes, which were like Joe's in color, there was very little of Joe in his looks. Since the age of nineteen or twenty Andy had caused a lot of seat shuffling in church. Girls arranged and re-arranged themselves with the purpose of sitting near him. His very quietness and reserve seemed to make them more eager. Now, at twenty-three, he was no more serious about settling down than he had been at eighteen, but the girls were. They also came to Bissets' on Sunday afternoons when Andy was likely to be there. It made Edgar smile to see them watching one another. Perhaps it was about a girl.

"How's things at home?" Edgar asked, and pulled out the kitchen chair for Andy to sit on.

"They're fine," Andy said absently, and then, "I'm here about something—a problem."

"Then I guess you'd better tell me what it is." And Edgar sat down on a chair that sighed resignedly under his weight.

There was quiet for a time while Andy got his words ready. Charlie had gone to sit in the cold front room until he was called, and Ralph was out in the barn with the last chores. The stillness made Edgar remember the vast and awful silence in which he had spent his childhood and youth, "souring," but the memory was still painful to him. Edgar sighed quietly. The chair groaned. If only there could be the same wordless flight into knowledge with people he loved that he had with the Presence. The Lord gave his Presence immediately and untranslatably. With this beloved nephew there was just the stillness and the dry chair sighing.

"It's about the service," the boy said, "about me goin' away and goin' into the service."

A sudden, blind cry of protest sounded in Edgar's mind. He took in his breath quickly and let it out slowly, repeating to himself the words of the Presence, "the hand to the plough, the plough to the field"—one thing at a time, forcing himself to stop all the words of defense, anger, impatience. He made his face neutral. He said nothing. Andy was looking at him and smiling.

"I'm glad I come to you; Pa would be stampin' and fussin' by now, but you just let the words rest quiet."

Edgar fought a desire to yell, "Is that false dream to go on forever!" After a moment when he hoped he might speak evenly, he said, "Have you prayed about this?"

"No, sir."

"Why not?"

"I don't know how."

"How you do it ain't as important as what you say. Do you want to try it together?" Andy looked stricken. "I don't mean like church, I mean that we'll both close our eyes and sit very still and listen for our needs and His answer."

They sat. Edgar could feel Andy fighting with his embarrassment and self-consciousness. His eyes were squeezed shut as though in pain, his hands gripping his knees.

"Sit easy," Edgar whispered. "You ain't hunting Him down like He was Jesse James. The Lord ain't blind in the dark. . . ." Andy settled a little and Edgar began again. His prayer begged the Presence to ease the pain of his love. It was this pain that made him want to cry out, to plead with Andy, Stay and be safe. He had seen the effects of such pain many times in many people but he had not endured it himself since the day he heard of Tempe's death.

The door opened. "What the hell are you two doin' sittin' there in the dark?" It was Ralph, in from the barn, fearful behind his clatter. "Ed, pull that chair in, I almost stumbled over the damned thing." Beside him, Andy sighed and stood up.

"I just came by to see Uncle Edgar, Grandpa, only for a minute."

"What's your hurry? You folks got your alfalfa in?"

"Yes, sir, and the broom, too. I should get back, though. Pa wants—" But the old man wouldn't let him go, and Edgar was relieved. He hadn't spoken or received from the Presence any word which he could give to Andy, nor was there any ease for himself.

"Hey!" the old man cried. "Ain't there no hot coffee left for the boy, walked all the way over here in the cold?"

So nothing would do but that they have coffee and some of the old man's leaden cookies. Ralph, who was never voluble when it was needed, talked for half an hour straight on weather, prices, and work. As Andy sat by in silence, Edgar had a chance to look at him, to study him in the light. It wasn't ridiculous after all, his wanting to go into the service. Somewhere between baling and bucking, as they said, he had grown up without informing them. Of course he would want to reach beyond the farm a little. Joe needed him, and the farm was to be his, but the dust had taken his youth, and now that the dust was over it was time for growing, changing, choosing.

Finally, Ralph was talked out and still nervous. He had stopped in the middle of a sentence.

"Grandpa," Andy said to him, "they're lettin' people into the Army now. Men are goin' all over the world and gettin' paid for it."

"You're twenty-three—you don't need to ask permission," Edgar said.

"Oh, that's a bunch of garbage!" the old man cried. "Your

job is to stay here and help get the wheat grown. Your uncle, here, went in the Army and it didn't do him no good at all." In spite of themselves, Edgar and Andy smiled at that. Andy opened his mouth to say something and then thought better of it.

After a few moments he said quietly, "I know I don't need permission. I want to do this right, to have you understand, you and Pa and Grandpa; to know that I am not quitting the farm or giving it up, or going away for good. I want to go with your good feelings and I want to send money back to help out until I come back to take up again."

How like Tempe he was, Edgar thought. Raised by Joe (foot through the wall and call it a door), and here he was, making reason come gentling down on them all, Tempe's way, and Tempe dead long before he could have learned her way. It was a sign of the mercy of God.

The old man raged and stamped, and Andy stood and waited. Charlie, standing by, watched them quizzically. Once or twice he caught Edgar's eye and, knowing that he could not help, looked away again. "Do you want us to be with you when you talk to your pa?" Edgar asked.

"No, it wouldn't be right to do that—it would hurt him too much, but after I tell him, I know he'll come here to talk about it with you. If you could only help him to see that it's nothing I'm doing against him or his way—"

"Will you do something for me?"

"Sure, Uncle Edgar, anything."

"Will you ask the Lord, let Him hear all your reasons, and wait for his answer?"

"I will."

"And beg his leave, not ours."

"I will."

Andy nodded, thanked them all with a kind of touching formality, and then took his hat and left. Ralph Bisset turned to his son:

"You're about as smart as a blind dog in a slaughterhouse. What did you say *that* for?"

"Pa, he wouldn't have listened to us. Maybe he'll listen to the Lord."

"And what help'll that be?"

"Maybe the Lord will tell him *no*."

"Oh, shit!" the old man said and stamped off.

Andrew Kornarens joined the Navy, as inland men are likely to do. His joining started a small trend in the towns around and the young men who had heard Edgar's cry asked the Lord what they should do. To most, He answered, "go," and they were not surprised. Andy was sent to California for training. He wrote noncommittally about boot camp and ecstatically about the land and the sea and the orchards and farms he had been able to see as he traveled between cities on his brief leaves. At first, he was assigned duty ashore at San Diego, and he sent picture postcards from there with scenes of the city, the farms, orchards, and the sea. Joe would bring the cards to Edgar, and he and all the Sunday guests would pore over them, studying, and arguing over details, marking with their blunted and cracked fingernails this or that feature.

"Look there, John, at the ground under this here tree. It's almost black. Do you reckon that's real or just the picture?"

"The photograph makes it look like that, don't it?"

"You reckon they color up these pictures an' make 'em look better?"

"I sure ain't never seen ground like that."

"And will you look at them trees!"

"That's 'cause the land is so rich they can plant 'em that close together."

When Andy was sent to Hawaii, the cards became brighter than ever, until they seemed not of this world at all. Joe said, "My mailbox has started to be a kind of dream machine. Every week or so I open it up and there's a brown woman in a grass dress or an island full of sand and palm trees just like in a movie—things better than movies—big waterfalls, and volcanoes, and stuff growin' so thick you got to beat it off with a sickle, else it'll grow up over your house!"

Joe came up almost every week. Edgar knew he would not come unless he had some particular reason, and Andy's cards gave him the reason he needed. Sunday, being the day of rest and visiting, he didn't feel that it lowered him to be away from the farm. The dust had done strange things to all of them. Some of those who had been dispossessed kept on moving, unable to root themselves again. Some of the men who had stayed were almost fanatic about their farms, keeping to their places as though in a day's absence the land would go back to desert again, the well foul, the cattle die. Joe's visits were routine now and people were comforted by the expected and dependable.

Because his boy was away, in the mythical lands of palm trees and coconuts, Joe found himself listening more to the news and weather reports concerning places outside the country. Because of this, Edgar and Ralph and Charlie got the news from Joe, who rode his car off the road and into Edgar's front yard on December 7, 1941, that the dream islands had been given over to nightmare.

There had been one last card, sent before the seventh, and then a long silence from Andy. They waited, caught in the tornado eye, while everything around them speeded up. There was no longer time for the old ways of long talk and slow decisions. It was all fear and wondering what would happen and people leaving for the cities and the war.

"I pity the Presence," Edgar said to Charlie. "All the prayers that used to be made by the season are made by the minute now. People are gabblin' like chickens."

Once, seeing Edgar alone and distant on the cold porch, Charlie came up to him and asked, "You been prayin' about Andy?"

"No—" And there was a moment when Edgar's voice was too husky to use. "I don't tell that to Joe, of course. He thinks I have some special line to the Lord and when he asked me did I pray about Andy, I couldn't tell him no—I let him believe I prayed for Andy all the time. I can't, Charlie, I just can't. The Lord will try to spare anyone He can, but how can I ask Him to go against the laws He made Himself? Bombs fall and where they fall the people die. Bullets and guns have the laws we made using His laws. Could I dare to ask the Presence to make time stop, or gravity go backwards, even for Tempe's boy?"

"What do you do, then? Do you pray at all?"

"Oh, I have to pray—you know that. I pray for us—just that He remembers us, all of us, on both sides of the fightin', as we were at the best times of our lives, and that those times make Him glad He made us."

"Both sides?" Charlie whispered. "*Both sides?* Them bastards started this war!"

"I didn't say *I* had to love 'em. I only talk to Him about his rememberin' his people. All of 'em."

"I never figured how deep a man could grow out here where there ain't water for shallow-rooted things," Charlie said. "I only hope to hell you don't go givin' them facts all around the neighborhood."

"I love God, Charlie, but that don't mean I'm a fool!"

At the end of the silence the Navy informed Joe that his son had been taken prisoner at a place that was unpronounceable to them. Edgar was afraid that Joe would blame him, then, for Andy's having gone into the Navy, or for the Lord's answer, a blasphemy that made him shudder. The worry was unfounded. Joe bore the news with stoic calm. Joe rested in the Lord, who had since declared the Japanese His enemy and who was only readying His arm against them.

People began to come to Edgar about family things. Their pains were no longer suffered for the land or the specter of starvation. Now the rains were even and well-placed and the crops came, loading every bin and silo, but the boys were away at war and the girls at war plants in Denver and Pueblo, and one heartsickness was traded for another.

"Is this a righteous war?"

"I think it is."

"Then the people who fight in it must be righteous."

"I don't know about that. They'll have good and bad choices to make no matter what the war is. . . . In the war I had, there were evil things done in the midst of good and good things done in the midst of evil. . . . War is always terrible . . . a terrible thing. . . ."

"How does the Lord judge it?"

"Ask Him, Duane, not me. He understands, not me. He loves and knows all things, not me. Not me."

"A boy sixteen, Edgar, and he could have stayed here like the government's been urgin' 'em, stay back on the farm, but he asked the Lord, like you said, and the Lord said to him, 'Go on,' and he went and lied about his age and got in service, and he wasn't but a week over there and he was killed."

"What do you want me to tell you, Rod?"

"I'm meaning to ask you if, after that, if the Lord has any mercy. . . ."

"It wasn't the Lord that killed him, Rod, it was a man like you and me, a man who could kill in blindness and ignorance without knowin' who the other man was or what his value was, or how awful the waste and pain was of what he was doin'."

"Edgar, you can't let all them people get you down so much."

"Hell, Charlie, what was I goin' to say to poor Rod, tell him it wasn't the Presence speaking to his son, but the boy's own wants roarin' in his ears?"

"You surprise me all the time." And Charlie looked quietly at Edgar.

"You didn't think I knew that could happen? That a man's own wishes could sing him lullabies? I'm gonna tell you about a vision, Charlie, and I know you'll hear it like it's meant to be heard. I was walkin' by the new flat, that kind of sandy flat the old creek left. And I seen a cottonwood growin' there, and I figured there was still water nearby, and sure enough there's a little spring or two there, just small ones comin' up like little fingers that sort out the sand and sift it a little to make a pool no bigger than the space a dog lies down in. It flows maybe three or four feet and then dries back into the ground. I got keen for a drink of that clear water and I went up to it, and the Voice of the goodness of the Presence said to me, 'Look there,' and caused me to look into the pool, and what I seen was like a miracle."

"What was it?"

"I seen the cottonwood, but with the sun through the leaves it made 'em look like church windows, only movin', and over the tree was clouds, white clouds, and the sky quiverin' like music. The Voice of the Presence said, 'Look closer,' and I did, until my face was up close and then so close there was nothin' else but my own face takin' up all the pond. I seen the message there as it was meant for me to see. The more I moved my will forward, the less place there was for anything else. The Presence ain't a liar, and He don't get boys to fool themselves. That boy was lookin' at his own face, readin' his own words, not the Lord's, yet what am I goin' to tell that grievin' man—that his boy lied to himself and was a fool in the bargain?"

"You're a smarter man than I give you credit for," Charlie said slowly.

"Ain't everybody?" Edgar laughed and nudged Charlie with his elbow.

"No," Charlie said, "not everybody."

It was a day in early spring. The April snows had evaporated except for patches on the slight northward falls of the land. Edgar was dressing the ground for a grass crop, a new strain. He saw a car on the road and sat up tall to watch if it would go by, but it turned into the Bisset place, so he groaned and headed back, arguing with himself. Why not let the old man handle whatever it was, or Charlie? It was always for him, and sorrow more than likely, and someone in bitterness accusing the everlasting mercy of God.

"Lord," he cried from the height of his tractor, "pass a miracle and ready my ground while I am gone!" The laughter came back to him before his words were finished.

"I am readying all the grasses. You do the ground and I'll do the seed."

The man had gone into the house. Edgar did not recognize the car, a Chevy with a B sticker on the windshield. When he went in, he was surprised to see that it was the Reverend Hummel. Edgar greeted him, and the pastor smiled at his slight hesitation.

"It's such a beautiful day, I've been dreaming up reasons for calls out of town." They smiled politely. Reverend Hummel was not a dreamer.

"Would you like to go out on the porch, Reverend?" the old man asked. "Or would that be too cold?"

"I'm afraid it might be," the minister said. He was a deliberate man, his speech slower and more measured than Roosevelt's, so that in town they joked about a conversation between the two of them on the party line. "What I need is some exercise, a walk, if Edgar here would take me around to your back pasture. I once saw some currant bushes there, and I'd like to dig one or two of 'em, if you don't need them."

For a moment Edgar saw a flash of play in Charlie Dace's expression, then his face changed quickly and Charlie said, "I'll take the tractor, Ed, if you give me the keys." Edgar threw them to Charlie, who caught them, and with the same gesture tipped his hat to the minister and went out the back door. The old man, after four or five excuses, muttered, "Whatever did I let you give them keys to Charlie for? You know he goes nuts on a tractor—just like a kid—" and he strode away toward the barn to find Charlie.

"Do you have a shovel and something to hold the plants?" Edgar asked.

"In the car." They went out to the Chevy.

"Enough of a walk when we get there."

"Yes," the minister said, and they got in together, but not like fishermen, or hunters, or friends going together to dig currant vines. After the lumpy drive, they walked from the back road to the dry wash, ducking through a culvert where some snow still lingered. The currant canes stood stark and dead-looking in the late winter light, but down in the draw it seemed warmer because the place was protected from the wind. When he parted the canes carefully Edgar saw that there was new green under the barky covering and green leaf shoots close to the ground. In the soft sand the digging went fast. Edgar saw the pastor looking at him in a quietly appraising way, but there was nothing to do but wait for him to speak. The earth all fell away from one plant and the net of roots hung weighted with new white shoots.

"You'll have to get that to water pretty fast," Edgar murmured, "before it dries up on you." The older man almost shrugged. He got three plants and then put the shovel upright in the sand, looking around, suddenly embarrassed because he wanted to sit down and there was no place warm or dry.

"Do you want to go back to the car now?"

"No," Edgar said, "I think I know the place you want. Come up the gully a little." They walked beyond the bend in the gully where Edgar remembered the two boulders, water-worn and out of the wind. They sat down on these, facing each other.

"I don't quite know how to start," the minister said. "No other kind of church work prepares a man for this."

Edgar was struck with a quick fear. "You're not trying to tell me somethin' about Andy? They would have told us first if it was Andy—"

"Oh, no, no!" And the man leaned forward and put a hand on Edgar's arm. "Please forgive me; it isn't about Andy at all. I'm doing this all wrong. It's about you."

"Me?"

"You know, don't you, that Mr. Linthicum and the two Empey boys and Joe Kornarens and Dilys Carbert have been planning to set up a meeting?"

"I don't understand."

"They're planning to leave the church and start a congregation of their own."

Edgar put back his head and began to laugh. It was a hearty, long laugh, one that resounded from the edges of the gully and broke at their feet on the noncommittal stones. "Edgar, I'm serious!" the pastor cried. Edgar shook his head hard and tried to stop.

"I'm sorry, Reverend, I had a thought of them four birds sittin' up there singin' 'From the Fount of Every Blessing' all by themselves, and how it would dry up every cow in the state and spook Taylor's turkeys clean out of their heads." And he laughed some more. "There never was four men for

singin' flat like them four. I tell you, they're a matched set."
He wiped his eyes and nose on his sleeve.

"Beg pardon, Reverend, I guess it's been a while since I laughed so hard. Have the four of 'em been blowin' hot air and someone picked up the words and went and told you?"

"This is not an idle thing, Edgar," the minister said.

"Well, Reverend, I'm sorry it got you upset."

"When are you going to call me John?"

"John, it's only silly talk. The Empey boys are restless stayin' home from the war. Old man Linthicum has never been pleased with nothin' thought up after William Howard Taft, and Dilys has put on a little flesh since the drought. I guess he wants to forget being left out so much when he lived at the sidin'. All the other sidin' men went off to Denver, and now he's gotten to be so solid in the community, I guess he's figured it's time to take on some airs."

"And Joe Kornarens?"

"Maybe he thinks he owes it to his old ma, now she's dead. She always wanted to do things like the Pentecostals did 'em—"

"These reasons seem to come easy to you," the pastor said.

Edgar laughed again. "It comes from knowin' everybody for so long. I guess they change less than they think."

Mr. Hummel looked hard at Edgar. "Then it wasn't your idea, the new church?"

"My idea—I think it's plain foolishness. We have six churches already, and we need another one like a drought needs sand."

"You know about the dance-prayers, don't you?"

"What dance-prayers? John, does this have to do with me?" His words sounded loud in the gully.

"They pray and then a vision comes to one or another of them and he tells the others what the Spirit has said. They pray outside, and they have a kind of dance they do, in a circle together, and then dancing faster and faster."

"What does that have to do with the church, with leaving the church?"

"I haven't been here long, as you know. It's been a little over two years, but people have been complaining that there hasn't been enough joy in our services, enough of the Holy Spirit. I've tried to get more hymns and get them sung with more brightness, but the service itself—well, there's the Order of Service and I can't change that."

"And Joe and Dilys and them, they want to break away?" Mr. Hummel nodded. "But why?"

"They say it was you who showed them the joy of the Lord."

"*In* everything," Edgar shouted, banging his big hand against the stone, "not apart from it, *in* it, sometimes in spite of it, not separate, not a church!"

"They've been having these dance-prayers for several months now, and you never knew?"

"I knew there was some kind of meeting to Praise. They asked me to come and I went once in the beginning, but people were comin' to the house so often in these months since—since—" he was suddenly shy and a little frightened, "since I seen things a new way—those times when they were away praisin'—I had those times to myself."

The minister smiled slightly. "You're not a saint after all," he said.

Edgar rocked backward, laughing. "Someone told you and spoiled the fun. I guess I've been careless about you, John, with all the people comin'. I didn't take the time to let you know how I felt. Say, John, is your hind end as cold as mine, sittin' here on these boulders? Let's walk a ways."

They rose and started slowly up the draw, following its switchbacks.

"They're a bunch of jackasses, and I'll tell 'em so," Edgar said.

"Maybe not so frankly."

"What's it to be if it's not frank! John, what they're doin' has nothin' to do with me, but if anybody askes me what I think, I'll tell 'em that leavin' the church is pure vain foolishness."

The minister bent and picked up a smooth, striped pebble from the sandy wash. "You know, when I first came here, I thought this place was the end of the world—a flat, bare, plains place, gray-brown in summer, gray-white in winter, and a stranger to spring and fall. A treeless, featureless, humorless place—"

"With the people as flat as the land—"

"Now that you mention it."

"And have you changed any?"

"A man's eyes adjust," Hummel said, and smiled. "I guess his spirit adjusts, too. In the time I've been here, the range of it all has opened wider than I could have dreamed. Shadows, for instance. On no other landscape I've ever seen are shadows so much a part of substance. In no other place is the color of light so rich or so varied."

"And the people?"

"I came after the worst of the dust, but the black dust and the red dust were still banking against the barns. Being young, I guess I thought despair had to be loud, and that joy had to be a kind of Sunday jubilee."

Edgar laughed. "Pastor, you're talkin' about the weight of this gift of mine—that because of a light, people don't think I should suffer darkness as uneasily as the next guy. They want me to be better than a man can be."

"And you, yourself?"

Edgar bent down and picked up a pebble and flipped it at the minister. "Stone the pastor because he knows too much."

They became conscious of the cold almost at the same time. The soft sunshine had gone. Edgar moved for warmth inside his work jacket.

"In this land it's hard as hell to believe in a God of law. The earth can flood, then dry to bone in no time, go from crack-cold to a heat wave from dawn to noon. Maybe we look at it and see the Lord to be all impulse and no law, all feeling, rage or love, and no thought. When Reverend Hummel tells us to live godly lives, maybe we go home and beat our wives and put our fists through things." They were walking back faster, cold now, and surprised at how far up the wash they had gone. "The Voice of the Presence once showed me—do you mind me saying it—does it embarrass you to hear me talk about it?"

"No," the pastor said.

"It was as though the prayers and the prohibitions were dark things, thick, heavy, bitter things, and the glory, a kind of whiteness, something light and sweet. The Presence showed me—tried to show me—that I should live each one fully, but with the flavor of the other in my mouth." They came in sight of the car, at last.

"And Lord, what this land does to a fine machine!" the pastor said. "Why, it's tearable," mocking the accent of the parish, which he did not realize he was slowly acquiring himself. They got in, grateful for the warmth of the car.

"Pastor, you've made a big mistake. Runnin' me home at just this time, you're sure to be asked to lunch, and but for the coffee, which Charlie makes, the food is pretty bad."

"Maybe a little heavy?"

"You don't understand how food could be heavy and flat at the same time," and he grinned at the minister, "like the people."

"If you knew, Charlie, why didn't you tell me?"

"I was waitin' for them to tell you. I thought it might be one of them big ideas that never gets anywhere, just talk."

"Why do I feel so angry, like I've been betrayed? I've listened to them all, and that's my trouble. People askin' my advice, comin' to me. I've taken on like some kind of minister or other. Church of the Nine Day Wonder, Church of the Holy Howling Humbug. It makes me scared, Charlie."

"Why?"

"Because what the Presence gives, He gives straight on. He never said to me, Go start a church and speak in My name."

"What if you did start a church? Not that I would join it—churches give me the dumb-fidgets."

"Start a church? With what? I wasn't asked to start a church and the Presence has given me nothin' to use, not wisdom or deep talk, or a flowin' beard. All I have is us, what's between us, the Presence and me, and what's been given can be dried up, pulled away, nothin' left but a sand rill to mark where sweet water once flowed. I couldn't stand that happenin'."

"Is that the way the Presence treats his own?"

"Maybe. I don't aim to play with it."

"You aim to go up there to Joe's back pasture with a holy shotgun and pepper their Christian breeches, not that it don't bear thinkin' about. What do you figure on doin'?"

"I figure on waitin' until tonight at nine or nine-thirty, unless there's bad news on the radio about the war." Grinning, he went off to claim the tractor from the old man.

Manure and white gypsum had been piled at the field side, and Edgar saw the old man with the spreader attachment coming down the row. He would load the spreader. It was heavy work for an old man. Waiting, he turned it over in his mind. The time he would be called would be nine-thirty, unless the war news was bad, and then it would be tomorrow early. Now exactly, how? He opened a bag of gypsum, grinning. The Hummels' neighbors were the Coopers, and they, no doubt, knew where the pastor had been this morning, and why. Because he had been successful, Mr. Hummel's mood would be good and his wife's mood usually mirrored his. The Coopers were close to the Heidenriches and she was Joe's sister, Frieda. With time out for lunch and doing up the dishes, the news should hit Frieda's by two o'clock and still be warm for Joe when he came in at five, since today was not his day in town. Joe would sit over it awhile, wondering. His new wife, Arla, was a capable woman. She would dissuade him from coming over right then. There was still a slight discomfort between the old brother-in-law and the new wife. Arla, a plains woman, as Tempe had been, was a woman to preach patience as one of the highest virtues. She would show Joe that he was not the one to go to Edgar. Old man Linthicum would be the one, or Dilys. Yes, Dilys was the one—there had been a special closeness for a while between Edgar and a brave, beaten Dilys, back before the war. Dilys had become a bit too keen on "betterment" since then, but there was still much sympathy between them and old man Linthicum was getting too cantankerous to listen to anyone these days. Dilys would come to see him tonight, maybe nine or nine-thirty.

The old man came up on the tractor. "What are you standin' there smilin' about?"

"What changes and what never changes," Edgar said, "and about you dyin' to know what the reverend wanted."

"I never said I was dyin' to know," the old man objected.

Edgar looked back over the track of the spreader. A third of the field was even and straight, the remainder hurried and out of line. "Pa, remember you used to tell me a man's furrow was a mark of his life?"

"Hell, that ain't now, that's when we used mules!"

"It was strange—it makes me shiver. I went up in your truck, Joe, since you have extra gas this month. There was only one light on in their parlor and Edgar couldn't have seen me. He was sittin' on the porch in the cold and I didn't see him there, and then his voice just said, 'Evenin', Dilys,' just like that. We went inside. I started to ask him how he knew it was me, but all he said was, 'We haven't seen you out here in a while, how've you been?' On the table they had a cup and saucer ready, and the can of evaporated milk was there, just like I take it. I was so spooked I could hardly drink the coffee, but afterwards Edgar said, 'Well, Dilys, when is the next meetin' for?' I started to tell him and he said, 'No, I don't mean the next meetin' to break with the church, I mean the next Praisin' Dance.' I told him next Tuesday night, eight o'clock, at your place, and he said, 'Am I welcome to come?' I said, 'Sure.' All the time I felt like he was lookin' down into my soul, and maybe a little sad for me. I asked him how he knew it was me come to see him, and he just laughed and said, 'I ain't nothin' but a big kid and couldn't help puttin' on a little.' "

The three men looked dignified, almost grave. It occurred to Edgar that they looked like elders already, or tried to. Had Joe ever been rash or fearful, the Empey boys no more than blurred combinations of their parents?

"Edgar, we've wanted to tell you all the while. What surprises me is that you don't jump for joy about it. This is your church, really. The beliefs and strength are yours."

Edgar laughed. "Just the time for me to raise my finger

like Moses in the picture book and say, 'The strength is the Lord's.' Whosever it is, it ain't mine. I never had one thought of leavin' the Methodist church. Ain't a Republican Methodist God good enough for you?"

"Blasphemin's no help, Edgar," Joe said primly.

"Was I blasphemin' the Lord? I had the feelin' my target was just a little lower. What got these doin's into your heads?"

"How could you think it was strange?" Joe said, grinding his fists as though to keep them from freezing up. "You know what church is like, you go every Sunday. Where's the glory in it, the rejoicin', the sense of the holiness? Reverend Hummel reads slow. We go through the creed and the hymn, the Bible lesson and the anthem, meditation and doxology, hymn, sermon, hymn, benediction, and out, and half of it's no better than a learned thing you can say in your sleep."

"You want me to argue with that? Why should I? The church is an anchor, a plow, plowin' the same field for a hundred different kinds of seeds. I'd preach a sermon myself, but you wouldn't want to hear it."

"Have you asked the Lord?" Sam Empey said with what might or might not have been simplicity.

"No."

"Well, why don't you ask Him the important things, the necessary things—"

"You mean, Sam, why doesn't He give me wiser messages, tell me wiser things?" Sam Empey had gone beyond himself and Joe was shocked. Edgar let his head go back in laughter. "Sam, I've asked the question myself, and the Presence answered it. What if He spoke great wisdom to me, would I know it? And if I recognized the wisdom, would I understand it?"

Joe, with a long, serious look, almost a stare, said, "We asked the Lord. We asked Him did He want us to leave the church, and He said 'Yes.' To each of us."

"To found a truer one," Edgar said with an edge to his voice. "Then there's nothin' I can say."

"But we want more from you," Joe insisted. "We want you to come with us, to lead us in the new church, to be our pastor, our leader."

The boy in Edgar leaped up and turned a handspring, but

Edgar kept his face straight. There was no way to lead and keep the vision. "When will you announce the new church?"

"At the Praise Dance next week."

"May I come and see then, see and talk to the people?" They looked at one another. It was only their vanity. They had wanted to know first, to be leaders in that.

"Well, sure, sure." Dilys, not having said much, was making up for it. The others had to agree.

It was late when Edgar got home. A grainy tiredness was pulling at his eyelids; his mouth was dry. He was feeling the cold now, too, not having taken his jacket, since the night had still been warm when he left. Going home, he had shut off his car lights, the better to enjoy the solitude of the night and the sleep of each of the four farms beneath the moon. There had been no light showing between Joe's place and his; he had passed no car or truck or boy on a horse, home from visiting a girl. There was only the earth, small and flat, a low line on his windshield. All the rest was sky crowded with its signaling outposts, each begging a blessing: "Here I am, Lord, your star."

"I hear you."

"What is your wish, Lord?"

"That you continue as a star and serve your nature."

"Amen, Lord."

"Amen."

"Enjoy us, Lord."

Too tired to laugh, it was enough to feel their light and the cold against his gritty lids. He thought his own house was dark, but when he got close he saw that Charlie had left the kerosene lamp on the table for him.

Bounded by the room, he left overlarge and clumsy, and went to the kitchen with the lamp. On the stove was a cup and beside it a pan of cocoa, kept warm by the slowly dying embers inside. Charlie. "Look what they are without faith," he murmured to the Presence. "Look at some of your naked ones, glory beyond reason, goodness beyond promise. They go without even the smallest road or light to mark a way. They say they have no faith, but they steer between heaven and hell so bravely and so well!" He drank the cocoa, which Charlie always made too salty, put the cup in the sink, and went upstairs, staggering with sleepiness, to the room that had once belonged to a sister now so long dead that if she were resurrected at that moment, she would not have known him at all.

9

The weather held; morning sunshine, afternoon rain, a week of glowing dusks in which the greening land was iridescent with its inhalation of the lightning. Everything took: crops, weeds, bees, moths, hoppers, forgotten watercourses.

"You can see the damn vine grow while you stand there," Linthicum marveled. "In a year like this my gelding could father a racehorse!" Linthicum said it because he was old and cantankerous. In the high plains, a farmer knows better than to waste his heart on optimism. They said, Good years are neighbors, disaster is kin.

"That Praise Dance should really be somethin'. There's a lot to praise this year, since the rain."

"Do they think we never praised before these dances?" Ralph said bitterly.

"What's the matter, don't you want to go?" Charlie asked him.

The old man put his cup down among the table crumbs. "I go to the church socials, one for each season. I go to the July Fourth doin's, Memorial Day and Christmas and Easter at church. I don't believe in the virgin birth, total immersion, total abstainin', the resurrection of the body, or the antichrist, but yet I'm a Methodist and a member of that church," and he glared at his son.

"It ain't Edgar's fault," Charlie said mildly. "He never told them people to have them Praise Dances, or to leave the church neither."

"I wonder," Edgar said slowly, "if it's a willfulness in me that hates to see this come. They told me the Lord had given them a sign. If that's so, it must be what He wants— why am I holdin' out then? I say all the time that I ain't a prophet, but here I am disapprovin', thinkin' that Joe and all the others should listen to me and not their own— 'Voices.' "

"Small wonder God give up runnin' the world," Charlie said, "seein' it was so much harder than runnin' the universe!" The old man sent him a withering look. He hated to hear Charlie talk blasphemy and loved to listen to it. Edgar caught Charlie's eye and smiled.

"Joe's been havin' them over to his place most of the time, hasn't he?"

"Havin' parties is Joe's idea of religion," the old man said. "Joe was always a great one for crowds."

"Of the two," Edgar reminded him, "his is the better way. A group is a law."

"And the law—?" Charlie looked up at Edgar with a faint glimmer of the old anguish. "The law cuts into a man."

"I know, but not as hard as no law does."

"You fixin' to wear your Sunday clothes to this?" the old man demanded.

"Nope!" Edgar pushed himself from the table and got up. "My clean shirt belongs unto the Methodists."

"You fixin' to take the car?"

"No, the Methodists get my gas ration, too. I'll just walk. If I go to dancin' too strong, I'll stay over."

"Charlie, are you goin'?"

"Hell no, the Lord ain't said a word to *me*." And Charlie got up and began to gather up the dishes. "And till He does, I'm givin' the Methodists and the Praise Dancers all the room I can."

Erosion after the drought had opened a gully on Joe's farm. It ran beside the six fruit trees he had had to restock two years before, after the drought and the dust. The new trees, five years old, still had the slender virginal look of new planting. He had thought this year to have part of the dancing near the trees, but they were still too fragile. There might be thirty people this time. They would dance in back of the house, which was larger than the flat place in front of the barn. If things went well tonight, he would keep that place clear for dancing always. It was something he felt he owed the Lord. Since he had admitted his mistake to Edgar and had taken Edgar's way, the Lord had been good to him. The land was prospering, the harvests good. The war had made Arla Daggett a widow and left her five children without a father, but the Lord had given Joe the courage and good sense to court her and the wit to ask her to marry him, and He had given her the conviction to accept Joe and to alter her faith to harmonize with his. Joe's new family revered him and he felt now like the true master of his place. It was time to thank the Lord.

Of course, he didn't hear the Lord the way Edgar did, but there are other ways to know the glory—Edgar had said that, too. He went up to the back-porch steps and called, "Arla!" She came immediately, her face red with supper preparations. "I'm goin' to fill the rain barrel and move it out where people can get some water easier. Tell Carl to bring out a dipper before the people start to come."

"I'll tell him, Joseph."

"We better be sittin' down soon—people will be comin'."

"I was just about to ring the bell."

Since they had discussed leaving the church, Joe and Dilys and the Empey boys and Linthicum had given much thought to what they wanted to do on Sunday, during the organized part of their service, but Joe saw now that if change was needed, it would have to be a thorough change. The table grace that Arla and the children said would need to be changed to fit the new way. How would a man show his piety, he wondered, with none of the ways made yet? He reminded himself that he had to be patient. Ways would come. They were coming from the Praise Dances, from the people themselves, rejoicing in the Lord.

They said the grace which Joe found newly irritating. He found himself thinking about a name for the new group. Should they call themselves Purists? Spiritualists? Separatists? He had thought to ask Arla's advice in this, but she had smiled wisely and said, "Prayer will teach us."

The first people came just as the family was finishing supper. They were new to the group, townpeople, and they came with an attitude more curious than reverent. Then the Empeys arrived, all stuffed into their big Packard, and the Carberts, Linthicum on his sway-backed mare, and Bucky Treece with his girl, Doris, and the Taylors and Van Bronckhorsts from west of town. The children had begun to form their own group right away, playing a game. The adults stood, or sat, on the porch, or walked up and down digesting their suppers until sundown. There was a reticence about the group, a formal courtesy, that would not free them to do so much as touch one another on the arm or rest a hand on a neighbor's shoulder. The men and women had segregated themselves naturally, as was the custom anywhere, calling across to one another occasionally, but sitting apart, except for Bucky and Doris, who stayed together and spoke to neither group.

The sky above them began to glow and the faces of the group took on a rapt look. The talk slowed, the silences ripened.

"Edgar's goin' to come tonight, he said he would."

"That's good."

"When we start meetin's on Sundays, I hope we won't give this part up."

"I don't think we will."

"Ruth, I heard you were expectin'."

"December, this time."

"Be nice not to have to carry heavy in the summer."

"Um-hmm."

"It will be good to have Edgar as leader—even though—"

The rose-gold darkened into bands in the sky, picking up clouds barely visible against the blueness and shooting them with light. All the surroundings—shrubs, barns, fences—

filled in with darkness. The first consciousness of chill caused the women to reach into coats and sweaters, happy for their warmth. They did not speak then, or wish to. The light drew down to gray and new people came, welcomed by Joe and Arla. Now and again, they caught each other's eye over the heads of others. Edgar Bisset had not come. Seth Empey asked about it before they began the singing.

"Didn't somebody say Edgar was comin'?"

"Said he was."

"Is that damn Charlie Dace comin' too?"

"I don't know, but I wouldn't think so."

"I don't know how Edgar puts up with that man."

They began to sing. They began slowly, touched by the consciousness of the King of Heaven listening to them. When they were finished, Catherine Empey's voice came intimately through the dark:

"The Lord called me yesterday and told me that He wanted all of us to call to Him tonight in the name of our Brian, who is away fightin'." It was a thing they had never done before. Before this, they had only prayed for the general good, danced praises and prayed. Joe struck a match to light the lanterns he had put out at the sides of the house.

"Let's Praise first," said Dilys gently. "Let's show the Lord our joy."

The dance began. Joining hands, everyone started to circle to the left. They sang familiar hymns from the churches they were leaving, but with a quickened rhythm, a stronger beat. At the end of each verse, they circled the other way and at the end of two verses, gathered into the circle's center. And they laughed. The hymns quickened. Some stolid ones walked, the quick and the graceful skipped or danced school steps, crossing their feet over before and behind. The children ran to keep up with the long strides of the farmers. They circled slowly until the joy took hold of them and then they danced faster, the women leaning back out of the circle until all steps were lost and they felt themselves flying outward too fast to catch breath. Gathering together, the group shouted and dissolved, joyful and winded. They felt themselves children again. They felt themselves children of the Lord of the Night.

Then Joe walked to the center of the group. "Now, let's wait upon the Lord. Let's wait on Him." They stood silent, resting, waiting for His sign. The tension built until it played over their heads like heat lightning and put their hands and spines in strange postures while the Lord hung them from his will. When they could no longer endure their own waiting, Ruth Carbert cried out:

"We ask your blessing, Lord!"

And Catherine Empey answered her, "It's comin', we can feel it now!"

"What does the Lord say?"

"He says yes to us, He says yes, yes to our prayers and our praise. He wants us to pray for ourselves and each other to hear his will for us clearly!"

"He is with us now. I can feel his presence."

"Lord, bless my boy."

"Bless him, Lord."

"Because he's away and in danger."

"He's blessed this moment. We can feel it. All of us. We can feel it."

The other men and women had joined them, clapping and stamping. Linking arms, they hugged one another close while the ring formed again about the two women.

"We are your apostles, Lord."

"All of us carry your word!"

"And your light, Lord, and your glory!"

"Glory!" The voices rose like winds bowing the wheat fields.

"Stop my fear, Lord! Stop all the fear."

"Strength to bear, Lord."

"Show us perfection, Lord!"

"—in our love, Lord."

"In your love, Lord—"

They had begun to move again, almost without conscious thought. They clung to one another, weeping for joy, exhausted with joy.

At sunset, Edgar finished his after-supper chores and, sighing, left for Joe's. Neither Charlie nor the old man was around. The beauty of the evening lulled him and he would have been happy except for the accusation of a row of unfinished postholes east of the house. He thought about them finished and the posts set in. He walked along half thinking, half praying. Idly, he thought he might go up to Joe's by way of Bitter Wash, but he remembered that the Slaytons had begun to farm up there again and had fenced much of it off. Of course, no one would mind, but he disliked crossing property lines, being beholden in that way, so he turned toward the road, the string-straight road that ran past his house and toward Joe's and town. How quickly the day turned downward once the sun had set. All the laws of light, the cooling of shadows, the night breeze from the west, picked up their rhythms.

"Lord," Edgar said, "you are surely a farmer, so savin' of your bounty, everything in its time." There were dandelions at the roadside, some still yellow-headed, and they glowed in the twilight and then were lost. It was quickly cool. Edgar walked faster. He thought, unless it was only imagination, that he heard their singing, that Praise Dance singing from Joe's, still a mile or so away. The slow wind perhaps was carrying it, making it sound more tuneful, richer than it really was. He did not hear the car behind him. He had no perception of it until it struck him. He felt, before thinking or even guessing, a blow, an explosion of himself that took his breath, lifted him into the air, and hurled him away. He fell in plowed earth at the edge of a field, hearing but not understanding the silence and then the sound of a door closing and the car starting up again. Soon the sound was gone. Something was keeping him from moving at all. His right side was half buried in the soft ridge of the earth. There was dirt in his eye, but he could not close his eyes. It confused him because he had always been able to close his eyes. His mind held nothing but a wordless wonder. He felt himself wanting to speak, and speaking, but he could not hear the sound. He said, "I love You," and he died.

Charlie

10

The body of Edgar Bisset was discovered on the morning of May 31, 1943, in the field of Gerd Longerich. It was first seen by Gerd's oldest son, Martin, who ran back to the house and summoned the sheriff. From the distance the body had been thrown, it was possible to place the speed of the car at between fifty and fifty-five miles an hour and the time of death at between 8:00 and 9:00 P.M. The other things were all the embroideries of guilt and love: that his hands were clasped in prayer; that he had written "betrayed" in the turned earth as he lay dying; that he had written "forgive them" in the earth or on a post with his blood; and most commonly heard of all, that he had appeared (flesh or spirit) at the Praise Dance and had spoken to many people there, telling each the special message which was needed, infusing each soul with its necessary particular comfort. These words were cherished and they formed the ceremony that was held by the group the following night at Joe's.

"But sure he was here last night—he came late, I remember, when the people were resting for the third or fourth time. I remember thinkin' he looked a little tired, a little sad. He greeted me the same way he always did, 'Hello there, Ruth.' I said hello and he said, 'Ruth, without hearers, the Lord can't speak. Have pity on the Lord, Ruth, and listen to Him.' I went to follow him, to ask him to explain, but he was talkin' to someone else then and someone had come over to me—it was you, Addie, wasn't it?"

"If it was, I missed Edgar, because I didn't see him, although I knew people were waitin' for him."

"Oh, he was there, all right. Come late, like Ruth said. I don't want to cause hard feelin's with what he told me, but I'll tell you what he said: 'I've always had a special likin' for you, Russell,' and then he smiled in that gentle way he had and he said, 'The men who endure—I love the ones who endure.'"

"I remember what he said once—I didn't see him at Praise, but I remember a long time ago when he and I was sittin' on his porch and he looked out at the field and he said, 'If we're hungry for love and for perfection, think how hungry the Lord must get—'"

"He couldn't have said a thing like that."

"Yes, he did. He talked about God in a funny way—sometimes it was almost like pity."

"Yes, I remember—when I had to close down the store and I told him that no man livin' had tried harder than I did to make a go of it, and he said, 'You can forget your failures. God lives forever, so his failures are eternal.' I said, 'How can God fail?' Edgar, he started to laugh. He said, 'Ab, look around at the humankind in these parts and tell me what you think.' I laughed too. I said I thought it was a pretty patchy job. Then he said, 'The Lord quit early on that sixth day. Quit without finishin' the job. We're stuck with finishin' the job ourselves like the nitwit partner in a hardware store.' I always thought he said that to joke a little and make me feel less like a fool goin' out of business when business was boomin' for everyone else."

"Remember when old man Dudley accused Edgar of blasphemin'?"

"What I remember was Edgar sayin', 'Don't curse yourself or suffer guilt for your mistake. It's a kind of cursin' God for his gift.'"

"One time I saw Edgar cry."

"When was that?"

"It was the day of the big storm. We saw clouds like cities, gray-black to the west, and the air had the kind of gray-green that it gets when trouble's comin'. Hail, we figured. I got the last of my wheat in and went over to Edgar's and he wasn't but halfway through. I asked him how come he had waited so long and he said he was bein' punished for somethin' and that was for denyin' himself to the Lord. I never really figured what that meant, but I won't forget the way he looked ridin' that reaper slow down that field, his face all streaky with tears."

"He come to me in a dream last night, and he said . . ."

So it went on, and people came and went through the vigil twilight and into the witnessing night. For the church people, things were not so easy. The funeral was to be held at Edgar's church, of course; the grave had been readied next to Cora Bisset, 1869–1919, At Rest; but Pastor Hummel felt that an ordinary service would not be enough. Something more was needed. He told the vestrymen that he had not been very close to Edgar; someone close should speak the eulogy, and the pallbearers should be special, representative, in a way, of the whole town's love. He had been thinking of the problem that morning and an inspiration had come to him.

"You're out of your mind," Charlie said flatly.

"But you were his closest friend, Mr. Dace, and probably his oldest."

"You ain't told this to anyone, have you—about me speakin'?"

"No, I wanted to check with you first."

"Lookin' up at the stars, Reverend, you stepped right into the cowshit. Edgar says—sorry, *said* that God protects the innocent. Well, He done okay with you."

"But, Mr. Dace—"

"I ain't Mr. Dace, Reverend, I'm Charlie, and that's the point. I drink and I don't go to church. I'm a hired man and I'll be that until I die and won't ever be no better than that. Worst of all, I know all the secrets of this town. I know what Methodist buys hard liquor and who ain't sleepin' with his wife. They wouldn't want me to talk about Edgar. In the last months, Edgar made 'em all embarrassed. Maybe just a little they wished he would go away and not embarrass them anymore."

"But the town loved Edgar. Everyone loved him."

"And when a whole town loves, Pastor, they don't want anyone to get in the way of that love, especially the one they are lovin'. Edgar's English wasn't no better than mine, and people want a hero they can look up to. Edgar didn't want no fancy new religion to make a new crop of heathens out of the ones the Methodists left over. Edgar *cared* for me. He saw through whatever keeps me like I am on the outside and he preferred bein' with me to bein' with just about anyone except the Lord. Now, that can't be forgiven—it's an insult to Joe and Dilys and all the people who came up here and had Edgar listen to their troubles. How would they like to know that after they were all gone, and the door was shut for the night, Edgar would tell me *his* troubles and listen to my ignorant, booze-drinkin', hired-man's advice?"

"What should be done, then? The town wants more than a simple service."

"Get the mayor to speak, and Doc Brantley, and Joe, if he'll set foot inside the church. I've got my own thing or two to say when I get drunk enough."

"I see how it is, and I'm sorry for bothering you. I only thought—I expect you miss him very much."

"I had no claim on him. After all, he wasn't kin."

The mayor's speech was simple and affecting. He traced the phases of Edgar's life, bringing in anecdotes full of the names and personalities of those who shared in them. Joe Kornarens was remembered as a young buck, courting Edgar's sister, Tempe, Joe's big family was all named, the years after the war were recalled when Edgar made a name in his own right working the family place. The mayor did not mention Edgar's vision or the change in his life directly, but told how, in the darkest days of the Depression, Edgar's strength and patience had made him a leader in the town. His faith in God was marvelous to behold in those testing times, and many could tell tales of the inspiration and courage that he gave. Dilys Carbert could testify to that courage. Dilys was looking for a place to settle with his family and could tell the many ways in which Edgar showed himself a good neighbor. "Edgar came to this church faithfully, but it's not his church attendance that makes him loved as a religious man. He stayed on his land and held when others left, but that's not what makes him remembered as a good neighbor. Edgar Bisset was a religious man and a good neighbor in many ways to many people. He was often more than those things, but never less, and the town and the farm and the county will miss him."

Charlie Dace had not really been expected at the service, but people noted his absence at the cemetery. Arla Kornarens said later that it had saddened her not to see Charlie at the graveside: "Someone so close to Edgar—someone almost kin. Probably didn't have the clothes to come, or maybe he felt it wasn't his place, bein' only a hired man. It's bound to be different for him now, just him and the old man alone on that place."

Joe shook his head. "Charlie Dace is one of them people who just don't know how to do."

He thought of taking a fifth or two out to the dry wash and getting drunk until he could no longer differentiate between night and day, vomit and violets. He found the whiskey a burden when he got there. Drinking was too much a ritual, too automatic a response of years—hand to raise the bottle, head to tilt back, mouth to receive—and it suddenly disgusted him that this day should be so like all the others. It wasn't true, really. Here he was standing alone in a dry wash in the middle of a day, no work at hand, listening to the coded messages of grasshoppers, heat, dryness, old age, and death. There had used to be water in this bed until the summer, but the creek that had run here was tied up now with a larger irrigation scheme and water would never flow here again. Another change. Everything changes, except one thing. He sat down in the soft sand of the wash and looked up at the strip of sky between the banks. It was bright blue and carried majestic processions of clouds in slow dignity, slowly because of their weight. The mayor would be at the funeral. The mayor's wife and all the greats in town. The

107

One responsible for it all never answered. Charlie looked out into the innocent-seeming blue space, seeking the One responsible. He thought for a minute to curse Him, blaspheme, and dare the Bastard to cinder him with a lightning bolt.

"Edgar could have done it," he muttered. "Edgar was big enough to rate lightning." He started to tell the Bastard, aloud, that if He had chosen Edgar, Edgar had chosen him, Charlie. He could not speak when he tried to. There were tears in his throat so that he only coughed.

All around there was silence. Fifty miles to the west, some farmer's field would be in shadow as that cloud moved past. Except for the grasshoppers' sound, like an echo of all dry years, it was the ordinary silence of any ordinary day. Charlie sat back against the side of the wash, watching the soft sand trickle down where he had disturbed it, and now and then he leaned his arms on his bent knees and shook his head.

11

There were people who expected the fervor of Praise Dancing to die down after Edgar's death. They were mistaken. What no one expected was the doubling and trebling of the numbers and intensity. People who came with time on their hands, to mock or make a holiday of it, were moved by the dance's simplicity and jubilant faith. In these Praises, all men seemed truly brothers, all wishes one wish in the end. People spoke of becoming completely men, of giving all and standing emptied, of receiving all again, a greater All.

And there were miracles. The miracles were not miracles of nature—the ones of the Bible—water into wine or the stopping of the sun; they were things that seemed to their beholders a thousand times more difficult—the unbinding of bound souls, the escape into love of locked tongues, declarations from throats dry as dust and spirits rusted shut. A young girl prayed at a dance for God's blessing and everyone heard his comforting "Amen." The girl said that she was pregnant and the dance heard with her suffering parents the Lord's injunction that she choose life. An hour later, her young man came forward into their blessing to stand holding the young woman while the dance went on around them. In the Praise the world seemed remade every day, "Perfect as Eden unless we are afraid." People confessed deep sins, wounds in faith, the absence of love, and all was seen, accepted, forgiven.

And there were healings also. Anyone who listened could hear how full healthy breathing conquered the asthmatic gasp of a struggling boy, could see the blue-skinned, heart-starved girl wrestle herself from her mother's arms to dance alone ten steps in the hanging dust of the great circle while people wept.

There was no preacher exhorting them. Brother Edgar Bisset himself had said that no man is the Apostle, that all men are apostles of the Spirit of the Lord. The Praise proclaimed it again and again, that the message must have no interpreter, the word no boundary to cross over between the mouth of the Spirit of the Lord and his completing part, his servant, his tyrant, his man.

Charlie was drawn to those Praises in spite of himself. He would stand aside, his battered hat pulled low like a gangster's, his hands in his pockets, and he would watch, greeting no one and making no comment. At first people tried to give him a place there, some special mark of respect as Brother Edgar's friend, but he was so poor in the role of grateful recipient of honors and so outlandish in his ways that people were more embarrassed than inspired by him and they soon left him alone.

Over the weeks and months, the Praises took form. People received word of God's wishes for them in the middle of their thanks, and Charlie would go home to the old house or over to the Pruitts' saloon and give Ralph or Bob Pruitt a muttered word or two on the progress of the faith.

"They're Apostles now, Apostles of the Spirit of the Lord, that's the name. Arla got it, straight from God." To Ralph, Charlie reported how Dilys Carbert had spoken out for splitting the Praise, now that it had grown so big. "A faith has to grow, he said, and it needs Praise leaders to keep some kind of order—not ministers or teachers, he said; elders, maybe. I stood there and heard him say it."

"Edgar always liked that sidin' man, though I can't tell why," Ralph said.

Charlie smiled slightly under his hat. Now Dilys and his family were making out that they had been special friends of Edgar's, but Charlie had never trusted Dilys and he had once spoken to Edgar about it. Something more than family land had fallen away from that bunch—they clutched at the nearest thing, clutched too hard, maybe. "Sure, you can see why," Edgar had said. "It's in the way of survival. If the dust weakens a man, that man is at the mercy of everything stronger than he is, including evil."

In Dilys's case, Charlie had said, the Lord would tell him exactly what he wanted to hear. "The Lord'll preach a faith that collects money and where friends of Brother Edgar will be elders with vests and watchchains."

Edgar had laughed and shaken his head. "What a defender of a righteous God you are, Charlie!" Charlie could remember Edgar saying that, but he was fast losing memory of the sound, the exact sound of Edgar's voice.

Charlie sometimes wondered if Joe was like Dilys, in his own, less greedy way. Even in putting a question to the Spirit of the Lord, Joe arranged his words in a way that made his own desires seem good. In a way he told the Lord what he wanted the answer to be. Do all men do that? Did Edgar? Charlie thought about the idea by himself for a long time. If it was true about Joe, it would show in the Praises. Joe was a careful, practical man—he was not a man of visions like Edgar, but he had prudence and good sense when dust and fear were not tormenting him. For Joe, God himself must be a God of good sense. What Joe wanted would be sensible and respectable and well-intentioned. It occurred to Charlie that watching "God" change was one of his reasons for going to the Praises at all. "That, and keepin' watch," he said, and uncapped his bottle. "Keepin' watch." He could now no longer see Edgar's face.

The Praises split and split again. Now there were nine— two across the Kansas line, three in the county, two in Arizona, and two more up north near Pueblo. Most of the Praises were held in late afternoon on Sunday and ran into the night. Daytime petitions, Charlie had noticed, were not the agonized, despairing ones of the night, when secrets were spoken in darkness, answered in darkness, beaten from their hiding places by the circling feet of invisible dancers.

The Praise Dancers themselves did not seem to notice this

difference. When he spoke of it to Joe, Joe waved it away: "Sure, people bring different things to the Lord at different times. A man's nighttime problems ain't the same as his daytime ones."

"Edgar never needed to get his neighbors' approval for what he told the Lord." He could see Joe looking closely at him, to see if he was drunk.

"You were Edgar's friend," Joe said. "You should be tryin' to help us, instead of snipin' all the time."

Charlie couldn't help giving one of his snorting laughs. "Edgar was my friend. What does the progressive, federated gen-u-wine army of apostles of the holy two-step have to do with my friend Edgar?"

"It was Ed's faith, Charlie, and you know it."

"Edgar's faith wasn't to take a vote on what God should say and *you* know it. Edgar used to go out alone and take his chances with the Word. He didn't have no growin' church, no payroll, no board of investors—"

"It's been a long day, Charlie," Joe said, and Charlie thought he must be almost as tired as his voice sounded. "I don't want to argue this now. Edgar is gone, but what he started can be saved. The faith is growin', and like anything else, will grow or die. Whatever grows has to have laws, a path to take, a way to go."

"Yes!" Charlie shouted. "But why does this have to grow? Does the world need one more sect of tree-swingers? Why does it have to be a faith at all? Why can't it be my memory of Edgar and yours, just that? Just the memory of all of us, to die when we die, just Edgar comin' in like he used to do, with some wild flower stuck in his hatband or lookin' over to us so damn happy because it was a good world that had *us* in it? Joe, I learned somethin' in all of this. You can't carry water in your hand and have it be the same sweet-tastin' water you took out of the creek. The holiness won't travel— it sours in another place. And all of Edgar's visions died when he died."

"You're wrong, all wrong," Joe said quietly. "You loved Edgar, but you never listened to what he said. Edgar wanted people to have what they needed—order, joy in life, the knowledge that the Lord hears them whenever they pray, answers their prayers. He would have changed his mind about the Praises if he had seen them, seen how happy and well-answered people were." Charlie's face had not changed its expression. Joe sighed and said, "We have to do the best we can."

"I don't recognize Edgar in anything you do," Charlie said flatly. "I know you ain't a bad man. If you was I would kill you and not be guilty, the Apostles ain't bad either—"

"Then why not join us, help us?"

"I can't do that. No, I can't," and he took off his hat, put it on again, and walked away.

After that, most pious Apostles left Charlie alone. He stood silently at Praises, ungreeted and invisible, but as the Praises grew in number and influence there was more curiosity about Edgar. Ralph and Charlie began to have visitors, "tourists" walking timidly or skeptically or curiously into the Sunday meal, the slaughtering, the haying, the hangover.

"Was this his chair?"

"What did he say, Mr. Bisset, about the death of children? I seem to remember once—" At the moonshine place where Charlie still bought booze after hours, he found himself joined, more often than not, by people asking questions. They stood him drinks, they sat with him in the old car while he drank more, beginning with talk of crops and weather and, with more or less subtlety, quickly changing to questions about Edgar, Edgar's youth, Edgar's visions, Edgar's genuineness. Charlie was always fooled. After the first few drinks, as the fumy warmth rose in him, Charlie would misplace the bitter facts of his failure and he would speak feelingly of "his" land, "his" place, stock, crops, plans. He was eloquent on irrigation projects and the certified insanity of the Colorado legislature. Then when he was grand, expansive, shining, his chest warm and his face just cooling in the light sweat of his last drink, the question would come as a complete surprise.

"Say, Charlie, what did Edgar *say* about them visions? Were they real? Did he actually see—" And then Charlie would remember his staggering loss and the impoverishment would make him remember that the house and the land and the problems and place and family and future were not his, that he was friendless. That Edgar was gone. Yet he found after a while that remembering Edgar gave his thoughts a focus, kept his mind from walking around like an old derelict poking at the burnt-out ruins of his house. He would tell the story about Edgar and the stolen hymn book, Edgar and the silences, Edgar punished for singing, Edgar going away to the Army, Edgar and the green-grown cows, Edgar and the cat-burr. There were stories he did not tell and some he changed a little to save Edgar or Tempe or Ralph or Joe.

While he was telling the stories Charlie was happy. The past was only words now, and couldn't hurt him, and he enjoyed seeing them all in his mind, Ralph when he was strong and young, Cora with that straight sourness of hers, going to the window to see if God had been merciful and brought back the hills, Tempe, like a flowering tree, Edgar, all eyes and ears, all silence and fear, a dreaming boy full of secret feeling. Yet, when he was done with a story, Charlie was dissatisfied. He had said nothing to the point, told none of the meaning of it—why would a boy steal a hymn book? It made Edgar sound like a pious little hypocrite. It hadn't been the religious part, but the music he had loved. Yet when Charlie would add later, "See, Edgar, he had a real gift for music," the people would nod and smile, visibly patient until he should get to something important, that mysterious secret important thing for which they had come, for which they had bought him all that whiskey. If he thought of more, remembered more, told more, would they find that fact. that happening, that glory?

It fell on Charlie to do because few people in town, or on the nearby farms, really remembered Edgar before the vision. When they combed their recollections for some hint, there was embarrassingly little. Edgar had been a member of the community all his life. The old people all remembered Cora, stiff and proud and miserable, riding in the buckboard to town, a woman so haunted by the silences of her farm that she had lost the way of easing her soul in talk. Cora they remembered, and Ralph and the strong competent Tempe, whom everyone respected, even when she was a girl. But no one could fill in the shape of that boy walking with them. What was he like? Might there not be in all their memories some ghostly stirring of the air over the head of the child, some trembling of the finger of God, impatient to come down into the story? He had seldom spoken, never played with the boys in town or been noticed by them. He had given no signs, and now so many years later when it had become important to know, neighbors asked one another:

"Did I see him in town? Did he stop by the firehouse or walk across my front lawn to get to the garbage dump?"

"Didn't he ever—"

"Was he the one—" Even the men who had been to the war with Edgar Bisset, intimates in filth and terror, who had starved and been rained on beside him, could not seem to place him in those years before the Lord put hands on him. Cora and Tempe were long dead, Ralph was dumbstruck with incredulity, Joe had blotted out the human part of Edgar, and Charlie alone was left to speak of that boy and that man whom the Lord saw fit to touch.

Perhaps there was a little hidden anger in Joe, because of the stories. Perhaps he felt put out with Ralph for keeping so much to himself, but Joe knew about Andy's rescue for three days before coming over to Bisset's with the news. The Army had taken back the Philippines and had walked right into those Japanese camps. There were pictures of the prisoners in the magazines, skeleton men staring out at their strong, competent-looking, well-muscled liberators with a kind of wonder. The men, said the Navy and *Life* magazine, were going to be taken to hospitals, first on the island, and then in California, and when they were well again they were going to be rehabilitated to the lives they had left.

"Rehabilitated!" Ralph said over dinner. "A good, happy man went over there and now he's comin' back a skeleton like an old man and how is he goin' to fit in his same life again? Them Navy people must think we're feebleminded!"

"The government means well enough," Charlie said. "They

juggle around with money and they think maybe they can juggle around that way with time, too. Anyway, they'll let them rest up and give them vitamins and good food till they're strong enough to make it on their own."

"It'll be a different person, a different person!" Ralph complained. Charlie wondered why the news of Andy's having been saved was making Ralph so fearful. Joe and Arla seemed only happy and grateful. They shouted their gratitude and prayers at five different Praises, and walked all over town "testifying" to their joy in it, never wondering, it seemed, about that changed skeleton-man himself. Then Ralph got a letter from Andy from a California hospital and in fear of what it might say he got Charlie to read it.

"Dear Grandpa, Uncle Edgar, and Charlie, I have written to Dad already and told him not to spend the money getting out here. The short visiting hours wouldn't be worth the trip and I am doing fine and will soon be home. Besides, I want to think of you there just the way you were when I left —doing all the things you always did. Life in the camp was very hard sometimes and the guys used to talk about their homes and families to make the time pass easier. Somehow they all liked to hear me talk about all of you, even about how much land we had in wheat and how much in broom and about our cows. The city guys, especially, liked to hear about you, Uncle Edgar, and us going fishing and how cool it was under the bank where the cottonwoods were. Me and Millard Moss talking about the snows of Minnesota were about the most popular talkers there. The city boys would talk about Times Square or the Loop and call us goat-ropers, but I think they did that out of envy. Those city boys will go back to New York or wherever and find it all changed—new buildings, new neighbors. I know they felt something special about the kind of land and people who never change."

"Dear God," Charlie muttered, "I hope that boy don't really believe that stuff about never changin'."

"Joe'll have to tell him about Edgar. It's a father's place to do that job. I done it once and I'm through. It's the father's place," and the old man went quickly into the front room as though Charlie would argue with him.

Charlie sat on the kitchen chair that used to be Edgar's. Had it been so short a time that Edgar had been gone? Poor Andy would have to get used to all the changes at once. And they would have to get used to him. Andy was twenty-eight now and a different man. It made Charlie feel old.

12

The call came from Arla in the forenoon. It was a morning in mid-August. The air was beginning to take on heat and there was a gassy glare over the fields. Joe had gotten a call from Andy at the station and had hurried to pick him up. She knew they would want to hear right away. Ralph hung up the phone approvingly. "Smart woman, that Arla." Then, absurdly, he and Charlie sat down to wait.

During the endless afternoon, they damned themselves and complained to each other about the stupidity of waiting. Andy wasn't fully well yet. It might be days, weeks even, before he was strong enough to come to see them. As to going to Joe's, they both felt shy of it, afraid to seem too eager, barging in on Joe's new family. Instead, they reminded each other that it was too hot to work outside and nothing urgent needed doing in the barn. They waited out the day.

"When do you think he'll tell Andy about Edgar?"

"After supper, I guess. Remember, he's got to break the news about his marryin' Arla and the new family, too."

"Of course Arla's kids are mostly grown. I don't think they'll stay on the place after they are through school."

"The place don't come to 'em, it comes to Andy. It's got to do that!"

"Of course it does," Charlie said, "no one ever thought different."

"I guess. I forgot about Arla, though. They was only just meetin' at church when the boy went away. Now it's as natural as breathin' to say Joe and Arla." Ralph clapped his mouth shut as though he had been disloyal to Andy at a critical time.

"I wonder how Joe's goin' to bring it up," Charlie said.

"In Joe's own way, foot through the barn wall, dead horse in the well. Subtle."

"I guess there ain't no way to be gentle or kind about the changes—Edgar dyin', a new family livin' on the place."

"Arla's a good woman, I always said so, but you never know what a woman'll want for her own kids. Here's Andy comin' back weak and sick and Joe so busy with his praisin' and the Apostles he won't be able to watch out for Arla's doin's. Charlie, we got to see that Andy gets his due, that that boy don't get eased out of nothin'!"

"Oh, I don't think there's any danger of that," Charlie said placatingly. "Why, if nothin' else, the Apostles would never stand for it, Edgar's own sister's boy—why, the Apostles would come out against it and Joe would never disobey what the bunch of 'em come out for." It was a new thought for both of them, that the Apostles might stand surety for someone they loved, that the Apostles might be some small bit of protection, a backing, however frail, to their puny, poor, old-men's dreams.

Ralph sighed. "Andy's goin' to have to see Edgar's grave up there to the cemetery. Them two was close, and it'll be a shock, that new grave."

"It's the stone does it—the big stone," Charlie said.

Ralph nodded. "I wouldn't have minded the Army one. The Army does it nice, bronze plaque close to the ground. Modest. I like that even if it only gives a man's Army things on it. I never met a man less a soldier than Edgar was. Army would have done it for Edgar all right, but then the Apostles took over and paid for the big stone and the big doin's—'Here lies, full of the Glory of the Lord, Founder Edgar Bisset, Apostle of the Spirit of the Lord.' Stone come all the way from Denver."

"All it needs is an angel up top spittin' water."

"Wait around," the old man said. "Five years and they'll set up a subscription."

In the evening, Joe came by. He gave his usual excuse, an errand, work to do. They pressed coffee upon him, "before you start back." He was spared, in this way, from saying that he needed to talk or to stay; it was because others wished it.

"It's been a great day, Andy comin' home," Ralph began. Joe told them the details of it, Andy's call from the station, their meeting, Andy's thinness.

"He couldn't hardly lift that duffle they give 'em, and sometimes I could see he wasn't really listenin' when I talked to him. We went out of town and parked up by the cemetery and I told him about Arla. Then we got out and walked some."

"How'd he take it?"

"Odd. We parked by them trees up there and got out and I left the door open to air the car out and Andy seemed more took with that than anything I was tellin' him. He looked around and said, 'Lord, what trust you people have.' I laughed at that. Anybody passin' by would know it was my car and that I'd gone to the cemetery. Anybody who passed would smile and know what was goin' on, that Andy was home, that we was payin' our respects. He said, 'Pa, the key is in the ignition.' I said, 'Where else would it be?' and he just shook his head again and again and said, 'The trust.' I swear that boy had tears in his eyes over my *car keys*."

"What about Edgar?" Ralph asked. "Did you talk to him about Edgar?"

"I didn't want to—the boy wasn't ready for it, but I knew I had to. Soon as he met one other person it would have come out. I took him up and showed him the grave."

"God knows you can't miss it," Charlie murmured. Joe gave him a hard stare. He had been a big contributor.

"Oh, shut up, Charlie," Ralph growled. "Don't pay him no mind, Joe, go on."

"Well, he stopped a long time. I guess it took a while for all of it to sink in. I thought he looked a little sick, pale, you know. We sat down and then he was okay. He asked how it happened and I told him. I'd wanted to tell him about the

Apostles, all the good things—about how Brother Edgar's spirit had infused us all, but I don't know, I just couldn't do it—it was all so new. After a while, we got in the car and come home." They looked at Joe, sitting a little forlornly over his cup.

"You done right, Joe," Ralph said, "tellin' Andy just what you did. Time enough to learn about the Apostles when he's ready."

"He's goin' to have to be ready soon," Joe said. "There's a Praise set for tomorrow and it's likely to be a big one— folks are due from Nebraska because there's two Praises startin' up there and they want to see—" he checked himself. Charlie's lip was pulled down a little. He had lately heard the phrase Founder's Praise, as though the Founder had ever blessed it, or given it its laws, or danced at it.

Ralph said, "Do you think we could have Andy here for a while, a day or two, maybe? It's quiet here and there isn't all the change. Except for Edgar, not much has changed up *here*. I think he'd like that." Charlie almost smiled. Everything had changed with Edgar gone. The joy, all the joy had left the house. But if Andy wanted quiet, God knows this was the place for it.

Joe paused to consider. "Well," he said at last, "I'll ask him. Arla has been waitin' for him—I wouldn't want to hurt her, and her boys took to him right away. Still, I'll ask him and see what he says."

"It would only be for a few days," Ralph said, bargaining, "till he gets his bearin's."

Joe rose to go. He was almost out the door when he turned back to them. "I almost forgot. He did ask me if Edgar talked about him while he was away or left any message for him before he died. Of course, I told him that sure, Ed had talked about him often and had many prayers for him. He only nodded though; I don't think he was listening. That boy's been through so much. Even the Navy's letter said so." He turned again and went out into the night. They sat in silence listening to the sounds of the car starting up and driving off. Then Ralph turned to Charlie.

"Come to think of it," he said, "I don't remember Edgar ever mentioning Andy after he left, and he never made any special prayers for him that I ever heard. Edgar never *asked* God to save any of 'em, now that I think of it."

"Nope," and Charlie shook his head, "he never did."

The next day at noon, Charlie got ready to go to the Praise Dance. This time, instead of simply telling Ralph good-bye and setting out, he took a bath and trimmed his hair a little, had a fresh shave, and put on a clean shirt.

"Now you're lookin' so splendid I suppose you'll want the car!" Ralph cried.

"No, thank you," Charlie said, "I wouldn't want to give the Lord's annointeds fits of shock at my reform. Besides, if I'm lucky I'll get Andy to bring me back." He clapped on his hat, winked at Ralph, and left.

Andy had come back a hero. Charlie could see it in the outright deference of the women and children, the subtle deference of the men. It was obvious, too, that Arla's tact had cleared a way for him to make his peace with his father's second family. He stood, leaning against the small corral fence by the barn, dressed half civilian, half issue. Charlie was glad that Joe had spoken of his drawn look and his thinness. Otherwise he would not have known Andy standing there, looking a decade older than the boy who had gone away. He had obviously been told something about these dances. Charlie was amazed at his own sudden shyness. He had to make himself go forward to meet this man he had known since childhood. He walked forward slowly. Andy was already tired with the strain of remembering old faces and names, of accustoming himself to the new order of days and habits. Every now and then he would breathe deeply as though to steel himself for the work.

"Andy, it's me, Charlie Dace." Clumsily Charlie put his hand out.

Andy took it and then smiled. "Hello, Charlie, I'm damn glad to see you. Pa told me he dropped in on you and Grandpa last night, but I was sleeping and he didn't think to wake me." Charlie was about to speak when Joe came toward them, big-voiced and smiling, with two men.

"Don, Fred, here's my boy Andy. I wanted you to meet him before Praise starts up. It's a fine afternoon for Praise, a wonderful afternoon!" While the men came forward and shook hands, Joe was greeting others; his large hand held up to wave to new ones coming, loud and happy. "Hello, Tyra, how are things over at your place? Luke, come say hello to my boy here!"

Many of the older people had brought camp chairs and stools or even peach boxes to sit on, and these had been put around the edges of the leveled and cleared space behind the house. When the people seemed ready, Joe went into the middle of the space and cried, "You're all welcome. Let's praise the Lord!" The milling of people stopped and the group formed itself into two circles. There was a gentle, friendly murmur of voices. The people still sitting at the side leaned forward, their faces alert. They were smiling. It could have been a square dance, a party Andy was seeing. There was even scattered clapping.

The slow, circling movement began, but even in its slowness there was a deliberation, an intensity that the witnesses could feel. Charlie and Andy were standing together, half leaning against the fence. Now and then Andy would give Charlie a searching look and Charlie had to work to keep his face expressionless. The Praising began.

It was a daytime Praise and the beginning was about practical daytime things.

"Thank you, Lord, for savin' our three sick calves."

"Thank you, Lord, for stoppin' our family wranglin'."

"Give strength to my mother in her pains, Lord."

"Teach my children the value of patience."

Back and forth the Praises went, almost in a rhythm, like an old poem. Then Joe's voice came out of the circle, seeming to Charlie, as he sat there, louder than the others. Beside him, Andy stiffened and his face seemed to draw in.

"I want to speak to this Praise about my son, a boy—man—who has seen death and known suffering." The circles slowed. "I want to thank this Praise for all the prayers it has given for this man, for giving itself so hard toward praying the good to come to him." The circles plowed on. People were turning toward Andy at the fence and reaching their arms out toward him as they passed. Joe broke out of his circle and came over to lead Andy in, his hand stretched forward in a gracious gesture of invitation, smiling. Andy had begun to tremble slightly. He was deadly pale. He reminded Charlie of nothing so much as a man before a firing squad leaning back into the fence because he could not trust himself to stand. Joe came and took him, victimlike, into the circles, both of which parted so that they stood in the center. Charlie was not aware that he had stopped breathing until he was forced to begin again, the sound harsh in his own head. "You saved him in the camp, Lord!" Joe was crying. "You brought him out alive!" People were swaying and sighing. The circles seemed to be moving fast. "You made him strong enough—strong enough to live!"

"Thank you!" people were shouting. "Thank you, Lord!" Now and then, in flashes between the dancers, Charlie could see Andy standing rooted in the center of the dance, head down, hair falling forward, his left arm loose at his side, his right held by his father. For a long moment Charlie hated as he had not hated in thirty years. Memories of his own despair came back upon him as immediate as wounds on new flesh. He began to sweat, his heart pounding against the rhythm of the dance footfalls. "Oh, Christ," he whispered, not praying but cursing, "Oh, Christ!"

At last the dance slowed. The dancers were breathing hard and the speaking stopped, so that all to be heard was the shuffle sound of feet and the hard breathing of the dancers. The next voice was low, a woman's, interrupted often as she caught her breath.

"I received word—during this Praise—concerning my son, Calvin Warren, who was killed on a beach in Italy." There was silence. The dance was slowed to a walk. The voice went on. "Since Calvin's death, as you all know, I've had many messages—the Lord told me that Calvin had loved us and that we had loved him." The voice recovered, went on. "The Lord told me that a man doesn't grieve for something without value and that our grief told us the value of Calvin to us. I can't tell you why, but those words from the Lord brought us comfort." The slowness of the dance took on a rocking rhythm, people swaying slightly as they went on in the rhythmic movements of their circle. "This boy came home, though, to his parents. When this Praise began, I felt my heart begin to ache. I felt that anger again, last year's anger when all my grief was raw. I hated the injustice of it all. I thought how this boy wasn't no better than my Calvin, no kinder, no smarter, or any more fit to live than my boy was. We started to Praise for him and the Voice of the Lord come loud to me, sayin' to me that some come back—some *have* to come back to move the generation on, move it along like the dance. The Lord doesn't think the livin' to be better than the dead; the ones that come back are not the Lord's own chosen ones, they're just the ones that have to go on and I don't need to hate them no more for my boy's sake."

Andy's head was still down. It seemed to be easier for him not to have to face any more than the dancers' shoes, but in his shoulders and arms there was a kind of tension that was not embarrassment. A man's rusty voice said, "Who here has dead, young men died before their time?" There was a murmur, a shuffling of the shoes. "Let's make a circle, us few, right now," the rusty voice went on. "Let's show ourselves to the Lord."

There was another small murmur and then Joe's voice talking to Andy over the others: "Come on back now, son. It's all right now. You can step back out of the circle." Andy's head came back and Charlie saw an expression on it that made him catch his breath. A sound came from him that Charlie could not tell was rage or sorrow, a great unformed cry that pulled his head up to face the wall of shocked eyes all around.

"No! I have my dead too!" And he began, stumblingly, to tell these neighbors and strangers in this dry, sky-conquered, flat and treeless, gray-brown land something about the camp.

13

Charlie stayed away from the next few Praises. He heard that while Andy was usually there he only stood aside, watching, after that first day. Sometimes he would come up to Bisset's, but he never mentioned what had happened, and Charlie felt in him as much repulsion as attraction for the thing, and a persistent quality of shame. Charlie knew how curious Andy was about the Apostles. He knew that Joe and Arla would say more than enough about the wonders of the Praises, healings, witnessings, and reconciliations, but the real question, how had it all happened, was Charlie's alone to answer. There was time.

There was work besides. They were putting in the winter crops and the cover crops before bad weather came. For Ralph and Charlie, the work was so hard that in November Ralph decided he would sell the two big fields that Edgar had won away from scrubland. There wasn't manpower enough to keep them. They were going back already.

"What the hell is it for?" he complained. "There ain't no family no more. I'd leave it to Andy, but Joe's place'll go to him now. It's bigger and a better place, too." After they sold the fields they found the diminished property still too large for them. They were shrunken old men moving restlessly in the outsized clothes of their vigorous days. It was harder to go into town and meet neighbors and shopkeepers, knowing that they had been diminished. When Edgar died Ralph had not felt old, but sale of those two fields had dried him up at last, inside his clothes.

Maybe, Charlie thought, that was why he seemed so jumpy all the time when Andy stopped in. There were many errands, the borrowing and returning of tools, gifts of food from Arla. Andy usually came on these errands now instead of one of Arla's boys, and when he did the old man would grow absentmindedly talkative, rambling on without listening to his own words. Once Andy came up with a girl, and Ralph launched into a long harangue on marriage and families that Charlie could see was embarrassing to both of them. She was a quiet girl, serious. Charlie had seen her among the spectators at a few Praises. Her name was Anne Currier and she was staying with an aunt and uncle, retired people who lived half a mile out of town on the paved road. Between jobs, she said, and resting. Something more, they said in town.

The pickup had been giving them trouble and the day after Andy's visit Charlie went into town with it.

"This truck ain't goin' to run for days," Connell at the gas station told him. "You better call home for a lift." Charlie was about to call Ralph to come with the old car when he saw Andy pulling up across the street. Going toward Andy's truck, he was relieved to see that the girl was not there.

"Hello, boy, want to take an old buzzard home?"

"I got some errands to do. Why not go into the Pruitts' and have a beer and order a second round for both of us. I'll be there soon as I can." Charlie smiled. Andy was the only man he knew who would let him stand for beers now and then. Most men were shy with Charlie's poverty and could not allow him to buy his own beer, let alone theirs. He walked slowly on, looking into the store windows he passed with the same casually incredulous stare for all the merchandise, his reflection staring angrily back at him.

It was well before noon when he stepped into the sudden dark of the Pruitts', but he knew the regulars would all be in their places along the bar, even though he was too sun-blinded to see them. He had the vulnerable feeling of a man being stared at by people he cannot see. There was also their surprise, a special kind of silence because Saturday, not Thursday, was Charlie's day and never before noon. Blind as he was, Charlie could rise to it.

"Hello, Manley," he said, "Tucker, Ab, Joe, Don."

"Don ain't here," Ab said. "Broke his leg."

"Didn't know that was enough to keep him away," Charlie said. They laughed. Charlie further surprised them by going to a booth and sitting there instead of up at the bar. He didn't want Andy to have to take him away from the talk there—it would change the level of their own talk. He ordered his beer and sat quietly drinking it. He would have preferred whiskey.

Andy came in, blinking from the brightness outside, and was only a minute finding his sight again. I'm getting old, Charlie thought. When Andy caught his eye, he came to the table smiling and Charlie signaled for more beer.

"Why do they make these places so dark?"

"Shucks," Charlie laughed, "I don't think men feel too good about sittin' up here drinkin' durin' the day. If they make it kind of night in here, it don't seem so bad. Bars are kind of hidey-holes anyway." The beer came and they sipped it for a few minutes, wondering how to get started.

"How's it been for you, Charlie?"

Charlie looked into his beer. "Okay," he said. "Of course, it's changed since—well, since Edgar went."

"I love Grandpa, but he's no cinch to live with," Andy said. "It must be hard."

"I'm used to it, bein' as I'm such a cinch to live with. We're two old geezers holed up on a broken-down spread, but I guess it gets to your grandpa worse than it does me." It occurred to Charlie that he had not been so personal since the distant nights when his friend Edgar would see the last guest out of the house and the two of them would sit, bodies tired and minds reeling, at the kitchen table, or out on the cool dark porch, and let the talk come, slow sentences, the silences between them as rich as the darkness between the stars.

"I been lonely," Charlie said, "godawful lonely."

"I've seen you at the Praises," Andy said, "standing back. Is that why you come?"

"I just can't stay away. It's almost like a sickness. I don't understand what they're doin', and I hear people, the ones that used to come up to the house, just to talk, droppin' Edgar's name to put themselves in a pious light. 'I see now how wise Brother Edgar was when he told me to crumble cornflakes in my bed'; 'Yes, yes, how often Brother Edgar told me that very thing.' "

Andy laughed. "I guess that's true—I don't remember many of the things they say he did, but I was away so long—"

"Is that why you been standin' aside, too?" Charlie asked. For a quick moment he was afraid he had presumed on friendship and gone too far. But Andy's look was open.

"I guess I'm scared," he said. "In that first Praise, I talked too much, and while I was talking I felt a kind of power, and there was a—almost a compulsion to it. While I was talking about the things I'd seen and done, it was as though I was dealing them out, like cards, giving this and keeping that, sometimes to shock, sometimes to be a master of the thing, sometimes palming off a statement like some kind of a cardsharp, to hold the people where they were, caught up in my story. Afterwards, I was sick with it. Because I had told too much. And the feeling you get in your gut is like the feeling you get when you eat too much."

"And it does somethin' to what the outside world looks like, too, don't it? Anythin' gets to be possible."

"Does everyone have that funny little hunger to tell more than he wants—more than what really happened—more than he really feels?"

"So people won't think he's a clod," Charlie said.

Andy nodded. "Or a monster. I know what those Praises can do—how good they can make people feel. I came back all cut up in pieces because of what I saw out there and what I had to do, what my friends did, and what the enemy did. At the Praises I see all the people here, all neighbored to one another. It's a beautiful thing and I love to see it—only, for me—"

129

"Too much?" Charlie asked.

"I'm going to become an Apostle, Charlie—I hope you don't think it's hypocrisy. I know how you feel about Uncle Edgar and all."

"I don't mind, if only you don't go all pious on me and start to quote Brother Edgar with a 'holy' smile on your face. Still, you said that all that soul-pourin' was too much for you."

"For me, not for others. I can join and be with them and be close and try not to let my own control get away from me. Maybe my listening is needed as much as their witness. It's appeared to me that I have something the Apostles need. I feel it but I'm not quite sure yet what it is or where it fits. Part of it seems to be in the way I have of listening."

"Lord," and Charlie grunted, "they'll listen you to death."

"There's something else I wanted to ask you, Charlie, something you can do for me if you would."

"What's that?"

"Did Uncle Edgar ever talk about me—I mean while I was gone? What I mean is, did he leave any message for me, any word?" He hadn't meant to ask the question that bluntly. Charlie could see that in the surprise on his face.

"You got to realize how it was—" Charlie began. "Edgar died sudden. There wasn't time to give good-byes or last words or the kind of summin' up that people do when they're gettin' ready to go. He died in the middle of a step, in the middle of his livin'. Of course, people was always at the house. He didn't have the time alone to say the things he wanted. People was attracted to that light of his, and he liked that and he liked the closeness, but he knew they didn't want to hear about his doubtin' and bein' worried. You could tell from little things, though, how bad he missed you. He never needed to *say* that to me. I know he felt for you."

"Charlie, there's something special I want to know, if you could think back. I want to know what Uncle Edgar was doing on April eleventh, 1943."

"This ain't some kind of bet, is it?"

"No, Charlie, it's serious."

"If you really want to know, there are some old account books that might stir my mind, bills and such. The wheat would have been green, but there was one year back there when we had a late frost—let me go find out if I can, only I ain't promisin' nothin'. April eleventh—"

"Look at the twelfth, too, since there's a time difference."

"I never could figure out about that—how Wednesday is Tuesday someplace else. It just don't make sense. But you say you need to know—"

"It would mean a lot to me."

"Some of the men in town keep records and I hear tell Dilys has a diary he writes in."

"How is Dilys these days?"

"Oh, Dilys is right prosperous. He bought out Sutter's feed and grain here not too long ago. They're what you call solid folks now. Very pious, Brother John this and Brother Bob that. People that don't expect to go to heaven don't keep diaries, but he does, and if he was keepin' it back then, maybe there's somethin' in it you can use."

"I'd be obliged to you, Charlie. You're a good friend to me."

"I don't friend easy," Charlie said, "but I friend long. Not many people in these parts are keen on the advantages of havin' me for a friend. If you and that Anne Currier get hitched, for example, you better be sure I'm welcome before you have me come to dinner."

"We're not at that stage yet, but I'm sure she would welcome you."

"Okay," Charlie said, "but best make sure of it."

The next time Charlie saw Andy he was with Anne. They came across the fallow fields from Joe's place, skirting the planted lands, running up the strips on either side of runoff places, playing tag in the road. They were laughing. The town had taken her measure and given its guarded yes. It was a pity, though, they said, with all the local girls around. At the last Praise, from his place on the sidelines, Charlie had heard an involved and complex discussion of all the possibilities. A nice girl, graceful and modest, but would she be a good Apostle?—after all, it wasn't an ordinary family anymore.

Looking at Andy coming toward the house, Charlie was

struck by the lie that youthful faces and bodies give to life's experience. He could have been any contented young man. It was impossible to think of him as a prisoner eating a rat, when he was lucky enough to catch it, begging water, stealing food from the dying and shoes from the dead, breathing despair. The two of them came up to the door with golden smiles.

"Hello, Charlie, just thought we'd drop in and say hi."

"I seen you comin'," Charlie said. "Your grandpa will be here in a minute. I'll get coffee up." It seemed as though it were springtime again with light coming from all the windows, light reflected from the walls and the ceiling, but it was only their faces, their voices, their game playing and teasing. The light took Charlie unaware and he could only motion them to chairs. "Sit down." They sat for a while, not speaking, and Charlie cursed himself.

"I see you got something going out to the west there," Andy said.

"Faffu," Charlie said. "Cover. A good grass crop."

"Does it come up green?" Anne asked.

"Not green like you think. I guess this part of the world looks pretty drab to someone who ain't used to it. It gets greener as you stay on."

"I always thought it *was* green," Andy said, "until I went away. When I was away, I remembered it as being green here in the spring, and I used to talk about the green wheat coming and the creek banks and the wild flowers at the banks of all the ditches, the big cottonwoods, and the juniper. It sounded like Eden, but I would have sworn I wasn't exaggerating. Coming back, I thought the land had all washed out before my eyes." They leaned forward a little, Charlie and Anne, listening carefully. It was the first time since the Praise that Andy had spoken with any kind of naturalness about his years away. They did not answer him, waiting for him to go on. "What makes this country special isn't what grows on it, like the tropics, but something else—the light— the way the light changes everything through the day and the seasons." They saw he wasn't going to talk about himself or the camp, so Anne said:

"It's a strange place for the starting of a new—" Charlie

132

saw that she could not say "religion" and did not want to say "cult" or "sect," "—a new belief."

Andy stretched a little in his chair. "I don't see why not. Over these long stretches, the light comes very strong and straight. We have shadows two miles long. A stone can cast a shadow longer than a man or a house, and if you feel like a dwarf all day, with the whole sky weighing on you, you can walk home at sundown and darken your steps five minutes before you get there. It's a good place for belief—we've got twenty churches in a county with barely four thousand people."

"And you're goin' to be part of it all now," Charlie said, "one of the twenty churches."

"You saw me make my declaration last Sunday—"

"Yup, I did. I'll give you this. It was honest and easy and quiet. Some of 'em I've heard can't make a declaration without a hysterical fit, like to shout down the Lord."

The old man appeared at the back door and excused himself. He had been out in the barn dosing a sick calf and he still stank, he said. While he washed again at the kitchen sink, he kept up a lively chatter.

"I thought you folks would be too proud to come see me now the Apostles have gone and got in the papers. A 'phenomenon,' that's what they called it, 'exuberance and fervor,' and Sophie Thiede standin' up there makin' more of a fool of herself than she usually does."

"Don't be hard on Sophie," Andy said with a little smile. "She's had to take comments from so many Apostles. She's a fairly new member and a lot of older members got their wind up because they thought they should have been interviewed instead."

"Just a minute," the old man said, "I got to get a clean shirt—I'll be right back," and he hurried out of the kitchen. When he came back he had the article. "Cut this out of the paper," he said gleefully and waved it before them.

"I thought it was okay for what it was," Charlie said. "They told about the dance without ridiculin' it, which I have a hard time doin' myself, and they told what the believers thought of it without takin' a stand either way. I thought they could have did a lot worse."

"They call it a movement, a phenomenon," Ralph said with delight. " 'Founder Edgar Bisset passed away in 1943, leaving a small following which has grown to upwards of seven thousand members in six states.' Makes you folks sound as big and important as the Methodists and Baptists, don't it?"

"You go on and laugh," Andy said, "but we didn't go to them with the article, they came to us."

"What do you think of it?" Anne said, turning to Andy. "You never told me."

"Oh, I guess I was as excited as the next guy—seeing pictures of the Praise, you and Dad and Arla and so many friends and our barn, and reading about people I know in a way that makes them seem important—but it's a little scary, too—formal, public—like a secret that's shared suddenly and too soon. It's something familiar that's been made strange, instead of the other way around."

"Sophie Thiede made strange, that's a hot one!" the old man cried. Then he found the place in the article he had been looking for. " 'I used to think of prayer as a punishment. Now it's my greatest joy. The joyfulness of the Apostles has changed my life.' That sounds like a laxative ad."

"It's true, all the same," Andy said quietly. "You can't see a Praise Dance and not see the truth of that. I know I haven't spoken out in the dancing since the first time, but that's not the fault of the Praise. I've seen it heal and I've seen it make people forgive each other and live with their own tragedies better." The old man stepped back a little.

"There are people I would have liked to forgive, healings I wish I could have had—where I was."

"And the Praises are doin' you that good?"

"They seem to be helping me forget."

"Then I'll say no word against 'em!" Ralph said, and banged the table with his fist. Charlie caught Andy's eye and Andy turned away to keep from smiling.

"One thing that bothers me is something Sophie said when she was up at the house yesterday," Andy said. "She didn't put herself forward for the interview and the other Apostles' anger upset her. She came up to the house and cried. She said that because some of the Apostles were angry at her, they might talk against her to the Lord—that they couldn't help feeling against her when they spoke to the Lord and that the Lord would somehow satisfy them against her." They sat still for a while.

"Crazy!" the old man said. "The old fool is crazy." Charlie's hand came up a little and he shook his head almost imperceptibly but said nothing.

"She said she was afraid that because she had tried to show the goodness of the Apostles—their joy—she might lose everything."

"But the Apostles don't do that," Anne said, "hound people with God."

"What did Joe and Arla tell her?" Charlie asked.

"They comforted her, of course—told her that the silly jealousy of a few people would die away, that the Apostles were a band of neighbors, friends, brothers and sisters, and that there was nothing to fear."

"Yes," said Charlie, "but did they answer the question?"

"What question?"

"Sophie's question: Can a man's enemies make God his enemy?"

"That's nonsense, Charlie," Andy said. "Of course not."

"I'm not so sure—the Apostles have started pushin' God to give advantages to their friends and to approve what they want to do."

"The other would be a sin," Andy said.

"Good you see it," Charlie said.

14

It was Sunday afternoon. Outside, they were having a Praise. From the orderly, slightly fussy front room where he sat, Charlie could hear the clapping and the feet of people and the drift of song now and then on the freshening wind. The room had comfortable chairs and a big sofa, but Charlie never felt easy in such places. Too many china cats, he said, too many ruffles on the furniture.

He heard Andy coming with coffee, two saucerless cups, whitened with evaporated milk, the way Charlie took it. He set the cup precariously on the arm of the sofa.

"We could use the kitchen," Andy said, "but likely as not Arla would come in or one of the women with a jar of jam or a baby to be cleaned up or something." He sat down and then they both stared at the floor for a while. Charlie was feeling strained and uncomfortable, as though this was a test he might pass or fail. He sipped his coffee. In spite of the milk, it was bitter. "Well," he said at last, "like I told you, I found some old bills. Receipts, really. April thirteenth, 1943."

"Nothing for the eleventh or twelfth?"

"It don't matter which one of them days it was," Charlie said, "because they was both the same for us. Edgar was sick both days, the eleventh and twelfth. We called Doc Fletcher for him late on the twelfth and paid on the thirteenth."

"Sick? Sick with what?" It felt better now, less super-natural. The front room was helping, too, with its dull, decorated coziness. He peered up at the whatnot shelves.

"I don't know," he said. "Goin' back to them days, I remember 'em good because they was pretty strange. On the ninth he was okay. The vet was up that week vaccinatin' all the stock for somethin' or other and I remembered all the beans was in, but the vegetable garden was in bad shape, and while there was time we thought we'd get a start to ready the ground. On the tenth we went out and done that, and that night we was sittin' at the table eatin' dinner when Edgar took some kind of chill."

"Did he have pain?"

"That come later, but then he just sat there shakin' and then went to get up to get a jacket or somethin', and he fell over in a kind of dizziness."

"You mean he was unconscious?"

"No, later on he told us he could hear us and see us, but he just couldn't stand or walk. We took him up to the bed, his pa and me, but we couldn't seem to get him warm enough. He was sick twice in the night, throwin' up and so forth, but it wasn't like any sickness I ever seen before."

"Was he ever unconscious or in some kind of sleep?"

"No, but he wasn't really awake, either. There was some pain then, and he'd keep shakin' his head with it, but yet when we asked him where the pain was, or if he wanted us to go for the doctor, he told us no, that it wouldn't help. Finally, after the second day, we did call Doc Fletcher, and he come out and told us he didn't know what it was, but just to keep Edgar in bed—give him lots of water and juice to drink. Charged us five bucks for that advice—water and juice. Edgar was in bed all that day and toward night there was more pain."

"What kind of pain was it?"

"He said it was in his hands and in his throat, a kind of pulling. He said he felt like someone was tryin' to pull him apart, and there was that chill, too. The night come and we set up with him, and in the morning we was thinkin' about gettin' the doctor again. We did the early chores and come in for breakfast and was thinkin' what to do when all of a sudden down comes Edgar all smilin' and says: 'Where's my breakfast—I'm as hungry as a hound.' "

"And he was okay after that?"

"Just like he was never sick at all. I seen people come out of sickness quick, throwin' up, a sick stomach, maybe, but this was—well, it was different."

"Different, how?"

"Well, I remember his dad and me, we tried to think if it was food poisonin', but we hadn't ate any different from him, and it wasn't fever or somethin' like typhoid, because the doc checked him out on all that, and yet to be so sick—the doc said he thought it might be some kind of injury to the brain, because of his shakin' his head and that thing with his throat, but there ain't no man suddenly goin' to snap out of that and go eat a big breakfast and do a full day's work, the way Edgar done." He said it with a kind of ingenuous pride that made Andy smile. It was almost as though Edgar's quickness at recovery was part of his greatness, a part seen only by Charlie and the old man and thus belonging to them. Charlie moved his thumbnail up along the edge of the slip-cover, leaving a little ridge. Then, seeing that Andy was watching him, he took his hand away guiltily. "Well, there it is. Simple stuff."

"And that's all?" Andy asked.

"That's all there was with Edgar. He was sick and then better. But that ain't all."

"What else happened?"

"What else is you tellin' me why you wanted to know about them three days."

Charlie saw Andy's look close up. "It's only fair," he said. "I suppose it is. I guess I'm not used to telling things without fixing them up in my mind to tell first."

"You told your friends in the camp lots of things," Charlie said. He knew he was pushing Andy and it embarrassed him a little. Looking around, his gaze wandered to the fireplace. Over it, a wide rectangular mirror inspected them. Sitting as they were, Andy was half out of its eye, but Charlie in his chair had been captured. He had forgotten, in Bisset's mirror-less house, how ugly he was, worse now that he was older, the jawlessness, wet gray eyes in the dark face, hair gone sparer and more colorless. When he was younger he had tried for the distinction of ugliness, but now he was far more nondescript than homely, a face that left no memory.

Andy cleared his throat. The coffee had been finished. He motioned to Charlie about more and Charlie shook his head. "I admire you," Andy said. Charlie gave a kind of bark. "It's true," Andy said, "because people are always asking you about Uncle Edgar and you never lie, never dress him up or make him into 'Brother Edgar, Founder Edgar,' even though that's the way everyone wants him now."

"That ain't true," Charlie said. "I always want to tell the truth, but it always comes out narrower, different, less than it was. People'll tell you now how the wisdom flowed out of him. It wasn't never so. It was hard for him, especially when he was a kid, all tied up and couldn't even begin. You'd see him standin' there wantin' to tell his ma or pa somethin'. They thought he didn't have good sense, and you could see the words spinnin' around in his mind too fast to catch hold of. Then, one day, one day after a storm somethin' was freed in him, the love he had and the joy of people, but I knew it was still hard for him to talk even then. Edgar wasn't a man for words, yet people trusted him and believed what he said. *Now*," and Charlie grinned, "they'll tell you about the *speeches* Brother Edgar gave and the *eloquence* and all of that. Horseshit! He wasn't never eloquent all his life. It always come hard and he never was satisfied with anything he said." Then he grinned. The mirror showed a face evil as a movie murderer. "Now, I want to hear Brother Andy be eloquent. He's goin' to tell what happened to *him* on April eleventh or twelfth, 1943. Lean back on the cross, brother, and let go."

"There was a man in the camp," Andy began, "the kind of guy nobody trusts. I don't know why or how, but some men have a way about them that makes you believe what they say almost from the start. Others you come to know one way or another, and some, one or two, are outsiders from the beginning. I've thought a lot about it since, wondering why it is that some men are like that, but this guy was, and he must have known how people took him because he never asked for anything from anyone and he never gave anything.

"It wasn't so bad in the early days at the camp because everyone was busy just surviving. It's hard to say it, but I think the best of us died on that first march into the camp. It was the helpful, cooperative guys, the guys who were moved by other men's pain or fear, who died. When they helped they fell behind, and when they fell behind they got beaten or shot. A man feels bad turning away from dying buddies to save himself, and in the early days in the camp we kept away from each other and didn't feel much like a group that had come through hard times together. When we did look for friends, it was on a small scale, two or three men who would go off to eat together, or rest after work together, or would trade off places on a labor detail to be together. After a while, there got to be three main bunches of guys. One bunch was always planning things, bribing guards, figuring escapes. They had more energy than the rest of us, I guess, and they used to argue and stew and make all kinds of plans, running between the barrack-tents when the rest of us were too tired to stand. I suppose you'd call them the heroes of the camp. The next group was the one I was in, more or less. We knew we were caught and weren't going to get away and make it through the jungle. We kept our heads down, did our work, and tried to live, and when we could, we made things."

"Like what?"

"Like wash poles or bamboo spoons or sandals out of fiber. The heroes wondered why we tried to adjust to the sickness and heat and starvation, and we wondered why they wouldn't. They called us 'the housewives.' Then there was a third group, a smaller group, who didn't fight and didn't fix. They did their work with a kind of glazed look, they stayed together except when there was trouble, and then they would drift over to the heroes for protection. They often stole from us and one or two tried to inform on the heroes. They were the dreamers, and sometimes we envied them, because they seemed to feel so little. Then there was Ronald Tilbury Bannister.

"He never had anything or made anything to trade for something else, never dreamed, never got involved in anything. All the guys went over each other for lice, but if anyone came up to him, he would walk away. Everybody went in on a big scheme to save the storm water. It used to come down in torrents, and when we tried to save it it would go bad. People were always thinking about water, but he never held up the water tarp we put up or had anything to do with the stills or filtering setups or burial pits or any of the other schemes we had."

"Man wanted to be let alone, serve his time, and keep his nose clean," Charlie said. "It's a man's right, I guess."

"Not in a camp like that." Andy shook his head, his voice sounding hopeless. "I wish I could explain to you—tell you about what's really so scary about prison camps—worse than the cruelty or the possibility of disease or starvation. It's the rumors, the fear and the rumors." Charlie said nothing. "As for the rumors," Andy sighed, "the good ones are no better than the bad. When there are rumors of rescue, you lose all the patience and the mental strength you've saved. You think, Maybe the soldiers will set fire to the camp and burn everyone alive, maybe the guards will put poison in the food rather than see the prisoners freed. The worst rumors are the ones you give and get about each other, about your friends and enemies, about Ronnie Bannister."

"I know," Charlie said, "and the wilder the stories are, the more you believe them, *because* they are wild, as far outside of you as control of your own life." He saw Andy looking at him, suddenly intent. "I ain't always been on Bisset's farm," Charlie said.

"The rumors about Ronnie started after a siege of rescue stories. The stories started early and they grew—not believed, then half believed, and then they became as real as men. They had shapes almost, personalities. But time went on and we saw we weren't going to be rescued and the rumors began to starve and shrivel, the way we were doing. Some of the guys tried to keep them alive, but they had no power. After a while, the Ronnie stories started. That he got water somewhere and was washing, that he got food somewhere and was eating, that he got strength somewhere and was living without our help and against our wishes. That story, too, got big and real and outgrew us. We watched him at night and fell asleep in our weakness, and we *knew* he got up and walked the camp. We knew the guards couldn't see him. Was he as thin as we were? We saw him as fatter, cleaner, less scabby. He took on powers we couldn't fight, he was dealing with the guards. For what? We never asked, we never reasoned out anything, but we believed everything. The rumor was taller than the man, stronger, more real. Late in March and on into the rainy season, some of the men began talking about killing Bannister.

"Most of the men didn't want to at first. Even though it was going to be an execution and not an out-and-out murder we hesitated. In our dim, sick way, we saw ourselves untied from the law. Beyond any considerations of Ronnie himself, we were afraid to touch him. We were afraid, too, of his power and our own hate.

"And then an odd thing happened. There were four guards in the camp that the guys knew could be gotten to. They had duty at various times and weren't often alone, but when they were, they could be bribed for bandages or occasional extra rice or ropes or tent stakes."

"What did you pay them with?" Charlie asked.

"A Carolina boy name of Wimmer used to catch frogs that sometimes came into camp with the rain. We ate the legs, but he would skin the things and then we would work the skins and they made up into a leather like baby alligator, a skin as big as my palm. We traded those. One of the guards was really interested in learning English, and if he was out alone at night a new Mother Goose rhyme or two could get you some coconut or a couple of squares of gauze. If not for those four, some of the men would have died, I think, since there was a lot of fever early in our stay. All of a sudden those four guards toughened up. It must have been some order from the Jap CO, but coming when it did in the wave of rumors, all those rumors about Bannister, which we believed then—how can I tell you now and have it make sense—there seemed to be a connection. We were sure there was a connection between Ronnie and the guards.

"Most of the men who wanted to kill Ronnie were heroes and the heroes had more say in the running of things than the rest of us did. Charlie, it sounds funny to hear myself say it, but I hated Ronnie as much as anyone else. I believed most of the things people said about him. By that time I'd been sick and had big ulcerating sores on my legs and feet and a kind of scurf on my scalp that was driving me crazy. Most of the men were sick or had lost teeth or had malaria, but Ronnie was in good shape, or so it seemed to us. We started—I don't know exactly how or who started it—we began playing with the idea of killing him, and this time it wasn't the heroes trying to convince us. Something had changed in our feelings. Maybe it was being in the camp so long with no rescue and no hope of it.

"Early in April, the rainy time, the heroes started going around to different groups of guys asking for votes to kill Bannister. Some of the men still said no. I said no without knowing why. Maybe it was that need they had for everyone's approval, spreading the dirt around, that bothered me—"

"Maybe you didn't believe in murder," Charlie said.

"No, it wasn't that. I hated Bannister and I believed the rumors. I wanted him dead and I was surprised at hearing *no* come out of my mouth again and again. I should have known what was going to happen. The people who wanted Bannister killed began to work on the ones who didn't and before we knew it there were only five men in the camp who were holding out for Bannister to live. The whole camp began to be against us. Some men even said that we were in with Bannister and selling out to the Japs. The pressure was terrible. I began to have nightmares, terrible nightmares, about being driven insane, and during the day there were times when I really felt I was losing my mind. The five of us were frightened all the time. We didn't dare meet or talk to each other for fear the others would think we were planning something. Then on a day that turned out to be the eleventh of April I was cutting brush in the space we had to keep clean and I fell over in a kind of faint. I could see and hear but I couldn't move or speak. I heard a man say, 'Take him up and put him in the sick hut,' and another said, 'He's one of Ronnie's boys, ain't he. Why not just leave him lay.' Another man said, 'Why not put him in the sun till he don't get up again.' I heard them and understood them but somehow I was not afraid. There was a kind of strength in me. I knew absolutely that I would live and be saved, and I knew for a certainty just then that Bannister must not be killed, that I must and would save him. I wasn't hungry or in pain or in any discomfort from the heat or lice or flies. I was perfectly happy and perfectly peaceful."

"And then?"

"In a few minutes I got up and went back to work and when night came I went around to all the groups of men and argued for Bannister's life. I was sure of myself and I had no fear. None at all. I walked around from group to group and everywhere I said something different. With some of the guys I talked about morals, with others about practical things. To a few I said that the killing would have to extend to the five of us and then to those who disapproved of *those* killings and so on and on into a hell worse than the march we had had to get to the camp. I was never so strong or so convincing before and never afterward; I was possessed."

"Possessed," Charlie said, and moved his tongue to suck at a back tooth. "Possessed by what?"

"I don't know, but now you tell me that on those days when I was suffering and I got that sudden strength Uncle Ed was weak and sick and in a kind of unconsciousness here at home."

"That ain't what I told you at all!" Charlie cried. "I didn't say they was the same days, *you* did. How can you be sure you got them days right—were they circled on some big calendar in the camp?"

"Of course not. I figured them out after—the days they must have been."

"Whatever happened to that valuable Bannister anyway?"

"I guess I had changed the minds of some of the men, because they decided to wait a day or two before they made a final decision about all of it, and somehow after that wait more time slipped by and after a while we began to see our own planes overhead sometimes, and the rumors started about *them* until we went half blind from looking into the sun. It was a kind of fever, that hate we had for Bannister, and when it was over we were left without any feeling at all. He came and went and worked beside us for the rest of the time. I don't remember anyone raising a hand to him or even saying anything. About three weeks before we were liberated he stepped on a piece of downed barbed wire and in less than

a week he was dead. He was the last casualty before libera-
tion, although there were a good many after. He was a
strange bird. After he was dead it was as though he'd never
existed."

Charlie stared out the window to the south. It gave on to
the low flat fields of Kornarenses' double section. The big
crops, winter wheat and other grains, had all been put in.
The fields of readied earth lay waiting for their changes: the
coming snow and then the crops. To the west he knew the
land was lying fallow, another shade of gray-brown beneath
beaten weed stalks and sparse clusters of yellowed prairie
vetch and gray sage. As Andy spoke a pair of magpies came
and settled in the fallow field and began to chatter. It was
a sound with almost human rhythms, rising and falling,
question and answer, accusation and denial. Something in
their voices made the day turn cold.

"It had a meaning," Andy said stubbornly. "It had a purpose and a meaning."

"What the hell are you saying?" Charlie brushed at something on his pants leg. "Are you sayin' that the Lord did that
or Edgar or who?"

Joe always kept his house too warm, but they were conscious then of a window having been opened or a door somewhere that had let the magpie-chill inside. There were low
sounds and a thump of something at the back of the house.
Charlie shook his head. "Lord says: I got a job out in the
Philippine Islands so I reckon I'll stir up some farmer out
in Colorado. Better yet, I won't tell either the Jasper in
Colorado or the Jasper in the Philippine Islands why I'm
doin' it this way or even what I'm doin'. It 'ud only upset
'em. Why didn't God just sweeten up old Bannister, or put
it in all your minds not to want to kill him no more, make
the rope break or the knife slip—any one of a thousand
things come right to mind instead of this, which, if it
happened like you said, was like scratchin' your eye with
your big toe."

"Charlie, I can't understand you."

"You share that with most people in the world."

"You don't believe in God or in the vision Uncle Edgar
had at all, do you?"

"I never had the vision and all I knew of it was the man who had it, and the only proof I ever had that God wasn't a fool was his pickin' of Edgar. How hard he prayed that I would get what he got and see what he seen and it wasn't no good. I wanted it, too—I tried like to die and it wasn't no good. Now I'm standin' out in the rain like a man trapped between locked houses. I can't unlearn what I know and get back to the way things was."

"Uncle Edgar was a good man, but he's gone now, and the Apostles have to try to carry on. Why not join us even without a special vision? All your ties are with us, Dad and me and even Grandpa."

"I know that. It's only that I ain't able, just yet, to forgive 'em."

"The Apostles? Why? What happened?"

"Nothin' *happened*, only Edgar wouldn't answer their questions. He was too ignorant for 'em and he didn't have what they wanted. They wanted God's Word brought down an' served to 'em." Charlie smiled. "There ain't many trees in these parts. Maybe you noticed that."

"Yes, Charlie, I have."

"Birds'll nest in clumps of grass or on fenceposts. You ever seen them feed, them little birds?"

"Sure, when I was a kid."

"The little birds close their eyes and open their beaks and the beaks is as big as their bodies. The big birds fly all day and on into the night gettin' food, but the little birds never let 'em rest, always cryin', those mouths always gapin' open. A thousand worms ain't enough, nor all the crawlin' bugs in the county, 'cause while them little birds is eatin', they are starvin'. Edgar's friends were like that. The Apostles are like that." Andy shivered and looked out at the blue air. "God is like that," Charlie said.

15

The wedding of Andy Kornarens and Anne Currier was the largest in the history of the area. Dilys, who had moved to Pueblo and started a group of Apostles there, came down with all his people on two flatbed trucks. The Nebraska Apostles came, groups formed by friends of Edgar's who were amazed at the numbers, liveliness, and youth of the other groups. The town came and all the farms, believers and nonbelievers. Anne's parents were dead and her aunt and uncle, faded with age and failure and astounded at the thought of their responsibility, gladly gave the arrangements to Joe and Arla. Joe went from errand to errand glowing with happiness at the stir. Years of holding Praise Dances and Apostles' meetings had taught him how to organize and delegate the work, how to figure food and space for numbers of people, and what unexpected things to expect. He had grown full size into the sureness and competence he had always yearned for, and he knew that it was his service as an Apostle of the Spirit of the Lord that had given him his strength.

"I'm no more than a farmer with his daddy's farm and a few head of stock," he said to Andy, to Arla, to Charlie, to Ralph, to the town. It wasn't vanity that made him say this. He was joyful in the service of the Spirit of the Lord, and this flowering of his family was the will of that Spirit and his competence and strength the gift of that Spirit.

The wedding went smoothly. There was a Praise which five years of tradition had invested with meaning. The bride and groom stood alone in the cleared space. They raised their clasped hands to the Lord and then were joined by their immediate kin, one by one, two by two, the close family, then friends and kin and the whole town were circling about, shouting wishes and prayers for love to the two in the center. The couple had steeled themselves for the moment when all eyes would be on them. They stood stiffly at first, their hands locked together. But slowly the rhythms of the Praise and their own innate modesty eased them. As the relatives and friends cried out to be brought into the new circle, Andy and Anne smiled at them, laughed a little, wept a little, and turned to each other now and then in that place between tears and laughter.

Outside the circle Charlie stood with his battered hat. Now and then in the space between the dancers, Andy saw him standing there. He had the furtive look that old vagrants have who do not know the names of the towns they are in. When their eyes met, Charlie raised an eyebrow and gave his quick, wry smile and the expression changed him. Many of the neighbors were openly scornful of Charlie for his lack of decent respect for his position as Brother Edgar's friend and his unwillingness to join the Apostles. Yet, by standing aside he had become as much a part of the circle as the most fervent of the dancers. It would have surprised him and them to know this, but Andy knew it and smiled for it. It gave him a peaceful feeling to see Charlie there.

Anne's old aunt and uncle sat on chairs near Joe and Arla. They still had the huddled look of people in constant expectation that an awful truth will rise and unseat them from the place of sudden honor. Their only living kin was marrying the nephew of the Founder, a kind of prince. They watched fascinated as their niece accepted the handshakes and good wishes of all her new relatives. It was a sight to turn their minds from the wedding supper that Joe and Arla were giving, where they would have to sit near the bride and groom and be watched by all those people.

Charlie had not been invited to the supper. They knew he

would not feel comfortable and would not come, saying he didn't have the clothes. He did not see the young couple for several weeks, but was never far from news of them. The town talked of nothing else for days. He knew about Anne's canning work with Arla, the new house near the older couple's, about how Andy picked his garden peas and when Anne hung the wash.

When people talked about the wedding they recalled Edgar and his mother, Cora.

"There's one sour face that girl never had to see. Now, Temperance, if she'd lived, she would have been a blessing to that couple, but that grandmaw of his, why, I can see her like it was yesterday, hair pulled back so hard it popped her eyes."

"She was a grim old harpy, whipping the world with Jesus."

"Makes you think, don't it—the Apostles never seemed to answer about Jesus one way or the other."

"I never heard Brother Edgar remark on that, on Jesus."

"Yet he was surely a Christian."

"Well, *sure.*"

Two weeks after the wedding Charlie had the chance to deliver some tools to Joe on his way back from town. Pulling into their yard he saw the new house framed up and busy with workmen. They had hired extra men from town, but Joe and Andy were also at work and Arla's boys were helping. Charlie noted that the groom seemed contented and the bride, while not radiant, was calm and steady. He had not seen her playful since the day she and Andy had come to the house the previous year. Perhaps the responsibilities of being a part of so important a family were weighing on her. Most brides followed their new husbands with their eyes, doted, glowed a little—or did they? Charlie cursed himself for the sketchiness of his knowledge. He had observed a little of Tempe and Joe as bride and groom, and that was all. How could he judge, knowing as little as he did? How could she be doting anyway, with the whole town measuring her—and him, too? Still . . . When he went back to Bisset's, Ralph close-questioned him for an hour.

"How's it workin' out, Charlie, him and her?"

"Well, they look good together—kind of a strength between 'em."

"Damn it, Charlie, that sounds like Linthicum and his mule, not a bride and groom!"

"I can't tell you no more than I seen. She ain't a farm girl, but she watches Arla close and learns. She don't have that special tone in her voice when she talks to him, but they have a solid look together—like friends do."

"Friends!" the old man cried out. "Who's talkin' about friends—I'm talkin' about a man and his wife, not friends!"

"I told you all I seen," Charlie said shortly. "What the hell do I know about husbands and wives—about families!"

In July, people at the Praise Dances began to tell of other Praises at which there was something called Racing or Running to Glory. The young people did it. They would break out of the circle and begin to run, arms outstretched, and they cried out when they ran, words that had no meaning. Sometimes they ran until they fell, sometimes they ran in circles around the outside rim of their parents' dances. They did not shout for the Lord's message or for understanding, but for something that the older people had trouble making sense of. It looked like some kind of test because the runners raced to the limits of their endurance and beyond. Sitting at the table, digesting the heavy meal, Joe and Andy listened to the guests who had come from Praises at Willow Springs and Portal to describe the running. The two men saw little to criticize in the action of the young people. You couldn't expect the young to key their steps to the slower rhythms of their elders. All over the country there were stories of young people leaving their parents' churches, leaving religion altogether, yet the Lord had shown his favor to the Apostles and the faith was growing, especially among the young.

"But they speak in tongues, gibberish. Brother Edgar never favored that, did he?"

"What did Brother Edgar say about runnin' till you faint?" The racing had not reached Founder's Praise, as they called

the Praise at Joe's, but if it was at other Praises, it was sure
to come to Founder's soon.

"—which is why I wanted to talk to you about it, Charlie.
The men who came to us asked what Brother Edgar said
about tongues and racing. Of course in Brother Edgar's time
there weren't the kinds of Praises that we have now—the
special ones for baptism, marriage, first enlightenment, and
death, but—"

"When did you start callin' him Brother Edgar instead of
Uncle Edgar?"

"Uncle Edgar sounds disrespectful, or as though I was
putting importance on myself."

"Why ask me about tongues or runnin' or any of it? You
know it wasn't Edgar's way, and if he seen it now it wouldn't
be nothin' he would recognize."

"I meant how does it sound to you?"

"Wrought up," Charlie said. "Right off it sounds all
wrought up, but what it really is is strange to me, I guess—
new. It ain't nothin' I understand. I'll tell you one thing,
mess like that will make hypocrites and liars easy as
breathin'."

"Why should that be?"

" 'Cause it's a contest, a race, and kids are more ambitious
than anyone else. Gettin' the Word is easy to fake, but up
to now there ain't been much reason to fake it. Now there
will be."

"I never thought about that—faking. You mean the emotion of it?"

"Anything a person needs to—emotion, messages—whatever is important can be lied about sooner or later. What does
the family say to it—Joe, Arla? What does Anne say?"

"Arla said the Lord wouldn't want her waddling around
chasing Him down. Then she smiled and said, 'He carries me
in his slower rhythm.' "

"Poor Arla never got over stoppin' school at the sixth
grade," Charlie said. "What does Anne say?"

"Anne?"

"Your wife."

"I guess she thinks of it as a special religious matter. I've asked her, but she doesn't commit herself. Coming in like this to a family like ours, I suppose it . . ."

"I know she's tryin' hard to be like Arla, a good farm wife—" Charlie said.

Andy nodded. "She looks up to Arla as a kind of model of what a farm wife should be, but a silence like that is—it can—oh, never mind. Now with a baby coming, I guess she's more taken up with herself, that's all." There was a look of loss and bewilderment on Andy's face. Charlie didn't know what to say.

All afternoon Charlie worked on the weeding of the shrunken garden patch. His mind kept going back to Andy's look. Racing and silences, speaking in tongues and not speaking at all. Edgar would have known the truth of it—he could have cleared away the unimportant parts and kept the truth. "Damn it!" Charlie shouted at the ground. "I know it ain't my faith and it ain't my worry. Let them pitch fits for the glory if they want—what's that to me!" He was amazed to find himself trembling and his eyes tearing. "Damn it, Edgar, they don't deserve it—it ain't right! It ain't fair!"

Founder's Praise soon learned how sheltered it had been from controversy. Two Sundays after Joe heard about the running, three hundred Apostles showed up at the Praise, most of them looking embattled. Many were strangers, but Charlie recognized quite a few early Apostles who had gone on to start Praises of their own in Kansas and Oklahoma. The Praise itself was too large to be properly done. People got in each other's way and felt constrained by the bigness from saying anything or thanking the Lord beyond the now-formal general thanks. When the time came, the visitors left quietly and without the usual joy. The ones who stayed were grim-faced. Joe went among them, recalling old days, remembering the names of wives and children, trying to loosen the mood. This ease of his always was a source of wonder to Charlie, who had stayed on to see what would happen.

"We're all good Apostles," Joe was saying, his hands open

before him in a gesture of conciliation. "The Lord gives us an answer that we sometimes don't hear."

"That's just the problem," said a woman whom Charlie knew but couldn't place. "The Lord has told us right along to keep our waiting times quiet, to let the Voice of the Spirit come in quietness. The silence, all of us together, is the greatest strength of our Praise. Now the young folks and a couple of wild people have started in on this running and tongues and falling down and they say the Spirit of the Lord has told them to do it that way. Our Praise is split. We need you to decide for us." Charlie could see that Joe wasn't happy with the baldness of the statement and even less happy when the other men muttered and nodded in agreement.

"It's not for me to decide these things," he protested. "It's the Lord's—Brother Edgar always said so—the Lord's Spirit only."

"The Praises will split," a younger woman said. "They'll all split and families who need to go to the same Praises will be split apart, and even the young people who may need the quieter way will feel they have to join the young people's Praise."

"With the Praises split into young and old, the young will never be a part of the older people's thoughts and feelings the way they are now."

"How did the racing start?" Andy asked.

"That happened in my Praise," John Seavers said, "up at Willow Springs. There are about forty of us there—we started with twenty and people came the way they did here. We even had some of the folks over the county line leave their churches and come to be with us and we were real happy until Laura Hoopes had the Word of the Spirit, she said, to show all her joy, like she said, joy beyond words."

"Young ones need to run," Joe said to them. "Why should we be against that?"

"In a circle a man sees people to the right and the left and all around. In the race a person is alone, and if he is quick he outruns his neighbors."

"But there's nothin' set about the Praises, that they need to be in circles, or any dance at all. We never really settled on the circle until after Brother Edgar passed on."

"We only wanted to Praise the Lord purely," Bill Blakely said, "not hamstrung and forced by a lot of rules. We aren't Apostles to win races."

"But the young people don't mean to race to win, I think," Andy said, "but as a kind of picture, a kind of example they understand about the Lord. After all, He gave it to them in their visions and so it's theirs and it must be true."

Andy began to speak quietly about the pride Apostles had. People were coming to the movement when all over the country and maybe the world religion was declining. The young of the Apostles didn't stay away from worship as they did in other groups. They were the more enthusiastic members. They gave the Apostles hope. He spoke matter-of-factly, never louder than a man would in ordinary conversation. Charlie watched in amazement. Andy's reasonableness had begun to soften the faces of the men around him. Some men even nodded as he spoke.

"Do you think it is a true vision?"

"Yes, I do."

"Then what will happen to our quiet Praise, our silences?"

"Why not have a race sometime during the Praise and then hold a special Praise later, in which people can use the running and the tongues—" Charlie saw them weighing it.

"That one race—should it be at the beginning or the end of the regular Praise?"

"As the Spirit of the Lord directs," Andy said. Again they weighed the words.

"We'll speak in our Praises—tell 'em what you said."

"Young people's Praises—no, maybe we'll just call them special Praises for special gifts—"

"Long as we save our silences I won't care what we call 'em."

When the men left, Joe looked at Andy. "Son," he said, "I never heard better, not even from Edgar, though I wouldn't admit it. How did you get that calmness that made them listen?"

Andy smiled. "I've been talking to Charlie here." There was a long, embarrassed pause. Joe's face showed shock and then disgust that he had praised Andy seriously and been rewarded with ridicule. Charlie felt stripped. Andy, too, read the silence and his face colored.

"Charlie's told us all about Uncle Edgar—Brother Edgar. Because of him, I know how. Uncle Edgar had a vision from the Lord. He had it without dancing, without petitions, or witnessing, or language, or the help of another living soul. He had it so whole that he never needed to find the ends of it or ask a question. Charlie told me how surprised Uncle Edgar was when people came with questions or contradictions between what they heard in church and what he told them. He never felt any contradictions. He never needed the questions. Uncle Edgar had the vision and the faith. We have the faith but not the vision, not whole, anyway, and there are people with us who don't have either but want both."

"What are you sayin', boy, that Edgar can't help us anymore?"

"The problems we have are problems he never needed answers for. I'm a keeper, a peacemaker, Dad, not a visionary. I found that out in the camp. Uncle Edgar had visions, but I can build churches."

"And Charlie taught you that?"

"I ain't taught the boy nothin'!" Charlie said angrily. "Hell, I'm standin' here wonderin' why those damn people couldn't figure out their problems for themselves." He walked away toward his car muttering, "Should have a Praise to ask the Supervision Spirit for a little good sense!" But driving home from Kornarenses' and after supper and again after whiskey and before sleep, Charlie saw the held moment, Andy's quietness, Joe's incredulous face looking hard at him for the first time in years, and he smiled his narrow, jagged, and unfamiliar smile.

16

They watched Anne carefully now that she was pregnant, and they saw how easily her pregnancy made her a part of the town and the farms. Charlie heard about the ups and downs of her condition from neighbors and storekeepers and the Apostles and even from men at the Pruitts'. She was quiet, seldom saying anything about herself or her condition, but neighbor women knew what a morning pallor meant, and the larger she showed the happier they were with her. Her body's statement stood against all secretiveness. Dr. Polk made her walk the mile to town to see him and another mile down the road. People stopped their cars for a word or two, men in the fields tipped their hats to her. They smiled and made her silence a virtue, thinking of her in the way they thought of Mary in the Bible, who also was silent. Sometimes she would walk over to Bisset's.

They waited for her the way they waited for water, with wonder and gratitude, because they were sour old men in an old and sour house, and that she should choose them, walking in the opposite direction from young neighbors and the busy stores in town to see them, was a miracle. They were almost reverent with her, making her sit down right away and giving her milk. They baked doughy cookies for her and washed and ironed the threadbare curtains. They mended all the kitchen chairs. They dropped their work when they saw her walking by the side of the turned fields half a mile away, bolting for the house to make themselves look idle so that she would not think she was keeping them from work. And they never said an unpleasant word in her presence.

"They make polite conversation like two schoolmarms," she said to Andy. Once she mentioned that Andy had caught his thumb in the truck door and Charlie had snapped:

"Now what's he gone and bothered you with that for!"

As the months went on and Anne started walking heavier, Charlie would hear Ralph at night roaming the house or slamming the icebox after a restless look for an unwanted snack. In the morning Ralph would be taciturn with self-disgust.

"Damn radio stories. TB. Spent all night worryin' about someone in the family gettin' TB. Fellow on the news was talkin' about measles. People can die of measles, did you know that?" Ralph never mentioned who might get TB or measles or be victim of any of the dozen other accidents or diseases that were suddenly so menacing, and Charlie never asked. When Andy or Anne wasn't at the house and when he didn't see them at the Praises, Charlie tried to keep his mind off them. He felt that helped to keep them safe.

Sometimes when Anne visited by herself, Charlie would defy Ralph's disgust and ask about some question raised at the Praises. He still went, still stood apart, and although Andy might trust his judgment, he knew that Joe would never speak to him about any problems. It was all Charlie could do to get a word out of Anne about the Apostles. Perhaps she thought she might be disloyal. Charlie counted it a victory when she said anything.

"There is a worry about Founder's getting too big again," Anne said one day. Charlie had plied her with bitter coffee and soggy cake and she was feeling freer that day, he could see. Patience and persistence had given him the victory.

"That's happened before," he said carefully. "People split off and get their own Praises."

"But this is different. There's talk about a building—something not so tied up with the family—and a place for the bad weather and older people to stay warm."

"What did they have in mind?"

"Well, Andy did mention some land across the road—" Now Ralph perked up. The acts of the Apostles were of no interest to him, but land was life.

"Farquahr's land!" Ralph crowed, "land he hasn't used in years."

"Do you think he'd sell?" Charlie asked him.

"I don't know. He don't think much of the Apostles—no offense, Anne, but I heard him say they weren't nothin' but a bunch of dancin' dunces. He probably wouldn't sell."

"I don't know—" Charlie said, and looked out the window at the sky. "He's gettin' on, Farquahr is, and his kids are grown and gone. He's bitter, but he ain't a fool. It hurts him to see land go back to scrub and weeds when it took so much to get it to give a crop."

"You're right," the old man murmured. "Every time he passes that field on his way from town, it tells him he ain't man enough to farm it." They caught each other's eye, Anne and Charlie. It occurred to Charlie that a person coming new into so inbred a community wouldn't know what is secret and what is not. Then Charlie turned away.

"No man is man enough to farm all that without lots of help," he snapped. They were silent until Charlie said, "It ain't the land, I mean, it's the feelin's. Farquahr's boys didn't stay, his girls married men who wouldn't farm. Now he passes that field of his and wonders why he couldn't keep them, what went wrong that not one of his sons or daughters saw fit to follow him. Maybe he's tired of that now and he'll sell the land off so it will stop hurtin' him on the way to town and back every time."

"Andy and Dad have been talking about that but they aren't sure how to approach Mr. Farquahr."

Ralph shrugged. They had come back to Apostle politics again, and he made a point of his silence. Charlie leaned back. "A group of men, older men, maybe, but not Andy or Joe, I'd say. Andy's too close to the age of Farquahr's own kids and Joe is too—too lucky. Anyway, it's better if Joe is only one of the bunch that buys that land."

After another silence Anne said, "I'll try to tell Arla what you said."

"Not that it comes from me!" Charlie said quickly. "Say it comes from the pastor or somethin'. She wouldn't credit it from me."

"Why not?" Anne asked.

"People don't."

"One person did."

"I know. The one that did credit me is gone, though."

"I'll try to tell Arla."

With a princely gesture he offered her another square of cake.

Edgar Bisset Kornarens was born on April 25, 1948, in the room and bed where his father and grandfather had been born. Anne was attended by a doctor, her aunt and mother-in-law, and several neighbor women. They said afterward that the birth had been easy.

The day was a Sunday, Praise Day. Charlie stood in his accustomed place and watched the eyes of the Apostles turning every now and then toward the window of the upper floor of the Kornarenses' house. He himself glanced up from time to time to the window where the shade had been drawn. Andy was trying to busy himself with the Praise. Once or twice he came and stood beside Charlie, resting.

"I'd go in, but they'd only send me out again. A man feels less than useless at a time like this."

Charlie nodded. "You're here if they need you and when the baby comes you'll be needed to host things—cigars and all of that." Andy was about to answer when the Praise came up and claimed him.

But the Praise itself was half alive to anything but the shade-drawn window. People gave thanks in dry, routine voices, stopping in mid-sentence for another look at the house as they turned toward it. Their steps were absent-minded and they sometimes bumped into one another,

159

bunching where there was a view of the upstairs window. In the middle of the second dance, Joe held up his hand.

"Folks!" he cried. "Folks—we ain't showin' the Lord nothin' like Praise. Now, I know we got our minds on what's goin' on in the house, maybe, and as a neighbor it makes me proud to see your care for us and know you're pullin' for Anne and the baby, but it can't take from what we owe to the Lord."

Curtis Ede spoke up. He was a neat, small man but his voice was extremely nasal and penetrating and people always flinched when they heard it. "I want to ask the Lord to make everything go right in there with that mother and that baby."

"I know it will!" someone cried. "The Lord has told me!"

The Praise suddenly seemed to have what it needed. The pace picked up and people began to smile. Messages poured through the dancers.

"The Lord has promised a beautiful child!"

"The Lord has blessed this mother."

"The Lord is smiling on this house, blessing this family."

"The Lord tells me this child is blessed!"

"The Lord is telling me the mother has his glory!"

"The Lord has declared his protection for them both!"

Charlie found himself standing up straight, watching and listening intently. The Praise was full of vigor. There was hardly room for the "Amens" and "Yes, Lords" to be heard for all the witnessing prayers that recalled the Lord to his promises.

Charlie found himself shaking his head slowly. "Somethin's wrong." He sucked at his lip, watching. It's all wrong. Can't they see what they're doing? Can't they hear it? The happy dancers swept around past him, and with his lip still tucked under his front teeth he turned toward Andy, who was standing beside him. Andy's eyes were full of tears and his breathing was labored. Charlie felt a deep relief. Andy knew what the Praise was doing and he had the words to tell people, the ways to make them see that they had changed from asking the Spirit's blessing to answering in its place. The boy would need comfort and support, though. Anyone does who is seeing something that others don't. "Don't worry," he hissed at Andy over the joyful noise of usurpation. "You can tell 'em later

160

when they calm down. You can show 'em what they done and they'll take it from you—"

Andy's hand found Charlie's arm blindly and patted it. "You're right, Charlie. I'll have to thank them later for this love they're showing—it is a wonder, all of them so full of the Lord's will for us, all so united in the Lord!"

When he told Ralph later, Ralph only said, "You shouldn't hang around them dances so much. As it was all account of my grandson, I ain't gonna see nothin' wrong with it!"

So Charlie continued to go to Praises and stood listening, or trying to listen, more carefully than ever for sounds of the change he had heard in that birth Praise. But the Sundays and the special night vigils came and went, and while there were sometimes hints of what he came to call Prophet-working, things seemed to have settled back to what they had been. Edna Farrier still toted up the family wrongs, Carson Oates still prayed for patience. Often, now, there were visitors from other Praises, and Charlie found himself listening to their problems with greater interest than before. Some of these people came from as far away as Iowa and Montana. Often they were Praise leaders and wanted to confer with Andy and Joe alone, but sometimes they brought their problems to Praise, and the problems they had showed how much the Apostles had grown and spread and to how many different kinds of people. How could a Praise be held in a city without its becoming a spectacle? How could there be outdoor Praises in places like Minnesota in the winter? What about Negro members? What about traditions of Christmas and Easter? Raising of money? Leadership? Special services or feasts— Brother Edgar's birthday or the date of the founding of the Apostles? What actually was the founding year? Many Praises were forming, breaking up, and re-forming over the problems of leadership. Because there were so many visitors, it was decided that summer to build a small guesthouse next to the new church.

A year after the building of Founder's Church, Ralph Bisset and Charlie moved into Joe Kornarens's house. The old man had fought the move for months, arguing with Charlie, with Joe, with anyone who would listen, that if he moved away from his homestead it would kill him. But even he knew that it was impossible to stay. The ground had never recovered from the bad years and the two old men weren't strong enough to keep the house in repair. On the day of the move, Charlie and the old man sat on their butt-sprung chairs while Andy and Joe picked among the tools and household goods for anything worth taking. When the old settee was moved, mice scampered away to seek other places. The kitchen bore years of grease—long tears of it flowed down the back wall behind the stove. Charlie hung his head with the shame of it. The kitchen and pantry rugs were so old and dirty that they had softened down and become one with the floor. It was his fault. He was the younger man, he was the one they would blame. "Why didn't Charlie keep the place up, clean under the sink once in a while, instead of leaving that slow leak to rot the boards like he done?" And the filth was years old, built up one year after another. It was enough to shame a man into muteness, and he sat silently while they went through the house, embarrassed at the poverty, the squalor, the evidences of loneliness. It was a relief when it was over and they could lock the house and go on to the barn.

Outside, they looked around for the usual extras that accumulate on old farms, nail cans under the porch, old rolls of wire. The farm was leached dry. The irrigation district had taken the water that had once nourished the place sporadically and diverted it away toward farms where storage arrangements had been made. Some of the ground had eroded badly in the flash floods of the past year. The air smelled of dust, a smell that Andy remembered as the smell of his childhood—death, hunger, regret, a smell of loss. He saw in his mind a white curtain pushed aside at a window, a woman's dress, a blue dress, dark blue with a small pattern in it of lighter blue, a step sounding grittily on a bare wood floor. Sunlight, a woman's voice, tired, a low voice saying— he strained to hear it but the words wouldn't come clear. He wondered if it might be his mother. He groped toward the memory again, but now he was trying for sensation and detail and the pictures wouldn't come.

Up in the barn, Charlie was poking among the old tools. Things were almost as bad here as they were in the house—splintering handles, rusted blades. A man fails when he can't answer the charges against him, when he's convicted by his own silence or by God's silence. Why should he want to stay here anymore? Why not leave it all, house and barn to the mice, generations of them squeaking and gibbering under the rotting boards, and let the walls sag until they were blown over by the March wind? All the nourishing memories were so distant and so old.

"Charlie, we got a dozen hay forks on the place and the oldest one's in better shape than that one. Put it down and let's lock up the barn. Ain't no one gonna steal anything."

But Charlie insisted. "I got to take this shovel. I got my own worn places on it. It knows me. That and the lantern, which was Edgar's favorite one, is all I want from here."

He was lying. He had bought the lantern himself not long after Edgar died, and now he watched them take it from him carefully like a relic because it had been Edgar's, and again he felt ashamed of himself. Ralph had scarcely spoken since Joe and Andy had come, but the mention of Edgar stirred him.

"What are we leavin' for? To sit up in Joe's big house like two old buzzards and sour the ground? Long as you're so keen on Edgar's things, why, this was his barn, that house was his house, his birthplace!" Everyone was stilled with embarrassment. It was true; they were all relics of Edgar, the Founder, and look at the care that had been taken of his memory here! No wonder Joe had been at them so long to come away. The house and the two old men had been a shame to everybody. Charlie took refuge in facts.

"Why, Ralph, this house wasn't Edgar's birthplace and you know it. Edgar was born when you was all livin' in the soddy —where I bunked when I first come to work for you." Ralph gave Charlie a disgusted look and they left the barn.

Leaving, they trailed a long plume of yellow-white dust behind them. This road would never be graveled and tarred now. The county was tarring the road past Dodson's as far as the new interstate. That would be where the coffee joints and beer places would be built, where the tourists might pass, looking at the flat fields without comprehension, on the way to somewhere else.

"Remember what I said about the house," Charlie said, "when the Ladies' Landmark Society comes around with a plaque to put on the door up there and charges half a dollar to people to get in and look at them mice!" Andy, who was driving, said nothing. Charlie, too, was quiet after that. Ralph and Joe were following in Ralph's old car. Maybe Andy had really seen in his mind the house repaired and kept, the land not farmed but given back to the thick, binding sod of the prairies of his imagination, cover-cropped and watered. The barn would be shored up and refurbished with its tools and kept as it was when Edgar had gone there to visit in peace with the Voice of the Presence. Why not? It had been done for presidents and historical figures. Why shouldn't there be a place for Apostles to come in future years and wonder at? Even now, the feeling of those days was slipping away. Farming itself was changing so much that the old people barely recognized it for what it had been.

They pulled up at Kornarenses' and the difference between the two places was so plain it was embarrassing. First and most important, there was water here. Andy's own house, freshly painted, stood behind the lacework of cottonwoods and shrubs. Not far away stood Joe's big house, built in the ample old-fashioned style, also newly painted and in good repair. On the north side, outbuildings, corrals, and runs made the place look like a settlement instead of a single farm. The ground had been watered down very lightly, but enough to wake the odors of growth and rich soil, and it made Charlie shake his head again and say what was always said in the presence of that incomparable smell:

"Damn country could be the Garden of Eden! the Garden of Eden if there was water enough."

When they got out of the truck and were all unloaded, there was a sudden stilted moment. The four men stood as if waiting, the old men wishing to go inside and be done with the change, the young abruptly aware of their own impatience. Then Arla opened the back door, Anne behind her, and shouted the welcome to all of them:

"Come on in now, there's hot coffee ready on the stove." Before they all escaped into bustle, Andy turned and saw that Charlie was measuring him with a long, unguarded look. The look surprised him, so that long afterward he found himself trying to remember it exactly. Perhaps it was the time of day or the fall of the light. It was a look of great gentleness, almost of pleading.

The two old men were living with Joe and Arla when Edgar Bisset Kornarens came to awareness. He was a placid baby and a loving child who accepted everyone genially and freely and loved to sit on Grandpa Joe's shoulders or to ride with his father on the tractor. He loved the huge suppers of harvest time when the big tables were set out under the trees. He, too, learned to lean back in his chair and sigh as the men did, and when someone noticed this and laughed, he laughed with everyone else. When he was sixteen months old, a sister, Corella, was born.

The family had become well known in the years of the Apostles' growth. People came to their Praises from all over the country and it was natural that the Kornarens children would be pointed out and made much of. That people showed special respect for his father and grandfather seemed natural to Edgar and that people paid special attention to him was to be expected. He took for granted old Charlie's silent patience. When Edgar was big enough it was Charlie who taught him to fish and play penknife games in the soft earth near his mother's vegetable patch. Edgar learned early that it was possible to devil Charlie in ways that would not be tolerated by other people. Charlie wasn't like Grandpa Ralph or Grandpa Joe. Even when Grandpa Ralph said silly things people listened and showed respect. Once or twice Edgar had sassed Charlie and not been punished for it, but he was not a cruel child and it soon appeared to him that he felt happier when he treated even Charlie well. Charlie was a strange person. The stiff deference he used to Anne always made the family smile. It was never mentioned aloud, of course, nor was the funny sweet-rot smell of Charlie's breath in the morning, nor the one time when Charlie's gentleness failed.

It was on a Saturday afternoon, one of the oven-afternoons of a dry mid-August, when Edgar was eight. The heat that day seemed savage beyond bearing; work was impossible, games palled, his mother and father waved him away. There was no rest in his house, which buzzed with heat. Corella in her boredom became whiny and contentious. Luther and Carl, Arla's boys, had grown and gone. Edgar was bored. After trying to find a cool place under the house he suddenly thought to go up to the attic room where Charlie stayed. Although it was hot under the roof, Charlie had once told them how he had rigged the window fan in such a way, he said, that tree-cooled air flowed through the rafters and was caught. Edgar had never been up in Charlie's attic place. It suddenly seemed strange that he had knowledge of every corner of both houses, every pen, outbuilding, barn loft, and toolshed on the farm, but not this little room on top of his grandfather's house, where his good friend stayed. Edgar left Corella in the hiding place under his own front steps, crossed the yard and the broken-through hedges between the houses, and ducked in at his grandparents' kitchen door. Just at the entrance his grandmother sat dozing in a big chair in the forlorn hope of catching a little of the breeze. Her breath whistled in and bubbled out slightly. He crept past her. Grandpa Joe was in the parlor, lying on the floor for the cool, his shoes off, his head under his arm like a bird. Edgar found himself furtively going up the stairs to the second floor and then to the big closet where the linens were kept and where the ladder was that led to the attic. He had been up the ladder almost to the top once, had, in fact, hidden on it in the dark, trembling with fearful glee while his sister and Arla's youngest passed below him in a game of hide-and-seek.

The house was utterly still. He was glad he couldn't hear them. The stillness was magical; not even the air moved. Slowly he steadied the ladder and mounted it with care so as not to flaw the perfect silence. When he was halfway up the ladder he thought he heard something. It was like the sound of steam escaping from under a pot lid. It came from

166

above him and ahead of him, from the attic room. For a moment he had a dizzy thought that the heat had set the roof on fire, that the air was burning with this hiss. He went up further, silently, savoring the strange sound. At last his head broke through to floor level. Now he saw everything from the dust-and-grit plane of the floor. Two inches from his eye a great puff of slut's wool stood motionless. He raised his head and blew it gently. It danced away across the floor. The sound came again. It was Charlie. He was lying on the bed asleep, facing the open attic window through which no breeze stirred the limp muslin curtains. Charlie's shirt was off. He was lying on his stomach with his face turned to the wall. Edgar didn't know why he kept his breathless silence. He wasn't playing with Charlie, coming upon him by surprise. He only wanted to keep everything as it was, to set no more dust rolling with his breath, or shadow any sunlight with his presence. Slowly he continued up until he stood on the top rung of the ladder. There was a little rail to hold and he held on until he stood on the floor. His feet were bare, hard-callused summer feet, but still sensitive to the uncomfortable heat of the boards and the gritty sand on them. No boards creaked. He moved a step or two toward the bed, thrilled with his own silence. He might have been bodiless. With Charlie facing away, it was impossible to call to him. Edgar looked at Charlie on the bed. His body was very pale, and on his back a lot of pinkish ridges crisscrossed each other. Edgar stared, fascinated. They looked like badly drawn furrows made by the old kind of plow and they pulled across his body from the right shoulder down to the left to disappear beneath his belt. Edgar could not take his eyes away. He realized he had never seen Charlie with his shirt off before. What surprised him most was that he thought he knew all about Charlie, knew him as fully as he knew the houses and lands of his father's and grandfather's farm and the secrets of a dozen Praises. He wanted to go over and touch the ridges to see if they were rough or smooth, yet the thought of doing it filled him with fear and revulsion. Then he realized he was trapped. He dared not sneak back down the ladder; the spell was gone from him and now the boards would creak, the ladder rattle. He could not go forward or speak to Charlie. He could only stand as he was standing, perhaps until the sun went down and he was hidden in the darkness. Then Charlie spoke, whispering something over and over, and Edgar realized that that had been the sound he had heard, a rapid, desperate whisper.

"Why can't it ever be light!" the voice hissed. "Why is there only this darkness!" Then, "I can't!" and the whisper sank beyond words. The captive feeling worsened in Edgar. He felt his vulnerability, his childishness. He was disarmed and guilty, far from the safe preserve he had left. As he stood by, a horrified victim, Charlie turned on the narrow cot, and then sat up, his head down, his knees spread, and his skinny arms resting on them. He was still whispering, then he spoke aloud.

"God damn! Hot as hell in here." Without raising his head he reached toward a footlocker that was standing by the bed and opened it, taking out a pint bottle of something clear. Edgar became aware of the hot, resinous wood odor of the walls. Charlie drank, tilting his head back, and his eyes met Edgar's in the wavery bottom of the bottle. Time suddenly became like the passage of a long, slow freight train at which Edgar looked, mesmerized.

"What do you want here, boy?" Charlie said. It was not a question and Edgar could not answer it. Charlie's hand came up to his chest and he perceived by touch that it was bare. He began to cough. The cough sounded as though he could not decide if what he had swallowed was liquid or solid. Word by word between coughs, he cried:

"Get out, damn it, and never break in on a man!" Edgar forgot to be careful. He turned and bolted, disappearing immediately from Charlie's sight, missing the first rung and falling against the ladder down to the floor below, where he lay half sobbing with his ankle bent beneath him. When his father noticed the limp later in the day, Edgar said he had tripped on the back-porch steps of his own house. Arla made him put his foot in wheat-water, and when Charlie came into the kitchen and saw Edgar sitting there, he looked away quickly and said nothing. Later in the week, Charlie made the comment that the boy was growing up and would soon be a man. Joe and Andy nodded proudly at the words, but Edgar heard something else. After that day Charlie did not muss Edgar's hair anymore or rest his hand on Edgar's arm or shoulder. Edgar sometimes saw him begin to do these things and then stop and push his own hair back or wipe at his own grizzled face.

Edgar

17

To a person living in the town its changes were almost imperceptible. In the abrading wind the newest storefront soon weathers to look like all the rest. If a street opens a little to the west it shrinks a little to the north, not growing or dying but only changing its position like a sleeper going deeper in his bed. Still, over the years the town had greened a little. Because the land was arid and the climate dry, people were careful to plant green things when they could and to treasure the few trees that would grow in a place too cold; too hot, and too dry. There were big cottonwoods next to the courthouse and one near the new bank, and when the old Methodist church was torn down they kept the tree that had been planted there to mark the end of the Big Dust. If a visitor complained of the cottonwoods shedding in their season, filling the air with fluff and banking the streets like snow, the townspeople looked away and did not answer.

The biggest change was the presence of Memorial Square. It lay one block behind the courthouse, a small square of unused land by the old railroad station which had stood vacant since the dust-bowl days. After World War II, the town council had decided to move the old World War I plaque out of the courthouse, mount it and the World War II plaque in suitable bases of the soft local stone, and set them both up together, leaving room nearby for whatever new wars were to claim county boys. Trees were planted around the park with mathematical exactness by the grade school and the lawn was sodded by the 4-H. The Elks had supplied four benches. It had been hoped, at the beginning, that tourists might stop.

There was one other monument stone on the east side of the park. This was the monument containing a plaque with the names of the winners of the Mohlencamp Scholarship Award, given each year by the county to its most deserving high-school student. Perhaps, in the council's mind, the award was also tied up with a war and so deserved to be in the memorial park.

In 1917, John Mohlencamp had left high school and joined the Army. When he was killed at Château-Thierry, his heartbroken parents had set up a fund to sponsor a deserving boy through his years at the state agricultural school. Over the years the bank had invested this money with such skill that the fund was able to send students to many Colorado colleges and universities.

The people of the prize committee and the Mohlencamp family, which still had its representative on the prize committee, were men of modest dreams. They did not see the scholarship educating an Einstein or sponsoring a Shakespeare. The standards had been defined years ago and were inscribed at the head of the list of names: A dedicated student who beyond scholarship exemplifies the qualities of leadership and service to his family, neighbors, school, and community.

The names on the plaque were names still in the county: Ambrose, Weile, Kornarens, Blodgett, Ede. The mayor in bestowing the scholarship had often remarked that to read the list of its winners was to show how well the committee's standards had endured. There were veterinarians, doctors, lawyers, teachers, one state senator, and two school principals. Many had seen fit to use their talents to enrich other communities, but a number had returned after their college years to serve the county and its people.

The award was, for the Mohlencamps, a triumph over loss and despair. Perhaps the prize committee felt, too, that the grief and failure of the dust-bowl days gave their monument a place in the park and that its presence there would teach the valuable lesson that sorrow, grief, and loss were meant to be transformed into something that the town might use. Like all farmers and the sons of farmers, they were men who hated waste.

It was almost time for school to start when Edgar's father took him and Corella to town to buy the clothes and school supplies they would need to begin the year. He was going to be in the sixth grade, the top of the lower grades, a year full of privilege and responsibility before being plunged into the bigness of the junior high. His mother had planned to go with them, but at the last minute she had gotten a headache and was upstairs in the darkened bedroom with a cloth over her eyes. The afternoon was warm and smelled of summer dust, and the three of them rode above it in the cab of the truck into town where Andy gave Edgar Arla's careful list of what both of them would need. Edgar sometimes wondered why it was always his grandmother who made the lists, supervised the trips, and criticized the results and not his mother, but something warned him away from asking anyone about it. It breathed a kind of disloyalty. He got the necessary money from his father, who was headed for the hardware store, and he and Corella started down the long street.

They walked from store to store, devouring the sights and passing in and out through all the open doors, up and down the aisles. Arla had called in to the dry-goods store ahead of them, and they were fitted from her list. They knew that only at the end of their shopping would they go to the five and dime. They were saving it for last because it was the best. Savoring was Edgar's way and he had talked Corella into it, although she was a child who loved the immediacy of good things. They had exhausted the dry-goods store and the drug and hardware stores, and the sun was streaming across the counters of the five and dime, before they went in. The late light broke across the bands of lipsticks and the rows of red mouthwash bottles. It glowed on the plaid ribbon that was pulled from the big spools for display. Corella went to the ribbons first while Edgar drifted to the toy counter and then to the hardware and slowly toward the school supplies piled against the north wall. The high-school things were at the back, mysterious graph paper and delicate glass slides of the wings of insects and the scales of fish. Toward the front were the great piles of paper and stacks of pencils for the elementary school. There was a first-day aroma from the wood of the pencils and the cool smell of the paper. Other schoolchildren were there also, drifting back and forth between the school supplies and the toy and candy counters. They greeted each other shyly and with formality, having been apart all summer. Edgar saw that friends had grown, and knew he had grown also; this, too, made them shy. Ansel Case was there with his sister, Annabel, a special friend of Corella's. The two girls greeted one another and began to talk. Edgar was holding his unneeded sweater and found that it was hard to balance the notebook paper, assignment book, loose-leaf, and pencil case, and the new pen, erasers, and ruler. He put the supplies on his arm and laid his sweater over them. Annabel and Corella had gone up to the front. Edgar followed them to the cash register where Mr. Lang waited to take their things. Edgar didn't hear Mr. Lang until he was close to him. Mr. Lang was facing Annabel stiffly and his voice was hard.

"You just watch your step, miss, and don't try to get away with things you haven't paid for." He scooped up the money that was on the counter before him, rang it up, and then wrapped the little pile of Annabel's supplies in brown paper. Annabel's hand was raised a little, the back of her neck a dark red, and Ansel was trying to say something that he couldn't get said. With a hard shrug, Mr. Lang pushed their package over to them and motioned them out of the store.

"Damn kids!" he said under his breath. Then he looked up and saw Edgar and Corella there. The other children had stepped back out of the path of his anger, leaving Edgar and Corella alone before him. Edgar saw Mr. Lang's face relax. As he watched, the eyes seemed to change their nature. The two children stood hanging in that moment, fixed on his great adult's face. When he spoke his voice had turned friendly and easy, as though by magic.

"Why, hello, Edgar, hello Corella. Getting ready for school,

I see. Now which of you is going to be first?" Corella went forward to the counter and put her things down, taking her sweater off the top of the pile. Mr. Lang rang up the pad, the pencil case, the crayons, and the notebook. Then Edgar's. He made the packages with care, tying a little fingerhole in each string and smiling as the two of them watched his fingers move. He even waved at them as they walked toward the door.

Corella was outside and Edgar halfway out when he remembered something and caught her arm.

"Corella!" She turned and her eyes opened wider at his frightened face. "We put things in the pencil boxes!" Another child had finished and was coming out. Mr. Lang was ringing up the orders of other children. Edgar motioned to her and they went back inside to the counter.

"You kids forget something?"

"We're awful sorry, Mr. Lang," Edgar said, "we both put things in our pencil cases—here, we'll show you." He began to work at the package string. The man only put his hand gently on Edgar's package and said mildly:

"Never mind. You just tell me what you've got and I'll add it here." He took a pencil and paper from somewhere behind the counter and added the prices of the pencils and erasers. They paid the extra money, thanked Mr. Lang again, and turned to leave. "Now watch yourselves crossing the street, you hear? Look both ways." They went out quickly to where the truck was parked. Passing in front of the glass window, they saw Mr. Lang from the back and the girl he was waiting on facing them. She was looking at him fearfully. His motions were quick and brusque and he tapped each notebook at the back, to make sure that nothing had been slipped into it.

"Mr. Lang was wrong," Corella said. Edgar did not answer. It was not the mistake over Annabel Case that he was thinking about but the difference in treatment between the Case children and himself, between all the other children and himself. It had often been there, a feeling of the difference, but never so clearly seen, never something from which he could not turn away laughing and forget. He had the feeling also that the difference was not because of his father or the

177

Apostles. It was for himself, he was sure of it, for himself. He looked up and down the familiar street. For a moment he was tempted to try out his known knowledge at the grocery, the hardware store. What was the difference? Did Corella see it?

"Corella—" She looked at him. "Annabel Case wouldn't steal anything," she said. And her face was puzzled.

When they went home and were asked about their afternoon they did not mention what had happened and the incident soon passed from their minds. That Sunday there was a meeting with Apostles from Texas, and Edgar and Corella were picked up and carried through the early part of the dancing by a huge, bearded man from their group. They were used to being pointed out and made much of by visiting Apostles and others wanting to see the family. Corella did not like the extra attention and she often cried or went sulky, or disappeared, but Edgar enjoyed being called over and introduced. The faces were friendly and the people often came from places hundreds of miles away. They sometimes had new jokes or little stories or experiences about their homes to tell, things Edgar had never heard before, and he would hurry over when he was called and answer the questions well. His behavior gave his grandfather great pride.

"Listen to that boy speak! Why, when I was ten, eleven years old, I couldn't answer to my own name in front of folks!" And if Corella balked at the continuous interruptions of her games and studies to meet and greet people, Edgar always responded with his natural and spontaneous joy.

His year in the sixth grade started well. His teacher, Mrs. McDonald, was a pleasant person with a liking for poetry and adventure stories, which she would read aloud in a deft, understated way. The projects and assignments interested him and he felt he was doing exceptionally well. Mike Anton, whom he had known since first grade, had become his best friend and he was happier with the friendship than he had been with all his other past "special" friendships, because Mike was witty and intelligent and perceptive and they could share more than the ordinary roughhouse with each other.

Then Mrs. McDonald began to change toward him. In class she stopped calling on him and seemed to grade his papers more severely than the others'. Whenever a group of boys was idling in the halls or talking after the bell had rung and he was among them, it was he who was singled out for blame, he who was sent most often to the office. Edgar was not a boy to question the reasons of other people—his life had given him no training in it and no purpose for doing it. He thought that she had stopped liking him for some reason outside himself. He grew cautious of offending her and tried hard to do his work well and be inconspicuous. As he succeeded, things went better and the pressure eased. His friendship with Mike deepened that year, partly because Mike was sympathetic to his problem and helped him to be quieter, less spirited, and so less often in trouble. He had realized by then that some of the others had grouped around him simply because of his already-present popularity. A popular person attracts more people and the popularity soon becomes impersonal, like sunshine or wind. Mike's friendship was personal, particular, and special. Had he been crippled or the son of drunkards, Edgar felt that Mike would have been his friend anyway. He had just come to a place in his life where that quality was important.

Mike's people lived past the town to the west on a small and dilapidated farm. The Antons were committed Apostles and long-time residents of the county, but unlike the Kornarenses they had no other pole-stars and no other success. John Anton was a man who was always backing out of ruin, pulling his coat up quickly from mistakes, bad luck, bad management, and impossible dreams.

Edgar loved to go to Mike's when John Anton's dreams were upon him. He dreamed eloquently, grandly, completely. Two years ago it was viticulture, and he had sketched for Edgar and Mike's other friends and whomever else would listen the great level sweep of the long land, gray-green under susurrous vines of a new drought-resistant strain. Their product would astonish the world, beggar California. And he proved it with charts of rainfall and runoff, soil tests, weather studies, graphs, and statistics.

"Boys, this county is going to change before your eyes," he

would say, and their eyes would get larger to accommodate the new things that were to come. He had laid out great tracts and set up the supporting frames and ordered the special parent plants from some special place. And then in the following months the flow of his talk slowed a little. He was working out the problems, he said. And then there was nothing more for a long time, and when Edgar would see him in town or at Mike's (with the vines toed-in but still not planted, the supporting frames stretching out the length of a long field but still unbraced) and would ask about the progress of things there would be a vagueness and long silence. Then there was a little flurry of the old passion, but all negative. The county couldn't support a big new industry like grape growing. Look at the condition of the railroad, the scarcity of water, the trickiness of the winds in the crucial growing months! By spring the supporting frames had begun to sag and some toppled, and the turned earth where the vines were to have been planted sank like old graves drawing inward. There was a month, two, three of silence from Mike's father, who moved like a depressed shadow from room to room in the house. Then, in the autumn, rebirth, a stunning sudden burst of genius and energy, and John Anton rose from his forgotten defeats with a new dream, a new plan, a new future—archaeology.

Sometimes the Kornarens men laughed at him a little.

On the last day of school Edgar stayed late. His mother had given him a small gift-wrapped box of her preserves to present to Mrs. McDonald and in the last-day confusion there had been no time to give it to her. He had hung back until the other kids were gone. Charlie was in town, he knew, and would give him a ride back home. He wanted to avoid the hectic, false gaiety of the last-day ride on the school bus anyway, so he had dawdled until the bus was gone and then walked back through the empty building. He found himself relishing the strangeness of a place that was familiar only when it was full of people and activity. The room echoed wonderfully. He knew the teachers were still there, sitting in their small lounge behind the school office drinking coffee. He got the gift from his locker and went toward the office.

He could hear some of them talking while he was still in the hall. The day was warm and all the doors were open. It was the mention of his name that stopped him from going in.

"The biggest worry I've had this year was Edgar Kornarens," Mrs. McDonald was saying. "I suppose I went a little overboard about it."

"Edgar?" (That would be Mrs. Greenough, the fourth-grade teacher.) "But he's such a lovely boy—you can't possibly mean *Edgar*."

"That was just my problem. I hate favoritism, I've always hated it, and it was all I could do to keep my feelings from showing and giving him preference all the time."

"Well, I suppose it's right to fight against these feelings, but usually it's the hateful thoughts you need to get under control," Mrs. Greenough said. "I suppose I favored Edgar when he was in my class, the other children knew, of course they knew, but then they favored him, too, and so I guess we all did. I wish his sister, Corella, had some of what he has, I can tell you that." She sighed and Edgar heard her changing position. "I wish I knew why certain children—what makes them have that special *presence*. It isn't looks or manners or brightness, not altogether—I wish I knew what it was, but Edgar is special in that way. Oh, do you want another piece of this cake? Mrs. Roy made it."

Edgar turned and walked very quietly back to the classroom. He left the package on Mrs. McDonald's desk and then went down the hall again, very quietly past the office, and out the front door. He never spoke to anyone of what he had heard, but there was a flicker of resentment toward Mrs. Greenough because of what she had said about Corella. Its presence in him surprised him.

During the next winter Brother Andy Kornarens went to Nebraska to visit other Praises. Some of the Apostles had begun to worry about the absence of formal religious training for their children. Few Apostle children knew even the simplest Bible stories, and there had been the question of a Bible or Sunday school. He left in January, between seasons. He stayed a week and returned in an excellent mood.

"Lord, they make it colder up there than it needs to be!

The Praises are fine and strong. There's a school that'll help with a Bible course through the mail for anyone who wants it, but the Nebraska Praises decided against a Sunday school and I agree. All the other faiths separate the parents from the children. I don't believe in separating the young." He reached over and mussed Edgar's hair affectionately. "We want you kids with us to share all of it. Grown-ups and kids should share the glory together."

Anne spoke from beside him where she was pouring his coffee. "You're not leaving again for a while, are you?" He looked up at her and Edgar had the feeling that there must have been some words between them about his having to go.

"Praises are always asking for someone to visit," he said reasonably. "I just wish you'd come with me and see how much they need the example of stability and patience that Founder's has."

Edgar began to say, "Why don't you go, Ma?" when he felt a sharp pain in his ankle. Across the table from him, Charlie was smiling serenely at him and making the smallest possible negative shake of his head.

"I couldn't leave," Anne said. "What about the children and what about the people who all come here—"

Edgar said "We—" and felt the pain again and this time Charlie's smile was sardonic, and he said no more. Charlie told him later that his mother's words had nothing to do with him at all but with his father.

"She don't have it easy, your ma. Your pa has a kind of a call and she married the call when she married him, but it ain't the same as having the call yourself." It was better to have a call, than, Edgar thought, to be the taken one.

The following year in the Apostle's bulletin, *Praise*, coming out of Oklahoma, there was a picture of the eight Apostles of the first college Praise. The bulletin was deluged with letters of joy. *Praise* itself had ushered in a new era for Apostles. The editors of this small bulletin apparently did not know how desperately their services were needed. Within two years, *Praise* was a fifty-page journal on glossy paper with pictures, articles, discussions, and a popular column on etiquette for Apostles. In the back it published a list of all the Praises in the United States, some 750 groups, mostly in the Midwest but with groups as distant as Oregon, Georgia, and upstate New York. And almost overnight, there were issues to debate.

Was the group Christian? Did the Apostles actively believe in Jesus? Seeking back across visions and all the way to Founder, they realized there was a surprising absence, a silent space which they had not missed until now.

"It was Cora who took care of Jesus around there," Charlie said. "When she got through, I guess there wasn't much left for anyone else."

"Yes." The old man nodded. "Cora was strong on Jesus. She wasn't happy out here. Too flat. She got to aimin' Jesus at people and I guess it got so's the rest of us just tried to keep out of the way. Why is it so important what Edgar thought about Jesus?"

"It's a question now, that's all. People are askin' it now."

"Why didn't they ask it then?" the old man demanded.

"I guess they're askin' it now because they didn't need to ask it before," Charlie said to him. "Edgar was walkin' in a desert; he was eatin' dust; he was down to the dry rinds of everythin' and he come on a stream of good, sweet water and he fell on his knees and put his face in it and thanked God for it. People now are askin' how deep is the stream and how wide, and how fast and does it run placer gold—"

Andy turned to him. "You're not scared we're going to set up toll booths on Edgar's path to that stream, are you?"

"Not you," Charlie said. "I'm not scared about you, but there's people waitin' to pan gold from the banks and there's nothin' in the setup to stop 'em."

"That's a little cynical, don't you think? Besides, what would they want? The money we collect isn't worth taking."

"It isn't safe," Charlie insisted.

"We're simple people," Andy said quietly, "modest people. We're not philosophers, there's no danger for us."

"Edgar was always in danger and he talked to God all the time—"

"Edgar? How could Edgar have been in danger? Edgar was with the Lord." Charlie shrugged and turned away. There was work to do. There was always work to do.

Everyone was working harder now and at more varied work than ever. Mixed farming was back and the stock which had been sold in the forties was being bought again for grazing. A man didn't make only one crop, but alfalfa, broomcorn, and one or two of a score of new strains of wheat. Bargains were being struck with the land. Men must compromise when they farm dry, high, windy plains because the plains will not compromise. A man may dam the water of his torrential creeks and slow streams, but the seasons flow over his head and laugh at him, and in their graves the dry bones of the dead measure the secret watercourses.

It was about this time, when Edgar was thirteen or fourteen, that the research man came to Founder's Praise. He was writing a book, he said, to be called *Religion in America,* and one large chapter was to deal with what he described as "the thousand groups and cults" which had no tie with the great central streams of the major faiths. He was a strange man, and his effect on the Apostles was stranger still. He listened to everyone with great seriousness, went to the Praises and stood watching with intense concentration, studied the Seeking and Bringing races with neither scorn nor condescension, and yet made no move toward Praise himself. The Apostles' faith was still a farm faith. Where there were Praises in the cities, they had been brought there like tied animals for sale; they writhed in the bonds. Indoors, the transplanted farmers found Praises suddenly too crude, sweaty, and undisciplined, when the Methodists had dignity and the Pentacostals joy.

The researcher's name was Hawkins and he went about with a small notebook in which he carefully quoted the statements made to him and reported the length of the races and the duration of the Praises. Soon people were asking him questions. Was it true that in the Mormon cities Praises were forbidden and that all the Utah Praises were held at night to circumvent the authorities? No, it wasn't true. Had he seen the Kansas Praises and were they bigger? Yes, he had seen four Praises in Kansas and they were somewhat bigger. Strangely, and no one could figure out why, his answers made them irritated and defensive, and they found themselves comparing their numbers and piety with Praises in other places. Still more tormenting were the comparisons they felt with other of Hawkins's thousand cults and sects. They had never seen themselves as one of a number. Young Apostles raced to find the Lord. So did the Sabbatarian Brethren. Apostles believed that no one could lie while Praising. So did the New Covenenters. Apostles had no ministry. Neither did the Receivers of the Spirit (Morganites) or the group which called itself Rooted in the Lamb. Listening to themselves in a list of outlandish names—the Sons of Light versus the Sons of Darkness, the Universal Watchword, the Way, the Truth, the Life—the Apostles of the Spirit of the Lord felt their own name go strange; their own gestures unnatural. They knew that most of their fathers and mothers had not prayed this way, and would, were they to see them now, find the way as bizarre as dervish dancing or snake handling. Once, after a particularly rich and varied Praise, a breathless old dancer brought her friends to the researcher and asked:

"If you was going to choose a Way, wouldn't you choose us?" Hawkins's face betrayed instantly the shock and incredulity which no amount of polite temporizing could wipe away.

"I—a person doesn't choose his faith, really. I am a student of religion in general."

"Can there be such a thing as religion in general?" the woman persisted, realizing that she should not persist but unable to stop.

"I suppose," said Hawkins, "some faiths are fuller, richer than others, but to me, as a student of religion, all of them are, must be, equal."

His statement was discussed by everyone. Most Apostles felt it to be profoundly insulting and could not tell how or why this should be so. The equality meant a freedom to Praise, to run races or sing or be silent and thus to fulfill the essence of Edgar Bisset's vision—to do whatever the Spirit of the Lord sent each man to do. There was no written commandment, lest it become a commandment only for one Apostle and not another. On the other hand, the equality carried a sense of interchangeability. Hawkins, who seemed to them a symbol or model of all the world outside the Apostles, was saying that the Apostles could be replaced tomorrow by the Sabbatarian Brethren, or Rooted in the Lamb, without any loss to the world or to the Lord either. It was a feeling that could not be banished. People began to demand a rite, some simple ceremony that would show, even to themselves, their faith in their own irreplaceability. Diaries, memoirs, collections, and the formal studies of Edgar Bisset's life, which would seem to later readers to be so joyless and sectarian and at the same time so eager to convince, were begun in earnest. The Apostles of the Spirit of the Lord had never had a martyr. Their lands had been bloodied, but not by them, their dead made no relics, and the wind scoured their arid land and blasted it clean each season. On such land, even the best-loved tree will be blown down if it is not rooted deep as the secrets of water and bones, the rock-knotted secrets of the forming of the world.

So, many Apostles, without conscious plan or decision, began to look back into what they yearned to call history, the old, old times. Times as old as 1938.

18

By the time Edgar and Mike were in their last year of junior high, the vine supports at the Antons' had all broken down and been blown away or gone back under. There had been another great enthusiasm, chiropractic, and that too had gone its way and been plowed in with all the other dreams. There was a new boy in their class, a dark, volatile boy who came to school the first day wearing a tall Indian felt hat with a shoelace tied around it. His name was Glover Castle. His mother, they later found out, was a Hopi woman, and his father did ranch work for one of the big companies that ran cattle on different spreads in six states. The school seemed ready to dislike and mistrust Glover, mainly because of his flair for the dramatic, but Mike and Edgar saw in the drama the gleam of his wry humor. He entertained them and they began to include him in their activities. Since they were leaders of the most popular group in school, Glover's eccentricities became accepted. As he became easier and less defensive, he was able, in the presence of his friends, to unearth the springs of a wild wit and sense of fantasy that fascinated Mike and Edgar. Mike, who had been hurled up and down so many times by family fortunes, tended to be serious and sometimes despairing. Edgar, as Founder's kin and namesake, was free in Praise, but the Apostles did not encourage fantasy or wit in their children or their converts. They did not ask it from the Lord. They did not thank the Spirit of the Lord for the gift of lightness; they thanked Him for plains virtues: endurance, health, and patience. So did Edgar. So did Mike. Glover's arrival woke in them a sense of fun that they had never known they possessed. His humor wasn't high-spirited, but the wry, self-aware wittiness that marks survivors. They were playful. They spoke their fantasies aloud for the first time and blew them up and up again like wisps of milkweed down that one blows to see it shimmer in the summer wind. Soon the three of them were inseparable and the town and the neighbors began to think of them as having always been together.

"What's it like?"
"Why not come and see."
"I wouldn't know what to do."
"We'd show you."
"But—dancing like that—I might bring rain."
"Come up to Willow Springs, then, where I Praise. We need the rain."
"Come down to Founder's, that's where you belong."
"Shirley Kinbote Praises at Willow Springs. I saw you staring at her yesterday."
"Inge Longerich is prettier and she's at Founder's."
"Then you don't think anyone would mind?"
"We'll show you what to do. Hey, why don't both of you stay overnight Saturday and come to Praise on Sunday afternoon?"

It was a good day for a Praise, not cold, but crisp and windy. The sky was a whitening blue, the earth long gone to seed, brown and crack-dry. The people had all the warmth and color there was between the earth and the sky. Their Praise was hearty and simple. For the good harvest, Amen. For the gift I received from my daughter, that she didn't want me to bear sorrow alone, Praise be. For the ability to learn things in school, Thank you, Lord. For my recovery from my recent sickness, Hallelujah. After the thanks came the petitions. Edgar and Mike watched Glover as voice spoke after voice. He seemed embarrassed at first, listening to the personal things people were saying, but as the dance went on and the petitions followed one another, they saw that he was interested, even moved.

"My sister is up in Pueblo in the mental hospital. Let her be remembered to the Lord by this Praise today and all them patients up there who are sick in their minds and can't hear the world's voice clearly."

"I need this Praise to speak with me to the Lord to help end the anger in my family—"

The Seeking and Bringing would begin soon. Edgar usually ran; he was planning to go out today. He liked the work of it, the action of his body, the resistance of the wind or the cold, the welcome hands held out of the circle to him, the happiness he felt and gave in his Witnessing. "The Lord loves us, the Spirit is a good light, a true light." These things had been said many times before. They were even usual by now, and no one took them as great revelations, but that they were said by a pious young Apostle made them true all over again, and that they were said with simplicity and conviction made them holy words. Next to him, Edgar saw Mike gesturing at Glover, who had been separated from him by more people joining the circle. They had told Glover about Seeking and Bringing, and he knew that he could run out, too, if he wished.

The Praise came to its second rest and Edgar saw Charlie coming toward the circle from the house. He went to his traditional place against the fencerail and leaned against it, watching, his face as always showing nothing. New people often remarked on Charlie, who seemed to belong so little to what was going on around him. To the older people he was so familiar that they did not see him anymore. Had he not been there they would only have felt some lack and would have been struck by it only in passing. During the third rest he left his place and went to where Edgar waited, catching his breath before the running.

"Your grandma and ma want them boys Mike and Glover to stay on for dinner. I'll run 'em home after."

"Okay, Charlie, I'll ask them." Charlie lit a cigarette.

"You aimin' to run out now?" He had a flickering look in his eye. On anyone else Edgar might have said it was a playful look. Charlie never said the pious words Seeking and Bringing or Witnessing the Glory. He never used any of the Apostles' special words and sometimes it annoyed Edgar. He said a little stiffly:

"Seeking and Bringing isn't something a person is supposed to plan for. It's what the Spirit urges on a person when simple Praising isn't enough." The words came out sounding too righteous and superior and he found himself irritated with Charlie for having drawn them from him. "It's a very holy moment!" he cried, making it all worse. Charlie motioned toward the now re-forming circle.

"You ever see Edna Farrier run in a dress that wasn't clingin' to her figure for dear life? You ever see Morton Empey run when Edna wasn't here? There's more fraud in kids than you think." Edgar snorted and turned back toward the circle.

The dance began again. Edgar had come into the circle between Mike and Glover and they looked at each other and smiled. The older people in the inner circle paced slowly, putting their full weight down with each step as though offering their rootedness and slow, sure rhythm to the spinning youngsters in the outside circle. Soon the young people were going faster, their feet barely touching the ground at all, and then came the moment, a yawning hunger for release, a kind of terrible yearning, took them and they spun off like sparks out of the circle, dashing outward into the horizonless field. Edgar ran blindly, feeling only the pure emotion of release, and when he began to be a little winded he looked around and saw that he was a great way from the circle and all the other runners. Glover and Mike had run also—he could see them as small and far away as the circle. It was exhilarating to have run so far and so well and to see young people all around, friends at the sky-blown, blue-white end of the world.

He began to run back, laboring toward the end, his breath sobbing in and out, toward the others and the welcoming

190

circle itself. He did not have the glowing revelations that some of the young people came back with. His Bringings were always quiet and not otherworldly, his prayers simple statements of gratitude for the ordinary, reasonable, good things of life. The circle was slowed, waiting for the Bringers. They reached out toward the runners, listening for the first caught breath, the Witness given in a winded sob, the revelation of great truths or simple thanksgiving.

Angela Reiter spoke first. She spoke haltingly of a vision which had answered a personal problem. She had been weeping as she ran. Two other Bringers spoke and the dance maintained its slow swaying, marking time until the runners regained their breath. Then Mike spoke, gasping a little, red-faced.

"The Lord gave me the joy of my friends today. In His presence there is no loneliness." The Praise sighed with approval. Other young people spoke. Edgar was the last to Witness. He was aware that he didn't want to repeat what Mike had said and it surprised him that he found himself having to prepare something to say.

"The gift of the Lord is not only the friendship of today but the strength of Praises and friendships in the past and the ones we look forward to in the future." The words sounded formulated and artificial in his own ears, but the Praise again murmured a little, its way of showing pleasure, and there were smiles for him, faces turned toward him with interest and approval.

When the Praise and the long, big dinner were over, the three of them decided to walk to Mike's house, and that Charlie could pick Edgar up there. A drizzle had begun. Joe said the boys were crazy to go in the rain when there was Charlie to take them, but they laughed and set out in the rain together. It was the elation of the day. They did not want to sit passively—they were full of joy and wonder and they felt like challenging something, even so tame a thing as the four miles to Mike's house.

"I never knew religion could do things like that to people," Glover said. He had sat at the dinner table, his eyes alive, his face shining, too moved to speak. "Is it like that all the time or just when the minister isn't there to lead the prayers?" Edgar and Mike smiled.

"We have no ministers," Edgar said. "The Lord tells each of us what He wants us to do. Sometimes the Spirit comes to a person and then He tells it to the whole Praise, and if it's a thing like an act of charity or visiting the sick or praying for a person's recovery, everyone feels the Spirit of the Lord moving toward the group. Then we all do that thing together."

"Older people are usually the ones who go on visits or get called to take up collections for special things," Mike added. "Sometimes everyone gets a clear call, the whole Praise at once, like we did after Winstead's fire—the older folks sewed and donated food and money and the younger ones helped rebuild and fix up the barn."

"I thought it was wonderful," Glover said, "the way people were so eager and full of happiness—"

"Well, that's Founder's Praise," Mike said, and smiled, "and that Praise is pretty pious. Usually I Praise at Willow Springs. Not so much piety, but not so many old folks either. Shirley Kinbote is there."

"Well, Inge Longerich is at Founder's—"

"You can't compare Inge to Shirley!" Mike shouted. They began to scuffle and laugh in the rain, swinging at one another, huge satisfying haymakers that missed by inches. The rain was washing out the separation between earth and sky, road and field, and before the boys knew it they were laughing and singing in full dark. The road was known, the rain would not beat upon them too hard, and in the ground kinfolk lay at peace.

Glover began to go to Praises, sometimes with Mike, sometimes with Edgar. He was an eager dancer who loved Seeking and Bringing and whose face lit up with joy at the Witnessing. The Praises accepted Glover comfortably although he was not formally a member and did not Witness for quite a while.

When he did speak in the Praise, it was hesitantly, in what Apostles called Self-Witness. It happened in the spring at

Founder's in answer to a young woman new to the Apostles who said she missed her old church only at Christmas and Easter—the clothing, the rituals and carols, the beauty in the church. Glover surprised the older Apostles by answering. He spoke not from the Spirit but out of his own experience. He said he was uncomfortable speaking from the Spirit as Apostles did, but he had been gripped with the power and intensity of their experience in prayer. He had seen at Forks a tormented father reconciled to his son and the urging forward of the whole Praise toward that wish. Surely that was as important as Easter Sunday services and women trying to outshine each other with new hats. He had seen cures performed and prayers for cures so passionate that everyone wept, and he knew that whether the cure was made or not, it must have been a source of strength to feel the spirit of the wish pouring from every member of the Praise. Surely that was as good as carols in the church. There seemed, he said, to be fewer social differences among the Apostles, too. He felt none of the stiffness between classes or generations that there had been in the churches he had gone to.

The Praise was deeply moved. It was one thing to hear such words from a dedicated old Apostle, quite another to have them from the mouth of a young person new to the Praise. After he spoke there was that familiar soft murmur of approval like a wind. Mike and Edgar were smiling at him.

They met after the Praise to walk him home again. "Well, it's your first time speaking in Witness. That's a big moment, really."

"I thought I'd be scared, saying all those things, but I wasn't. It seemed as though I'd been doing it all my life, as natural as talking to you."

"People took it well," Mike said.

"I know." Glover's eyes widened and he half smiled. "They looked at me then the way they always look at Edgar—that 'special' look."

"What special look is that?" Edgar asked, feeling suddenly as though there were some danger waiting in what Glover was saying and in defying it by saying more.

"You know, the special way people look at you—a difference."

"I guess they do think I'm a little of a celebrity at Founder's. I'm Brother Edgar's great-nephew, after all, Founder's namesake."

"Half the young Apostles in the county are named after Brother Edgar," Glover persisted.

"Yes, but I'm Founder's kin. There isn't really anything special except for that."

"But there is, Ed. You must know it, must have seen it, and not only among Apostles. Mike, you've noticed it, haven't you? When we're all together, all three of us, people give it to all of us—a special look, a special attitude as though we were more than just three kids." Mike was silent, his face set. Glover reddened. "I didn't mean to make you feel bad, I just thought you knew—" he ended lamely. "Maybe I'm dreaming and it's all in my mind. Maybe I'm just used to being treated like nobody at all."

They didn't answer him. The three of them walked, heads down, their hands in their pockets. It was something Edgar had always known. It was part of the unsaid reality of his life. Why did it sound so strange and make him so nervous? Beside him, Glover walked stiffly with the truth of what he had sensed. "Maybe it's true," Edgar said. "Maybe there is a special way people treat me—us."

There was a palpable relief in Glover; even Mike relaxed. Now that he had admitted the truth, Edgar wanted to hear more. Did everyone know about the difference? Did his family see it? His school friends? His teachers? He remembered Mrs. McDonald three years ago in grade school. What was it she had said? He remembered standing near a door and the voices of the teachers talking about him, but he could not make out anymore what the words had been. It was something about that difference, though, something about what everyone knew.

Not alone or in fantasy, but in the darkness with his friends beside him, Edgar began to feel a strange elation. He kept his voice level and thanked God for the covering dark, but his mind was racing with an odd kind of fearful joy. He was special, had always been special, he had indeed been singled out, and for praise, not blame. The looks were approving, not condemning, the smiles warm. People liked him and trusted him. They always had, but he had taken it so for granted that he had never asked why.

"Did you ever see it happen?" he asked them. "I mean, was it a feeling, or did you really *see* it?" He kept his voice quiet and ordinary, and was glad his face was hidden.

Glover made a movement, a shrug maybe. "I saw it."

"When?"

"Lots of times."

"When was the first time?"

"I guess the first time was the day we went into Seen Bean's after fruit crates."

"That was back when you first came here. We weren't even close friends then."

"I know," Glover said, "but that's when I noticed it first."

"What happened?"

"You know how tough old man Bean is. When I first moved here I stopped there to get some crates to keep my boots in and for shelves for my magazines. I knew he'd charge me for them and I expected to pay because he didn't know me. With me, he kept his head down and talked into the floor. We were both embarrassed and I felt like a beggar, although I paid for the boxes. When you were with me you said, 'Hi, Mr. Bean,' and he looked up."

"I remember," Edgar said.

The old man had asked after the family and joked with Edgar and then had taken them to the back of the store and let them choose among his crates and boxes for the cleanest ones. When they offered him something for them, he had refused the money. As they were leaving, he had held out to each of them a ripe peach.

"You see, it's simple," Edgar said. "C. N. Bean grew up with Grandpa and worked in the store when my great-grandpa bought his goods there. Pa remembers getting candy from old Seen Bean's when he was a kid. That's why it's easy for me. We go back in the county, that's all."

"I don't believe it," Glover said. "I don't think you do either, all the way. There's more. I think there's more."

Edgar turned to Mike. "Is there a difference in the way people treat you when you're not with me? Is there a way they look at me that's different from the way they look at other kids in town?"

Mike grinned. "To me you're the same simpleminded oaf you've always been, your pointed head, walleyes, and runny nose still make you a standout at every party—"

"I don't mean different from what I was, jerk, I mean, different." He felt himself digging for something he wanted from Mike, but he had begun and couldn't go back now.

"I cannot tell a lie," Mike said, and looked at the ground. "I've seen things sometimes, many little things in school or in town, at Praises now and then. Don't make me say them, you know what they are. It isn't anything you do or say, or special thing you have. When Glover and I are with you, whatever it is seems to spread to all of us. I don't know, but I feel strange talking about it. There isn't anything wrong with it, it isn't a sin to be liked by people, but it makes me feel funny. If we analyze it or talk about it too much it will become something else—"

"Hell," Glover said, "Ed didn't ask for it, it's nothing he demanded—it's just there, part of the way things are. Why shouldn't he enjoy it if he can? Why shouldn't we all enjoy it if we can? People are nice to us. Is that a sin? What do you do about it, ask them to stop? At Burkett's they never give kids credit, but Burkett gives us credit because of Ed. Do we tell him we don't want to be treated differently from anyone else? He'd probably deny that we were. It's there, it's a good thing, and why don't we let it be?"

Edgar hadn't realized that Burkett's gave him credit but never the other students who ate there and had sodas and pop after school. He knew that it was true and always had been, but he had never really noticed it or asked himself why.

"Okay," he said, and noticed himself smiling in the dark. "We can all use credit at Burkett's and that's no sin." He heard his voice smooth and noncommittal. He did not like watching himself from the outside. At Glover's house they parted with the usual friendly horseplay, but Edgar's mind was busy observing them.

The next day, as usual, they went to Burkett's after school. The three of them sat with their group in the back, the biggest single group in the place, greeting new arrivals. Edgar liked the banter and the jukebox. He liked coming in and being greeted even by the senior-high tables. This time the three of them laughed and joked as usual, but they were listening to themselves and to their friends with care, hearing their own ease and wondering how it had been built, year after year, these questions, these answers, without their knowledge. As they watched and listened to themselves, the time began to stretch out to a length they had never experienced before except during the dullest of school sessions. They sat and joked, laughed and flirted, grinning endlessly. Had it been this way all along, since fall, when they had jumped joyfully into the tradition? Edgar wondered if perhaps it wasn't some kind of an illness, a blighting of their real joy because they had for an instant looked at the sources of it. Was it a sin to look at the sources of joy? He did not know. Sin was a word Apostles never used.

They left at last, earlier than usual, and wandered back toward Memorial Square, where they usually separated to go home. They did not speak until Mike said:

"I'm sorry I was such a wet blanket in there. I've got things on my mind. I couldn't think about laughing and telling jokes today." Edgar looked at Mike in surprise. He had not noticed anything sad or troubled in his best friend's face or voice. He knew it was because he had been busy listening to himself. Now he saw that Mike was struggling against tears.

"Hey," Glover said, "what's up?"

"Oh, Christ!" Mike cried. "I'm not going to bawl—oh, Christ!" He began to choke, half laughing then because Edgar and Glover were pounding on his shoulders to stop the choking. When he quieted a little they walked, eyes down, embarrassed, and afraid to speak for fear of driving him to tears again. After a while he said, "It's a new dream, a big new plan. New lives, he says, new lives, for the tenth time."

Edgar said quietly, "Your dad?"

Mike nodded. "I don't know why I can't be fooled this time, too. Always before it made me feel hopeful—a new start—and he's so happy and Mom gets happy and the house is full of noise and building and he goes around whistling.

Guys in the barbershop listen, he meets people on the street and smiles and tells them about the plan, and it's always so good to be where he is. Only this time, this time I can't care. I can't be fooled. Last night he asked me what was wrong and why I wasn't joining in—"

"What is it this time?" Edgar asked.

Mike burst out, "Oh, hell, it's *turkeys!*"

Without knowing why, they all burst out laughing. Edgar had a picture of ten dozen turkeys looking as surprised to be in business with John Anton as he was to be in business with them. Beside him, Glover was almost doubled up and Mike was holding his side, his face red, his eyes running.

"Our lives are changed all right—now our whole lives are turkeys. Pens!" He gasped. "Thirty pens. Feed. By the truckload."

"You'll have a turkey tenement!" Glover said. "A city of gobblers." They wheezed.

"And this time—" Mike was still laughing, "when Dad was asking me what was wrong, all I could think of was, Do turkeys get hoof-and-mouth?"

They roared again but now a little too much on purpose, too loudly, to keep Mike from his distress.

"They get diseases," Mike said, "just like the fancy pheasants Dad tried a long time ago, and the special nut trees before that, and the closed-system model farm that broke down all at once, and the other things, all the other things that went bad or died or got sick or fell apart or never came up at all. I figured I could live around it this time—do what I was told and just stop caring so much so that it wouldn't change my outside life, school or friends or anything like that—"

They didn't speak for a while, then Glover said, "Could we help you? Is there anything we can do?"

"Chores, maybe," Edgar asked, "to help you until the thing blows over?"

Mike shook his head. "We started talking about the way people treat Ed and how they treat the three of us when we're together. I guess I've known for a long time that people laugh a little behind Dad's back. Oh, they like him, but they laugh, too. I don't want that anymore." He shook his head again. "No, I don't want that anymore."

"I was the one who brought it up," Glover said. "Ed's specialness, our specialness. I never meant it to give anybody bad feelings or start you guys staring into your soup for noodles to spell out messages. You guys are my friends—"

They sat down on the nearest bench. For a long time they did not speak. Edgar had a quick premonition, in the air, of summer coming and warm weather. He turned to them and said quietly, "It's the three of us, whatever happens. Turkeys or Mike's dad or chores or school or anything, it's the three of us."

Glover said, "The Three Musketurkeys." They smiled and then sat for a while. Around them the town was slowly closing for the night. They could see cattycorner across the street to where Ron Ede was locking up the jewelry-and-gift store. He was too far away to hear, but they knew he would be singing the tuneless hum he always did when he wasn't speaking. In the fading light Mike looked calmer, Glover relaxed. "The three of us," he said again, and they watched the dark come down on the town.

That night at supper Charlie said, "I seen John Anton in town today. He's got a idea to breed turkeys."

Joe tried to sound as though it were any other man about whom they were talking, but there was an odd smile on his face. "Well, there's men raisin' turkeys here. Ab Coombs does, Orval Dresser. I did once myself back a while. Land's not hurt by it. Expensive, though, if you got to buy feed."

"Interestin' man," Charlie said. "He talked to me like he never did nothin' all his life but raise turkeys. He had me seein' acres of pens, yards of turkeys, breedin' places, dressin' places, all clear as day. If I'd a had a dollar I would have gone in with him!" They laughed, sitting around Joe's big table. The two families often ate together, usually at Joe and Arla's. Edgar wanted to laugh, too, but couldn't out of loyalty to Mike. He looked at Charlie and suddenly thought about Brother Edgar—Founder Edgar. He had always seen Brother Edgar in his mind as a cross between Jesus and Lincoln, a tall, spare, ascetic man, larger than life. Was it possible that such a man could have Charlie Dace for a friend? Could they have talked to each other after the day's work was over about anything more than work? Charlie's grammar was so bad it made him wince sometimes. He drank a lot and days would go by when he didn't wash. Of course, Brother Edgar was *everybody's* friend. Still . . .

When Charlie went out to do the last chores and the locking up, Edgar was waiting for him in the barn. Working silently, they watered the calf that Joe had penned there as an experiment. As they were leaving Edgar said, "Charlie, were you really a friend of Brother Edgar's?"

"Yeah, yes, I was."

"What was it like, being his friend?" In the dark he could almost see Charlie's eyes looking at him, measuring.

"There was a lot of waitin' to it," Charlie said, "you wait a lot when you have a friend. It was worth it, though." They left, Charlie going over the little gully bridge to Joe and Arla's, Edgar to his house. Charlie waved to him once as they turned away from each other. It couldn't be true that they had been real friends. Waiting. It couldn't be true.

19

The boys began to be seen together at different Praises; now at Mike's at the Springs, where his married sister Praised, now at Founder's. No one spoke to them about it since there was no rule about having one particular Praise. Technically, an Apostle could go from Praise to Praise and never be considered an outsider. It was only that few Apostles had ever changed places of Praise without special reason, marriage or moving or a family upset, and none had ever gone back and forth. The other dancers did not know what to say, and so said nothing. It was good to have the boys at their Praises anyway; they seemed to make the Praises young. By the end of the summer it was an accepted thing that the boys came and went the way they did.

The August 23 Praise was held on a day so lowering that there was talk of taking it inside, but the air was cool and snapping with the threat of lightning waiting behind the fast-moving rack of clouds that shut out the sun. No one would have gone in on such a day.

The early part of the Praise went by quickly. People were anxious for the drama of Seeking and Bringing to match the wind-whipped color of flowing hair and blown clothes, the shadowless luminescence of the air before a storm. Edgar, Mike, and Glover moved smiling in the circle, calling out responses to the prayers of thanks and the petitions for help.

The Praise at Willow Springs was a younger Praise than Founder's; there were many Apostles of their own age and the pace was fast. Most of the dancers ran and somehow because of this the metaphor of the Seeker was changed.

Edgar had often felt the metaphor as he ran. It did not come to him consciously or in words, but as a feeling of his being a participant in a scene wider than itself. There was a moment in the Praise when everyone knew it was time to run. The young Seekers flung themselves away, tearing outward from the circle, arms wide as though to embrace the sun. They ran headlong, crying or shouting or biting their lips in the pain of their joy. They were free of the past, the law, their parents' generation, and they wanted to run forever. They could only run to the field's end, where they found themselves alone and in silence except for the sounds of their own spent breath. Looking through sweat-stung eyes, seeing themselves all at once so far from the turning circle, they knew the loneliness that their freedom had also given. Then came the visions and the Presence of the Spirit of the Lord. Then, too, came the sudden gift of the strength to tear back, crying out what they had seen. At Willow Springs there was less of a center to return to, sometimes only four or five old people, not the happy dancing majority that lured and beckoned the Seekers back at Founder's. Still, Edgar was glad for the quickness of the dance and to face Barbara Jenson, whose black hair whipped back and forth like banners against her pale, delicate face. The people had begun to shout the chants: "He wants Gladness, He wants Joy" and the "Glory Four" set to the steady beats of their steps, four silent beats, a syncopated fifth, and then a shouted "Glory!" The Apostles had few hymns as such besides the quiet hymns of their cast-off churches which the young people took up sometimes at a campfire. Their souls were in their chants, which could be intricately rhythmic and could give spirit, it was said, to rocks and Raymond Clitheroe. The circle quieted and broke, rested, and formed again. Some spirit of special joy was in them all. They didn't want to rest one more breath than caught breath itself, then back again to the circle where the consciousness of God's presence made them tremble, half weeping, in the chant. The moment came and the dancers spun away, fleeing to the outward places, the lone, unpeopled edges of the world. They ran to the horizon.

Edgar ran hard because he was healthy and high-spirited. He had learned the week before that some of the more mystical young Apostles saw the outward journey as one of suffering and loss, and he felt a slightly embarrassed pity for Kenny Brewer, who had come back to the circle and wept and spoken of something like exile. People shouldn't admit to things like that in a Praise. Others remember it afterward; they can't help it.

At last he was winded and spent and knew it was time to stop. He looked around and saw Glover near enough to shout to, but Glover's head was down and he did not see Edgar. There was an unspoken rule at Praises not to speak to other runners during Seeking and Bringing. Edgar turned and started back with a head-down doggedness, pushing against the wind. He had had no special message and he began to think of what he would say—something in thanks, familiar to the Praise. He began to pick up speed so that he could come back into the circle at a full run. It was as he was building his speed, pushing actively against the wind and his own body, that a sudden thought came to him with the intensity of revelation: Could I fail? Would they let me fail? What if I came back and said something stupid or evil? Would they listen and nod and say it was from the Lord or would they be angry? Would the Praise turn against me? Could it? Could I *make* it happen? Then the chill quality of the day came down on him. He was conscious of the sunlessness, of the danger of being struck by lightning, as though it must choose him, alone and upright in all the vast flatness of the land. Where had such a thought come from, that kind of blasphemy? With a conscious effort he turned his thoughts, first toward his own running and the breath whistling to get out, then toward an effort to think of something he could say to the Praise. When he was close he put on a final burst of speed and broke into the circle, arms and legs moving, received back gladly, one of them.

The runners slowed the dance while they got their breath. There were no questions asked of them, but silences were left, the tacit places of entry for the Bringing of Witness, through which the dancers waited a little tensely. In the first of these silences, Rodman Brown spoke. Rodman was only fourteen, a worried, weak boy small for his age. He was always forcing himself to run although it brought him near to fainting.

"When I ran," he gasped, "He told me all the way that He wanted me to be brave." The approving sigh closed around the boy who had been brave and spoken. Other Bringers spoke. Then, to Edgar's great surprise, Glover broke out of the circle and went to the middle.

"The Spirit of the Lord called me out there," he said. "The Spirit of the Lord said to me, 'I want you to stop being alone. I want you to belong to these people and this Praise.' I want to be an Apostle."

Perhaps it was the day, brisk and cool, or the wind, or some quicksilver mood in the people, but without warning or special reason the Praise erupted in a great roar of joy. The circle began to spin again. Some people were weeping with the intensity of their hunger for something they could only define as God. The definition was a limit, yet the Praise had broken its limits. As Glover spoke the few simple words required of him, the Praise chanted back at him. Caught up in the irresistible rhythm of statement and answer, the feet of the dancers pounded on the gray-yellow earth. The dead woke up and pounded back from the ground until it trembled and the sky vibrated with the beating. The living circled until they could run no more, walk no more. Then they stood shuddering like heat-struck animals, sides heaving, the breath whistling back and forth through their faces. This was the way it must have been in Brother Edgar's time, the clean exhaustion, faith without mixture, question, or interpretation, no past or future, only here and now, whole and perfect as the Spirit's Word.

No one left until the cool rain began to fall, and when they went, bemused and silent, to their trucks and cars, it was without the ordinary words of good-bye that relatives and neighbors have for each other.

Glover, Mike, and Edgar were also quiet on the long drive back to town. The rain had turned solid and caused the fields to overflow the roads. When Glover got out at his house he said to them, "I knew it was the right move, I knew it would be just right today."

They began their first year of high school without the fear many students have of new people and new ways. If anything, there was a sense of the inevitability of it all that sometimes whispered over their shoulders as they wrote their themes, and gave a soft groan as they sat in Burkett's with Cokes after school. The habit was to outshout the groan. They played the jukebox at full blast so that they had to scream at one another over the sound of it. They played western music that made romance out of loneliness and boredom and the stoical silence of tradition.

One afternoon in November, Edgar came home and to his surprise found his mother not in the house. It made him anxious. His mother was always there when he came in. Apostles praised her for her wifely and motherly ways, but her own kitchen was a refuge and the family knew it. The silence of her absence thrummed in the house. He walked across the footbridge that spanned the washed gully between his father's house and his grandfather's. Arla's cat had killed a bird and was self-absorbedly eviscerating it on the front step. He went around to the back, creeping almost, part of the silence. The back door was never locked. In the yard the truck waited, but the car was gone. He went up the back stairs and opened the door. He found himself tiptoeing through the kitchen guiltily, as though he had broken in. At last he could bear the stillness no more and he cried up the stairway, "Grandma! Grandpa!" A chair moved in the front room and Charlie said, "What are you yellin' for? Just a minute!" Then Charlie came in from the front room. He had obviously been dozing in the rocker and was embarrassed to have been caught at it. "Where's Corella? Wasn't she with you on the bus?"

"I didn't take the bus," he said, "I stopped at Burkett's. I guess Corella stayed after school for a club or something."

He found he had a boyish tone in his voice that he hated. "No one is home. Where's everybody gone?" He didn't like a situation so far from his own knowledge and control.

"Well," Charlie said, "your great-grandpa died during the night last night and they're all out seein' to things." Edgar said nothing. He felt strangely ashamed. He had not thought about his great-grandfather for some time except in a very routine way. The old man had been ailing and was often too ill to come to the table. Sometimes Edgar and Corella would be asked to take a tray up to him or a hot drink or a newspaper. Edgar had done these errands automatically, without thought.

"Dead?" he said.

"Seems sudden." And Charlie shook his head. "It's funny how surprisin' it can be. He was an old man. I should have knowed it was comin', but I didn't. We was in the room up there together last night. He started rememberin', goin' on about this and that, makin' out like the old place was a paradise. Forgot about all the creeks out there bein' dry, forgot about the house bein' gone. He started in about how we was gonna move on back there. I told him there wasn't no house no more, no more than a ruin and the barn was stove in. He got mad at me. Got so mad he fired me. Told me to get off the place." Charlie's face had the look it must have had in the darkness, as though it had been slapped. "For a minute I didn't understand, and then I seen he didn't mean *here*, but *there*; he was firin' me from off the old place that wasn't even a place no more."

Edgar nodded. He and Glover and Mike had gone out there one idle day last fall in Mike's father's truck. The house was gone to ground; only the outlines were left and a bit of the chimney like a broken tooth, standing no more than knee high in the cricket-popping broomgrass. All the outbuildings were gone, too, except the old soddy smokehouse and that was broken in on one side. The rain runnels had eaten scars into the bare places. The place had reminded Edgar of an old cow fallen on its knees in death. The boys kicked at the shards of broken glass and the half-buried, half-burned trash of campers' fires. They had stood about uncomfortably.

All his life, Edgar had heard about Brother Edgar, a man larger than life, and certainly larger than death. Yet the house was gone, the land going its way. It was no longer possible to raise in the imagination the picture of a family living there, farming the land. That someone still remembered it that way filled Edgar with wonder. And the man who had made that land his own had died while Edgar was sleeping or getting dressed for school. "I guess I should have come and seen him more," Edgar murmured, "asked him, maybe, how things were back then."

"Oh, hell," Charlie said, "he wouldn't have told you the truth. He'd want to, but he couldn't. Things change and the person who's livin' it don't see it change, really. He'd have told you about the big trees they had around the house. Them trees blew down in the thirties and they wasn't never really big. They got big in his mind because—"

"Then how come you could see them and remember them like that?"

"Because it wasn't my place," Charlie said, "and it wasn't my family." In the gloom he had the self-satisfied look of someone who has made a telling point. They went into the front room to wait for Corella. Edgar did not mention the thought that came to him. It was a memory of late last summer. He had come up on Charlie dozing in the warm sun of the back porch and had begun to wake him to call him to the table.

"Charlie—Charlie—" Charlie's eyes had popped open, his hand had come up, and a look of joy had rushed across his face like a spasm.

"Edgar, boy!" And then his eyes were suddenly stripped to their shallow, blue bareness and he had turned away.

They sat waiting. After a while Charlie sighed. "You try to figure how things'll come out, but you never know." He seemed to be talking to himself. "Old man was a little bitter about Edgar. You couldn't blame him. All the glory flyin' around like water shook off a dog—glory to strangers, enemies even, the livin' and the dead and none for the old man, nothin' but his same dried-out farm. That and *me*, and I didn't have no glory either. Now thousands of people all over the country have the glory in Edgar's name—his words about the glory—"

"But?" Edgar said. Charlie looked down.

"But not the law. They don't have his law or the awful things there was to make him strong, and it scares me. It ain't their fault. They didn't have his times or his silence or his folks or his years over there in the war or the beatin' he had from the dust. The vision was cut for him special. He was *special*, don't you see?" The word was jarring to Edgar, but he kept looking down and said nothing. Charlie went on more quietly, "I never figured I had a place in all this except as his friend, no reason to be where I am, gettin' old enough to bury everyone that knew me when I was strong. Did he want me to guard somethin' for him, the way you'd set a mean old dog to guard a treasure? The dog can't understand the treasure hisself, the treasure don't mean nothin' to the dog, only the master means somethin'. Maybe that's why I'm here, sufferin' for a family that ain't mine and a faith that ain't mine. Is that why I'm starvin' to death in the middle of the fattest years in memory?"

Edgar was frightened. He had never heard questions of this kind. Always when people asked the unanswerable questions of faith they stood in the warm sun of Praise and the answers were triumphant and noble, God's joyful "yes" to all his loving children.

Charlie had raised his head and was looking at Edgar. "Don't pay me no mind," he said. "So many times I guess wrong. I once thought someone was gunnin' for Edgar because we was friends and I was sure he was gonna get killed, and instead he was out in Stavren's Gully gettin' good news. It's the story of my life." In the kitchen the phone rang harshly. "It's the folks," Charlie said, and patted Edgar on the shoulder clumsily. "You take it."

Ralph Bisset was buried next to his wife, Cora, on a day of mud and sunlight. The funeral was well attended, but because of his longevity the remarks made at the grave were mostly by people who had never known Ralph except in old age. Joe, in the role of closest kin, accepted their words.

Charlie stood by silently and shook his head to himself now and then. After the funeral, Edgar slipped away and got a ride to Mike's.

A new kind of feeding setup was being put in on some of the coops and the boys were helping Mike to renovate them. Edgar had often helped at the beginning but the project had grown beyond him. In the beginning there had been two acres set aside for John Anton's intensive turkey operation; now there were acres of fenced runs and dozens of buildings but only a few were in use. The wiring for some of them was lying around, the attachments still in their boxes. The ungraveled areas of the runs ran mud. It had been a year since the beginning of this latest dream and the dream was beginning to curl at the edges.

He found Mike and Glover working on one of the large coops in the center of the compound. They had been told to dig a trench around the coop and were working steadily, following John Anton's almost-surgical measurements. Edgar joined them without a word and the three of them continued down the line, the sun warm on their heads and backs. Now and then they would murmur to one another about the work, where to turn or how deep to dig. The companionable silence was soothing to Edgar. Once he found himself about to whistle and stopped abruptly because he didn't want to lose the silence and wasn't sure how he should act on the day of his great-grandfather's funeral. He could see that Glover and Mike were uncomfortable and did not know what to say. When they came to the place where the trench turned they took a break.

"I'm sorry to hear about your great-grandpa," Glover said at last. Edgar felt a twinge of resentment at the old man for dying and leaving them all so wordless in the face of it.

They were standing in the center of all the equipment— coops, runs, storage buildings. Mike looked out at the spread of it. "When the bust comes," he said quietly, "this sure is going to be a mess."

"He won't just let it go—will he? With the grapes, well, that was different—"

"Yes, he will," Mike said, "and probably soon."

"And you let me do all this work?" Glover cried. They all laughed. Glover picked up a garden fork and dug it into the ground. "You know that scholarship they give—the one they talked about at the last assembly? We should fix it. We should fix it so Mike gets it."

They all waited for a minute. Edgar said, "How could we fix a thing like that?"

"Why not? We've admitted that we're special, that you're special, Ed, and all of us are when we're together. We've said we're a team. Why not use that specialness and that teamwork to get Mike out of the hole he's in? Look, Mike, if you've got college to look forward to it won't matter what your dad does or doesn't do. All we need to know is what that committee wants the winner to be and we can make Mike *be* just that thing."

"It's nuts," Edgar said.

"Why not?" And Glover walked to a feedbin and sat on it. "It's in a good cause and it's going to be easy. We see that he covers all the angles; we tutor him, get good notes to him before tests, help him with the social stuff, the community work. . . ."

"My math is rotten," Mike said, "I'll need more than good notes in that."

"Can't you see that doesn't matter!" Glover cried. "Who remembers later how well his neighbors did in school? People don't trust the superbrainy ones anyway. Football and school count because they give people an excuse to pick whom they like. The thing that counts most is that specialness, the way people think about a person. That and the community work he does, which is only a bigger reason they give themselves for picking him because they like him."

"It doesn't sound right, somehow."

"Somebody has to get the Mohlencamp our year," Mike said. "And why not one of us, one of the Musketurkeys? We wouldn't have to compete against each other when we were seniors—"

"Sure," Glover said, and walked back to the ditch. The air was cool now that they were not digging. "Knowing who we're going to back will stop us from having all that upset later, and it's efficient, too. All the others will be working for themselves. It will be three against one. We'll have it made."

They went back to work and said no more about it, but every time Edgar raised his head to look around at John Anton's grandiose place he thought about what Glover had said.

On the day after the funeral Charlie went up to the barn when he knew that both Joe and Andy would be there working on a piece of machinery. When he saw them he took a breath and said loudly, "Now the old man's dead there ain't no need of keepin' me on. In case you was thinkin' how to raise the subject of me goin' my way, I'm raisin' it now."

They looked up. Andy was winter-pale and had greasy smudges on his face. His blue eyes went wide as he turned to Charlie.

"What brings this up right today?" he said. Joe looked up, too, pained.

"Oh, hell, Charlie, no one's askin' you to—"

"That's the point. No one's asked me because it ain't proper. I don't want one of you to get the other out in the milkhouse and say, 'Hey, why don't you tell Charlie to go,' and the other one say, 'Well, no, I know him better and it's your place.' 'No, it ain't my place; he likes Anne, let's get her to do it. If she won't, get Arla—' "

"Charlie—" Joe stood up, cramped a little from having been on the hard ground on his knees. It gave him a slightly apelike gait as he came toward Charlie, his big hand out in front of him, his face full of sympathy. "Charlie, there ain't no need to feel like that at all. Nobody can think of you goin' anywhere else, you're too close to us here. You're part of us, like family. We couldn't think about you leavin', not Brother Edgar's helper and friend. You was Founder's steadfast servant and I won't never forget that. A friend to Brother Edgar like you was, you got a place with us as long as you want it." Charlie sighed, his shoulders fell a little, and then he straightened them, muttered something, and turned and walked away. Joe looked at Andy, who had not moved. He shrugged and they went back to their work.

"We been at it all day and it's no better. Would you come out and take a look now?" They were amazed at Edgar's understanding of motors and engines. Joe had learned, step by step, specific things to do to specific machines. Andy knew the general principles behind the differential and transmission, but Edgar, having grown up with every kind of power attachment and engine, had the kind of bone-and-sinew knowledge that men had once had of their horses and mules. His knowledge came to him wordlessly and naturally, and because he had never learned, he couldn't teach his father and grandfather what he knew.

"I'd better hurry," he said. "It'll be dark soon. They don't give you much extra time in high school." The thought crossed his mind that if he, Mike, and Glover went on with the plan to get Mike the scholarship there would be even less time. His life would be ordered to the minute. Still, what a challenge it would be. He had been thinking about the scholarship all day, turning the thought this way and that—his specialness, his friendship with Mike, the simple excitement of trying something so big, and a faint discomfort at the secrecy of it. That it was to be a secret he did not doubt, and more of a secret than simply not telling anyone about it. There would have to be strategies made, plans of concealment, a studied casualness in important classes, a false nonchalance toward their other friends. This, too, attracted as much as repelled him. Looking at his father and grandfather walking beside him, he found himself smiling. It would be a relief to bend over a motor and let the nice, fumy stink come back up at him. There, at least, were clear questions and direct answers and the hands did the work without worrying the mind.

"I tell you it was a sight to see. We was workin' on the thing all day—you seen us up there, Charlie—and when he come home we called Edgar up. There was maybe half an hour of light left. Edgar, he just sticks his head in the thing, rattles somethin' around, tightens this and loosens that, listens here and there and then tells us to connect the thing, and it starts runnin' smooth as silk."

Edgar felt himself reddening. "Come on, Grandpa, it wasn't any kind of miracle. You and Dad had the right idea all along. It just needed a little adjustment, that's all." He saw that they were taking an even greater pleasure in his modesty, not believing a word of what he said. He decided to change the subject. "I went over to Mike's yesterday—I told you about Glover and me helping out over there. Mike and Glo wanted me to tell you how sorry they were about Grandpa Ralph, you know, to give condolences. They didn't either of them have grandfolks, and it's kind of special to them, our family, that we do." It came out so clumsily that they all smiled.

"Well," Joe said, "they're good boys, and good friends." Nothing was said for a minute. There was a pause where previously there would have been some comment about John Anton's newest project. Out of respect for the friendship there was silence now, but no one knew what to put in its place.

"Everyone well up at Antons' and Castles'?" Andy asked after a while.

"Fine," Edgar said. "Of course, I don't see Glover's people much. His dad is gone a lot on his work and his mom keeps pretty much to herself." There was another slight pause because of Anne.

"Does she?" Corella said. "Or does Glover fix it that way?"

"What?"

"Does Glover's mother keep to herself or is it Glover who sees to it that you don't visit up there?"

"Corella!" Anne said, half whispering in her high, nervous voice. "That's not a nice thing to say."

"I know, Mama," Corella answered automatically, "but which is it?"

Edgar was surprised. "What have you got against Glo?" he said.

"I don't have anything against him," Corella shrugged, "except that I don't like him and I'm trying to figure out a reason." There was a rustling of surprise at the table. Joe looked from his end down the length of surprised faces to where Corella sat.

"Hate ain't what you are meant to feel, child," he said. He spoke gently, a gentle surprise, an even gentler disappointment. "Whatever has the boy done to you?"

"Nothing," Corella said, "nothing. I don't trust him, that's all. He's always watching people watching him. He always says just the right thing at just the right time. All the good things and all measured out just right to the last drop and no more."

"Corella!" Anne was genuinely shocked. They all knew how much Anne hated discord. For years they had disallowed it at the table, to spare her. They had grown out of the habit of arguing, and so they all sat still and did nothing.

"Glover is my friend," Edgar said at last with what he hoped was quiet dignity. "His mother is Indian and very shy. She doesn't speak English well and so I guess it's easier for her to stay home, where she won't be embarrassed. Glo hasn't invited us up much, that's true, but I think that's because *she* is so shy, not he. You've never tried to get to know him or you wouldn't say those things about him." Andy had listened to Edgar, and he nodded slightly.

"One thing our faith teaches us," he said quietly, "is that God is love. Most people *say* that, but we really try to live it, to mirror it in our Praises and all our actions. Of course there are lots of people you don't *love*, but it's sad to see a young person go so far over to the other side in judging people."

"I'm not on the other side—" Corella said. Her lip was beginning to quiver very slightly, her face to redden. She got control of herself and went on, "I didn't say I hated him, I said I didn't like him. I guess I mean I don't trust him." She said suddenly, "I'm glad I'm not God—I don't want to be all love," and before the open eyes of their shock, she left the table.

Edgar, as stunned as the others, looked around from face to face, seeing his surprise mirrored everywhere, until he came to Charlie, who was looking after Corella without any surprise at all, but only that intense gaze of his, measuring, measuring.

214

20

They were at the memorial park a week before school started their middle year. They had met to discuss the strategy of getting Mike the scholarship, but the morning air was iridescent, the sun trembled in it, and the cottonwood fluff was seen away down the morning wind, light glowing on its undersides. So they played. They laughed and joked about nothing and everything and Mike's name on the memorial plaque bigger than the others.

"Because we're special," Edgar laughed, "because we're special people."

"Because *you're* special," Glover said, and got a hammer-lock on Edgar.

"Prove it!" Edgar shouted, choking.

"Let's," Mike said. "Let's prove it." Glover changed his hold, and Edgar fell and was pinned. They got up, dusting him off.

"How are we going to do it?" Glover asked.

"Ask people, take a poll." They laughed.

"It would be fun, though, seeing it work."

"Seeing if it did work."

"I'll bet it does, though," Glover said.

"I'll bet it doesn't," Edgar answered.

"How much?"

"Ten bucks."

"You're on."

"How'll we do it?"

"I'll let you know," Edgar said. "Something will happen that we'll all agree on, something we can use."

"Done," Glover said. They shook hands.

Discussing the scholarship, they saw the idea get simpler as they talked. Mike's freshman grades hadn't been bad. With tutoring and notes in math from Glover, and Edgar's work in social studies, Mike could easily get A's and B's. The biggest thing would be psychological—deferring to Mike in school, their subtle acknowledgment of him as their leader, their seeing to it that he covered the bases socially and in clubs and football.

"Look at the way they groom the top man on a basketball team," Glover said. "They do all the teamwork around him and it looks as though he's the one who's doing the work."

"We can't forget the community part, the social part," Edgar said. "I've been thinking about it. I Praise at Founder's and you guys often go to Willow Springs and the Forks. Why don't we rotate the Praises? That way more people get to know us better. Why not do it according to a plan?"

"And after Praise we cram Mike and plan the week for him. It sounds like a good idea."

"Why the Forks?"

"The prez of the school board Praises at the Forks."

"Amen," Glover said, and they laughed. "Remember, though, I want to hear from you about that bet."

"Never fear," Edgar said, and went to where Charlie was waiting for him in the truck.

That week, Corella, smoking in bed, had burned two large holes in the bright red blanket. Anne had cut up the blanket and made it into a skirt for Corella and a jacket for Edgar. She had gotten some old metal shank buttons from Arla's button box, polished them up, and used them on the jacket. Edgar complained that the outfit was too fancy, but Anne looked so wounded that he wore it to school, expecting at least a word or two in fun. Instead, some of the girls commented that he looked good in the jacket, and so he wore it two or three times that week.

Within two weeks the school halls were aflame with a dozen shades of red and two dozen varieties of silver and gold buttons. The local catalog store got four hundred dollars worth of orders for red wool flannel and the five and dime had calls for more metal buttons than had been ordered since its opening. Glover and Mike wanted to pay the bet but Edgar was against it.

"It was nothing I planned or picked. It just happened."

"Be honest," Mike said. "If Weile or Joe Dresser had worn the thing they'd have been laughed out of school and you know it. It was *you* wearing it that made it good, that made the other kids want to get one."

"I don't want your ten bucks. It wasn't the bet we had. The bet we had was for something we'd planned, something that couldn't be mistaken for fashion or style."

"Have you thought of what it should be?"

"Yes, this morning."

"What is it?"

"Remember when we used to call ourselves the Three Musketurkeys?"

"Don't remind me," Mike said. "We have about thirty turkeys left, and they're for our own eating. It's a ghost town up there now, a smelly ghost town."

"Do you have any feathers left over?"

"Feathers? Any kind, any color!"

"I just want three, please, medium size, medium color. Bring them in tomorrow, but don't show them to anybody."

"What are you going to do with turkey feathers?"

"Wear them."

"It's crazy, it's too crazy."

"I know it's crazy," Edgar said, "but how crazy? I want to find out how crazy."

Mike brought the feathers to school the next day and Edgar slipped them into his notebook. The red-shirt fashion had not made him feel as good as it should have. In fact, when he thought about it, the sudden appearance of all those red shirts and jackets with bright buttons was disquieting, hinted at a power in his hands, which he could not measure or control. That afternoon, after lunch, he went into the bathroom. When he came out, he had a longish mottled turkey feather in the pocket of his red jacket. Some of the other students asked him why it was there but everyone took note of it. To those who did ask he only answered, "A pocket feather."

The pocket-feather craze hit the school before Thanksgiving. No one knew how or why the school kids suddenly started wearing feathers in breast pockets or what they meant, but by Thanksgiving vacation there were dyed "steady" feathers, "available" feathers, bleached and perfumed feathers, modest and flamboyant feathers. The gun club and the Moose and Elks started to wear them and the storekeepers also, to show "town spirit" or "Thanksgiving spirit." At school, the student or teacher without a pocket feather was an asthmatic.

"You've done it, you actually got the town, not just the school, but the town in *feathers!*"
"I can hardly believe it myself."
"The ten bucks is yours. Spend it on one of those old raccoon coats and start the town wearing them. Paint yourself blue, for crying out loud!" Glover laughed.
The three of them were walking off a huge Thanksgiving dinner which the family had given for fifty Apostles. It was cold and they had served the dinner in the church. A fire was lit in the fireplace and the woodsmoke smell followed them down the dusty road past all the parked cars and trucks. The earth lay weed-blown and crack-dry under their feet. There had been a Praise and then the big dinner. They had too much strong coffee, and now they were exhilarated, breathing hard, getting a kind of oxygen euphoria that they knew was not joy but some chemical change in their lungs or blood that pushed them into exaggerated talk and dizzy, charged gaiety.
"I want you to know," Mike cried, "that I am very grateful for what you guys plan to do for me, that in helping me to get the Mohlencamp you are saving me—no, I mean it— saving me from a lifetime of sweeping out my father's old turkey coops. I will go to Ags with that money. I will go to Ags and be a vet, and the vet you will get is a vet in your debt." They laughed. "No kidding," Mike said, "it'll be free

for you two—free vet service for the rest of your lives. I plan to sign a paper about it—I mean it."

"Hell, Mike," Edgar said, "you don't have to do that. You don't even have to feel so grateful and get all bent out of shape over this. We're friends. I don't need the scholarship and Glo says he doesn't want it, but we both want you to have it—it's as simple as that. If we can help you get it, why not?"

"It's not that," Mike said, "it's that I wish we could all—all together—"

"All together what?"

"I wish there were three scholarships, three chances, that all three of us could have. Then I wouldn't feel funny about what you guys are doing and there still wouldn't have to be any competition among the three of us. If only we could make them give us three—"

There was a silence. Edgar was about to speak, to try to comfort Mike, to tell him again that what they were doing they were doing simply and happily as his friends, but Glover, who was wearing a long turkey feather, took it out of his shirt pocket and held it up in his left hand, flicking it with his right. It sailed up in the brisk wind and circled his head, falling in a spiral and landing gently in the weeds ahead of him.

"Why not?" he said. "Why the hell not?"

"You're out of your mind!" Mike said, but there was awe in his voice. He turned to Edgar. "He's out of his mind, isn't he? I mean, it's *impossible!*"

"Why?" Glover asked flatly. "Why impossible? For a town in feathers nothing is impossible. Look, we have two years to do it, two years to show the town and the committee that they *want* to do it, they *have* to do it."

"How?" Edgar said. "By going up and pleading?"

"No, by making ourselves inseparable, by making ourselves like one person and that one person indispensable to the town."

"Indispensable," Edgar said, "I'm not that even at home—"
But he thought about the motors he had worked on and stopped.

"Oh, come on," Mike said, "kids our age are the most dis-

219

pensable people of all—we're not cute little kids and we're not grown up enough for jobs and that's why we're in school so long. Indispensable!"

"I've been lots of places and lots of small towns," Glover said, "and what we are is the spirit of a town. What we are is a sign of whether a town lives or dies and you know it and people know it. Why is there such a fuss about young people staying on after high school? Why are people so scared of us going off to work in Pueblo or Denver? We're life, that's why, and for a county like this, a town like this, we're all folks have to look forward to—"

"You've thought a lot about this, haven't you?" Edgar said. He said it with admiration, but there was fear there, too. Or was it excitement making a slow, coiling feeling in his stomach and legs that tightened his blood vessels so that he had to breathe harder? He was suddenly cold. Three scholarships—the three of them together at Ags. What could be wrong with it? Could it be a wrong thing to do or to want? Glover looked at them levelly.

"Yes, I've thought about it, and here's what I've thought. This town needs us and we need the scholarships. We pay them back anyway. It's not really a scholarship at all, but a loan, an interest-free loan. The good we do will be for the town and the county as much as for ourselves. And like Mike said, there wouldn't be that rotten competition between us. The worst that can happen is that it doesn't work and we lose out to some grind with an uncle on the committee."

"We'd have to plan it, every day, every hour, practically."

"The thing would have to run like a watch," Edgar said. "All the grades at least B's, all the clubs, the football and basketball, all the community-service things, the Grange and the 4-H. We'd have to be good Apostles, too, not missing Praise or any of the special projects that come up. We'd have to do all that and still keep up with chores at home—"

"That's the beautiful part of it," Glover said. "You, Ed, and I go out for football and basketball. Mike is not all that hot on those things, he can do the clubs, history and drama, something that has plenty of public contact, debating maybe. I don't have much to do at home and that means I could cram for you—type up notes and all that. It's the same with Mike. We've got it in the bag, I'm telling you!"

Edgar wanted to say that somehow he had felt better working the plan for Mike. This was something that meant more than three boys trying to work harder in school and get a scholarship. He couldn't form the thought clearly enough to give it words. He looked at his friends. For Mike it meant getting away from the responsibility of their gift. He had an open, relieved look on his face. Glover had the wonderful enthusiasm that Edgar loved in him, the feeling he sometimes radiated that he, and by extension they, were special beings, living at some greater height. The secret would add to the size of the challenge. They would still go to Burkett's after school, still sit for their mandatory Cokes at exaggerated leisure, feigning the idleness of grown people with no boring chores at home and no schoolwork to do. It was the game all the students played, but for them it would be a double deception; they would be cramming in dead earnest in order to play the part of easygoing, popular good fellows. Mike and Glover were watching him.

"Okay," he said, "we'll try." How could there be any harm in it when the other two smiled so happily and with so much relief? They began to pound one another on the back and laugh.

That night Charlie had some trouble getting up to his place in the loft. When Ralph died he had moved back up there and none of the family's pleadings or reasoning could get him down. With all the room downstairs, they said, it was silly for him to stay up in the attic baking in the summer and freezing in the winter. He let them reason with him until they were tired and went his way. This evening he had finished his chores late. The Thanksgiving feast had settled at last. It was time for another pull at the bottle. He headed back to the big house tiredly and let himself in. Arla and Joe were watching TV in the front room. He could see the blue glow on their faces although the sound was turned low the way Arla liked it. He tiptoed past the room and around and up the stairs and then to the storage closet where the ladder was that led to the attic loft. It pleased him that he could do all this without a light, even avoiding those places where boards creaked. He was on the first rung of the ladder when a voice said:

"Charlie—"

"Who's that!"

"Charlie, it's Edgar."

"What the hell are you doin' there, boy? What's the matter?"

"I've been waiting for you."

"What is it? You should be home in bed."

"I want to ask you a question." Charlie's heart was slowing, the air that had gone tight in his lungs released itself.

"I don't know no answers to anything," he said. "Your dad, he's the one to ask, or your grandpa."

"I can't ask them—I don't want to. I want to ask you."

"It's your misfortune then. Ask away."

"I read where a man said, 'Power corrupts.' Is that true?"

"I guess so, but don't think weakness don't corrupt just as bad. The difference is that power can use its power and weakness has nothin' to use but its weakness. Is that what you wanted to ask me?"

"One more thing. Charlie, can you make good out of evil? I mean can something good come out of something—well, not good?"

Charlie's laugh came gravelly against the musty softness of the dark closet. "Make good out of evil? What the hell else is there to make it out of!" And he stomped up the ladder to the dust-thick stillness of his loft.

They threw themselves into the plan like dreamers or gamblers. They joined the history club and the French club, went out for sports, debating, Future Farmers, Young Apostles' Service Group, glee club, drama club. While Edgar and Glover were out in athletics practice sessions, Mike would make copies of all the classroom notes. He wrote abstracts of books they might not get a chance to read, and outlined papers for them. When Mike was gone for evening meetings, Edgar and Glover did his work. Not a moment was wasted, not a movement made without purpose, farmers' virtues—husband the strength, harness the will, plow in patience, waste not. They learned the other arts easily. They learned to talk low and slowly so as never to appear hurried but they never stood still. While they greeted friends they moved along toward the next class, the next appointment, the new plan, taking the group of smiling acquaintances with them as they went and leaving the group at the door, the gate, the truck, the house, charmed and awed by their ease and relaxed good humor. It must never be seen in their easy camaraderie that their true attention was elsewhere, that they were following a rhythm like jugglers attuned to the dozen balls in the air, the height, the fall, the toss, and the catch.

After three months Mike began to look harried. The basketball season was at its height.

"We can't meet after school," Glover said, "Burkett's is too important."

"We'll have to meet before."

"I'd have to get up at four in the morning!" Edgar protested.

"I'm doing double the work and sometimes triple!" Mike cried. "And when is it going to stop? I thought, okay, it'll ease up after football, but it wasn't two days from the last game before the basketball practice started. A once-a-week meeting just isn't enough. I have chores, too, and it's getting so I can't sleep anymore. I wake up in a sweat in the middle of the night scared there's something I've missed!"

"Mike," Glover said, "it's no easier on us—games most weekends and lots of nights—all the study we have to do on top of it—"

"You guys are used to having me prepare everything for you—Mike, make me another outline, Mike, sketch out an essay—besides, I have to cover all the clubs that aren't athletic clubs, and don't think *they* don't take preparation, too!"

"We're working as hard as we can. What makes you think we have it easy!"

"Wait a minute—" Edgar said. He looked from one to the other of them. Mike was pale and his hands were clenched at his sides. Glover had a sullen, removed look. "We're all working eighteen hours a day as hard as we can and we're still only barely managing. There's something wrong here, there's got to be."

"What's wrong is Glover running everything."

"What's wrong is Mike thinking that some dumb debate takes more time and energy than a big game!"

"Hey, wait a minute, you guys. I told you there was something wrong and I really believe it. Give me till Wednesday to find out what's happening to us, why we're so overwhelmed, and don't do anything at all until then. Take assignments but don't work on them. Nothing till Wednesday, okay?"

"Okay," Mike said. They left for their houses bitter and silent. For the first time there was no code word called back, no secret message of their faith and solidarity.

The next day Edgar hailed Glover on the school steps. In the minute before others came up he said quickly, "I think I have the answer, but I need proof. I have a lunch meeting with the student council and our advisers. Do this for me, Glo. Go to the school library and get all the yearbooks you can. Look up the scholarship winners and see what clubs they were in and what sports they went out for. Write it down, all you can."

"I'll have to miss lunch, but that's okay because the library is less likely to be busy then."

"Okay. This is important." His face changed and his voice opened up. "He says he gets twenty-seven miles to the gallon!"

"Fourteen is more like it!" Glover chanted back at him. Others had joined them.

"You guys talkin' about Buster Crail and that new car of his?" Doug Empey said. "Nine is really more like it."

They met on Wednesday, hurriedly.

"I've seen all the school records," Glover said. "Every winner of the Mohlencamp Scholarship got A's and B's in all his classes. Every winner, every male winner, played football *and* basketball and usually did track and other sports, too.

Every male winner was up to his butt in clubs and social activities."

"It's not possible!" Mike shouted at them. "It can't be done!"

Edgar smiled very quietly. "I know."

"How then—"

"The difference has to be in the grades. They must be grading the athlete differently, at least during the season." Edgar grabbed Mike's jacket. "You'd better go out for basketball, Mike, before you flunk out altogether!" He began to pummel both of them, laughing.

"It isn't true!" Mike shouted. "It can't be!"

"It is, you clod. You've been grinding for nothing—dance on the ceiling and we'll still get A's and B's until the season is over."

"Is it a lie, then? The grades—are they really fake? You *can't* have practice every day and still do homework and write papers—it's a goddamn dirty lie! It's like the lies my father tells—dreamer's lies, believer's lies. Why do they do it?"

"They do it everywhere," Glover said. "I should have known it was here, too. Sports are so important, even the high-school teams, that they have to help anyone who isn't a total moron get A's and B's."

"What would happen if we asked the principal, asked him if the grades were fixed—do you think he'd admit it?"

"I don't think so," Edgar said, "not that it was a lie, anyway. The point is—"

"A believer's lie. Won't I ever get away from believers' lies!"

"The point is," Edgar insisted, "that we're onto it. Because of what we're doing, we've gotten in behind these things."

"The point is," Glover echoed, "that we've gotten in behind these things and now we can use them."

"I nearly killed myself for their damn lie!" Mike said. He was trembling and a little pale.

"There were times when one more thing would have broken me," Edgar said.

"But we won't break." And Glover smiled a hard smile. "We won't break now."

21

Because Mike was not good enough for the basketball team he stayed in dramatics and debating, where he had to make real grades and do real work. Edgar had been correct. Even when they were late with papers or reading they were not marked down, the A's and B's kept coming. They soon found that it was too demoralizing to turn in no assignments, read no books. For their own needs they were forced to keep some semblance of faith with the school records. They did this with a certain clinical detachment. There was no longer any joy in the work, but no pain either. After a while, they felt themselves weathering under the work. It made them feel heroic, outlined a little starkly against the background of school, home, and Praise.

Despite all the calls that were made on their time, the three of them knew that they must never miss a Praise. They often went Seeking and Bringing together, happy in the drama of it, careful of the words they used and the impression they made. It was exciting to run and Seek for the Spirit of the Lord, finding at the end the delicious secrecy of their triune wholeness, a unity surely as blessed and special as any single blessing the Lord bestowed on the other runners. It excited them that they could share subtle hints about what they could not speak of to the Praise.

There were times when Edgar looked around and saw his father gazing at him in a puzzled way. Andrew Kornarens was principal elder now, a man whose goodness and strength of character made his presence at the thirteen hundred Praises in the United States eagerly sought after. He reconciled dissidents, inspired leaders, called forth young people and enlisted them in the service of the old, the grieving, and the poor. He was unfailingly patient. Edgar admired his father, and when the two of them worked together they seemed to be happily and matter-of-factly at peace with each other. It was at other times, at Praises or picnics or at a football game, that Edgar would be aware of that gentle, questioning look.

Edgar knew his father had many problems. For years the Apostles of the Spirit of the Lord had succeeded in keeping peace between its factions. There were cures experienced in Praises but some Praises wanted to become completely involved in curing. Some Apostles wanted to speak in tongues, some wanted to codify the flexible, natural order of service into which the Praises had grown over the years, some wanted hymns, some a collection of the words of Founder Edgar now that the original bearers were dying and the greater number of Apostles had never seen southeastern Colorado or been alive in the dust-bowl days. Edgar knew that his father was seeing him as a Praise leader of the future. Founder's Praise, with its 250 regular members, had a power and influence far beyond its numbers and in spite of its geographical isolation. A word from Founder's changed Praises all over the country. Edgar knew that his father needed him, was proud of him, loved him. The trouble was that Edgar had no time for it. No time at all.

The three Praises, Founder's, Forks, and Willow Springs, had long since gotten used to seeing Edgar, Mike, and Glover in three-week intervals. Each of these Praises had its own personality and special qualities, but in attending them all the boys were widening the number of people who saw and knew them and thought of them as sharers in Praise. Sometimes Andy or Joe would ask the boys how things were at Forks or Willow Springs. The boys always answered "fine," because for them things were fine.

One warm day in March, Edgar had slipped out of school a little early. He decided he wouldn't go to Burkett's or any of the clubs or meetings. Burkett's was becoming more and more of a strain, the laughing and talking an ever-more galling waste of time when homework had to be done and cram sessions worked. He had ducked out just before the last bell and was hurrying to get away before people started leaving. He had ridden his bicycle from home and he took it from the rack, quickly got on, and pedaled off down the street. The air was dry and sweet and smelled of new roots and the moisture of melting snow. He had gone past the memorial park, away from Burkett's and the main places where people went after school, and he was thinking about what he would do with the hour or two of unguarded time he had stolen for himself. He was thinking so hard that he did not notice a girl walking up the street toward the park. They collided and the girl fell. Edgar was embarrassed and shaken. He helped her up, apologizing. She hadn't been paying attention either, she said. She was a girl from school and an Apostle who Praised now and then at Willow Springs. He had forgotten her name.

"What are you doing out of school so early?"

"I had to pick up a few things and if I don't skip study period I miss the bus."

Abruptly he said, "I'd take you home, but I don't have the truck today."

"I see that," she said. He shook his head and they laughed. "It's pretty far anyway," she said.

"Living at the Springs, you miss all the after-school activities, don't you—the clubs and sports and that kind of thing."

"Yes," she said, "we do. Lots of the kids think we Willow Springs kids are clannish, but it's just because we're isolated in a way and don't really belong to the school the way the closer people do."

"Maybe you're lucky," he said. The statement was properly casual and offhand but he was shocked at hearing it come out of his own mouth and full of anxiety at having said it. What must she think when the most popular boy in school said things like that? Would she talk about it to others, tell it to

228

the Willow Springs kids on the bus? "I forgot your name," he blurted out, at least changing the subject. She didn't seem at all surprised.

"I don't think you ever knew it," she said. "It's Martha Wyer."

He saw Ansel Case coming down the street toward them, waved at Ansel, and said, "I've got to go now."

She smiled. "Good-bye."

He was half a block away before he allowed himself to look around. Ansel had stopped and was talking with Martha. He smiled because he had never seen that happen before. Martha was not a very pretty girl and Ansel only talked to girls who could "do him good." He turned toward home.

Andy was doing some bookwork at the kitchen table when Edgar came in. Anne had baked them some cookies and had set them out with milk, as she usually did. Also as usual, she had gone down to the cellar to iron or sew, and to watch the old TV down there.

"Sit down a minute, son," Andy said. "I'm just finishing here but I want to ask you about some things."

Andy never said "talk to you" but always "discuss" or "ask." He was careful about being considerate to his children. Edgar sat down and waited. The cookies were floury. Anne never did have Arla's light touch with dough. Andy sighed and Edgar, automatically defending his mother, said, "Ma sure tries to please us—cookies or cake almost every day—" This too was a thing he or Andy often did. It was a form of which they were barely conscious.

"I wanted to ask you if you knew anything about the Willow Springs people wanting a special baptism," Andy said. The question was simple but Edgar found himself completely adrift in it. He had been at Willow Springs one week in three for the past year and yet he knew little or nothing about the spirit of the Praise. He had not been listening carefully to what the Witness was or to the petitions or even to the thanks. He, Mike, and Glover had been so busy with the impressions they were trying to make, the exactly proper words they were to say, that they had lost a feeling for what was going on around them.

"Special baptism?"

"Yes, there was a group here today, young people, five or six of them, and they were talking about how ordinary the ceremony is in which we welcome new Apostles. I suppose they have a point, although I don't really see what more we can do. It's been a sore point right along that there's nothing 'official' because there are no 'officials' to, well, 'officiate.' " He smiled. "They're coming back Sunday after Praise to talk more about it, but I wanted to know what was happening in the Praise, what you felt about it. Praises have personalities all their own, young, old, tight, loose, reverent or rowdy, and sometimes, I think, healthy or sick." He sat back, looking quizzically at Edgar. "What's it like up there?"

Edgar answered from memory, from what he had felt back in the days when he had first started to go to Willow Springs. "It's a young Praise, much younger than Founder's. Most of the people aren't thirty yet—it's smaller than Founder's, too, and of course there aren't the numbers of new people, visitors, outsiders that Founder's always gets." He felt he was only moving the air, not really speaking. He wasn't saying anything that his father didn't already know. Why couldn't he tell his father what should have been so simple? Why wasn't he able to give something better than a census? He saw Andy's head at a questioning angle, his eyes widening a little. "I never heard anything about special baptism, though," he concluded lamely. He knew he might have heard and not even paid attention. He couldn't be sure. Andy took another cookie and bit into it.

"I'd be pleased if you'd stay at Willow Springs for a while, just stay there and watch what happens, see what the mood of the Praise is like. I know you've been visiting the different Praises with Mike and Glover, trying to get the broadest experience you can, but I have a strange feeling that that Praise needs our help." Edgar nodded mutely. He didn't know that his father had put that construction on his Praise-jumping. He was suddenly reminded of one time during a Seeking and Bringing when in the middle of a run he had begun to wonder whether he could come back to the circle with something blasphemous or obscene and still be listened to with the same "special" feeling there had always been. If he told his father now why he, Mike, and Glover went to the different Praises, would Andy be angry or disappointed? Would he believe it? Would he be forgiving?

But Andy had finished the doughy cookie and had taken a swallow of milk and said, "The next thing is closer to home, a family thing, and I need your help in that, too." Edgar mastered the little jump of fear before his father saw it. "You must have noticed," Andy said slowly, "how upset and unhappy Corella's been these past few months. I've spoken with her, your mother's tried many times, and neither of us, and not Grandma or Grandpa, has been able to find out what's bothering her. Being her brother and close to her, we thought you might know, that she might have confided in you. I wouldn't want to break that confidence, of course—only to get an idea if there's some way we can help, something we can do."

Edgar had been amazed at the question about Willow Springs. He was floored by the talk about Corella. Confidences? Closeness? What could his father be thinking about? He saw Corella only at meals or riding the school bus. What had they ever talked about in their few shared moments waiting for the bus or sitting in the truck with Charlie going into town? He searched in vain for a single remembered comment, the barest statement of facts or thoughts or feelings. He could see her sitting at the supper table, moving in a Praise, getting on and off the bus, and it was true, now that he thought about it, that there was a closed quality about her, a discontent pulling subtly at her features so that they looked slightly pinched and narrowed. And, of course, she wasn't very popular in school. The girls she went with were all plain. When she walked into Burkett's, there was no big greeting, no chair pulled up at the favored table. She sat in the back and in the corner with one or two of the plain girls, had her Coke, and left.

His father was watching him closely for his response. He had hidden his confusion with a furrowing of his brow, drawing up his lip as though pondering the whole thing. All he really wanted was time to make up something, anything at all.

"It's a big question," he said. Andy nodded. "I know she's not very happy," he went on, "but I've never been able to get her to tell me what's wrong." He was pleased with that. It sounded adult and concerned.

Andy reached out and patted his arm. "I'd be happy, it would be a great relief, if you would try again—not to force her or break in on her privacy, but only to get some idea what's made her so unhappy. Even the teachers in school say it about her, that she hides away in herself and doesn't want to open her feelings and her thoughts to anyone." He shook his head. "How strange it is that we Apostles find so much spiritual strength in opening our hearts to the Spirit of the Lord and yet with all that fine background of freedom, a lifetime of freedom, our own girl is so hesitant and afraid. You must have noticed how seldom she joins the Praises lately. Now she spends the time standing next to Charlie, looking on, not even talking to him or anyone else."

He hadn't noticed that either, but he nodded as though he had, and thought to say what Andy always said to other people whose kin or children had stood by instead of joining in. "Watching is a form of prayer, too. Everyone stands back now and then." Andy sighed deeply. He had said it himself too often. Edgar knew he was thinking that from their family more was expected—should be, had to be.

"You will talk to her, won't you, son?"

"Sure, Dad, I will."

"I don't mean for you to spy on her or anything, or violate any confidences."

"I'll just try to find out what the trouble is."

"Thank you, son. I know you'll do the right thing."

The problem was when. Even as he turned away and went up to do his homework, Edgar realized that days would go by, weeks perhaps, before he would have the time to get Corella off by herself. When they saw each other it was only in passing, annoyed because the other one was talking on the phone or taking up the bathroom. He would have to make the time, to make a special effort to talk to her. When? The days were solidly filled, every hour from waking to sleeping carefully planned, orchestrated to the rhythm of their work. Community service was what he was supposed to be thinking about now, the community program that he, Glo, and Mike were supposed to get in on, something public enough but not glaring. People hate showoffs and young showoffs worst of all. His father's talk sank away and was forgotten.

It was when he was planning to leave for Praise at Forks that he remembered his father's asking him to stay on at Willow Springs. He called Mike and Glover and told them to go on without him, and to come to the later Praise at Founder's and stay for dinner. It would take extra time but it was urgent that they get together. Both of them sounded puzzled but they said they would come by later to see him.

"You're not changing the plans, are you?" Glover said. "A lot depends on keeping things going just as they are." Edgar said he wasn't. He was so irritated at having to take the extra time that he ground the gears on the truck as he started out on the highway.

His first Praise alone at Willow Springs astounded him. Without Mike and Glover, Edgar found himself listening closely to what the dancers said and watching the running with greater care. He had realized before this that he saw Praises mostly in terms of the three of them. Would Glover run now or later? Would Mike answer a dancer's question or wouldn't he? In this Praise he sensed, or thought he sensed, for the first time a definite break between the generations of dancers. The young people ran, Seeking and Bringing, and afterward they spoke out. But their elders did not reply to their questions or add their assent, the "supplementary evidence" in a Praise Witnessing. When the elders spoke, the young listened with barely concealed impatience. Both sides were polite, too polite, but neither spoke to any point raised by the other group. Edgar watched himself do what he, Glover, and Mike had always done at Willow Springs. He gave a conservative, simple Praise, answering no one from either group but thanking the Lord for general things, crops, the ability to work, for friends and special people in the community. Because it might have been a potential cause of conflict, the choice of what to praise the Lord for, he, Glover, and Mike had spent a good deal of time discussing subjects of praise. Their planning and skill had paid off. No one knew their politics or preferences. They did not favor any group over another and they spoke to the older people with respect but not deference—just enough to be winning, not so much that the younger people were put off. He did the same thing now, going easily into a friendly concern for Mrs. Price's brother after her petition and seconding Jamie Cogburn's Witness with a careful statement of his own. People always approved when he spoke. Edgar tried hard to keep the same tone, too, friendly, open, and neither young nor old. He watched carefully as he spoke or ran, measuring the effect he had on all of them. He could see he was doing well. After he spoke there was the sigh of approval he had learned to listen for. Watching himself doing all this, he stopped caring about Willow Springs.

He did notice the girl he had bumped into near school, Martha Wyer. At school she always looked a little shy and out of place, but among the small group in the Praise she had a simplicity and directness that Edgar liked. He did not speak to her, but he noticed her and watched her, and wondered why he had not noticed her before.

That afternoon Glover and Mike arrived early at Founder's and went up to the barn. Edgar saw them and slipped away between dances. He didn't mention what had happened at Willow Springs, how much different the Praise seemed without the three of them together, or his surprise at seeing people more richly and fully than before. They had a lot to talk about. There were notes to be exchanged, book reviews to be gone over. Mike, who liked to read, read for all of them, and in the case of novels and plays told them as much as he could about the plots. They used cram books for history and math. Luckily, the school had dropped the foreign-language requirement.

"What have you thought up for the community-service idea?" Glover said. Edgar shrugged.

"There hasn't been time," he said.

"Time? It's April already and we need to be in people's minds during the summer. Basketball is over, football hasn't started yet. Now's the time to plan, to start the summer thing going."

"Well, what, volunteer at the hospital? It's too far away," Mike said.

"It wouldn't get to the important people anyway. It has to be seen."

"Hire ourselves out somehow?"

"Not with work at home," Glover said quickly. "That would really be a losing shot. The people around here are very strong on family chores coming first."

Suddenly Mike said, "The fair."

"The county fair?"

"Sure, why not. Something to raise money for the town and the county."

"What do you have in mind?"

"Nothing, I don't know, it just seems to be the only way we can do something without attracting the wrong kind of attention."

"A booth," Edgar said, laughing, "we could set up a booth and pose in it. 'Send these boys to college, fifty cents apiece'!"

"Be serious."

"What could we do, let people hit us with softballs?"

"Something we organize—"

"No, something else, something the county or town does, but something that will get us known, the three of us together."

"A turkey shoot," Mike said slowly, "a turkey shoot, with muskets."

The fair committee was delighted with the idea. Of the thirteen or so antique-gun clubs the committee contacted, ten responded with great interest. The committee wrote to the president of the Colorado Muzzle Loaders to work out the arrangements for space and safety and to set up requirements for the targets. Live turkeys had long since been outlawed but there was a dazzling array of targets, moving and still, and the fair committee worked hard to have the best contest it could. The gun clubs put general invitations in their magazines and newsletters and the committee received requests for information from musket clubs and blunderbuss brigades all over the county. Edgar thought the three of them should ask to run the event, but Glover advised against it.

"I've been to enough of these things to know. We've suggested the thing and helped to set it up. One more suggestion about costumes for the judges, maybe, and then we step back and let the committee get its innings. The judges should be respected men, we'll say, older men who will be listened to in case there's a dispute. Of course we'll volunteer to do any backstage work people want, cleaning up or setting the targets or anything that keeps us out of the limelight."

"Why? Isn't the point our getting seen?"

"We have to make sure that no one mistakes our ideas about our place here, and no one thinks we are trying to put ourselves forward or show off in any way."

"Just three innocent boys," Mike said, "brightening the corner where they are." Glover and Edgar laughed at this. They felt sophisticated enough to enjoy the cynicism.

The Frontier Musket and Muzzle Load event was the high point of the fair. Many people came in groups and many were costumed. The Cumberland Mountain group turned up in Daniel Boone regalia, the women leaving campers and trailers in poke bonnets and calicoes. The Kansans marched to music, the Oklahoma men did close-order drill. Eighteen turkeys were awarded, live or dressed, and most of them were eaten that night by the winners and their friends. A concessionaire made three hundred dollars plating and mounting turkey wishbones as trophies. After the fair the boys were exultant.

"Mr. Bowen saw me working in the store," Glover said. "He hadn't ever taken much notice of me when I wasn't with you two, but this time he called me by name and was downright friendly. He said that the shoot had gotten more people and raised more interest than anything else at the fair. I think they're going to plan it as a yearly event."

"If they do, they'll have to get the turkeys someplace else."

"You mean your dad got rid of all of them? Not even a coopful of the best birds left?"

"Didn't you know he donated the birds and they were the last ones we had? After all, 'it's impossible to raise turkeys on a large scale in eastern Colorado.'"

"All that energy—all that planning—won't you be able to save anything?"

"No," Mike said. "Actually, we kept that last bunch longer than we've kept anything before."

"What's coming now? Anything new in the clouds?"

Glover had turned away. They could see that he was uncomfortable talking about Mike's father. There were still moments when Glover felt all too keenly his place as outsider, even now when he was a leader of the most popular group in school. What was it like, Edgar wondered, to want to belong so much that you couldn't be sure even when you did?

"Mike—" Edgar began.

"Listen," Glover interrupted, "while this turkey shoot is still in people's memories we should have another thing planned, something for the fall and winter, something that goes on and doesn't end the way the fair did."

"Glo," Mike said, and picked his teeth with a straw, "where do you get all your energy?"

"Don't you see, this is the last clear summer. If they're going to give us the scholarship next year, they're going to have to know it this year, know it and plan for it. I've looked at this year's seniors and the only one they could pick would be Betty Harrison. She's a girl and they don't pick girls unless there's *nobody* else. We have to make them see us coming, all three of us, and we have to be strong enough so that they'll not give the award at all this year because they're saving it for us."

Edgar had a dreamlike sensation then as though he were walking under water. Where did Glover's knowledge come from? In the back of his mind he saw the possibilities too, a big thing, something that would unify the town and with which their names would be associated.

"We'd have to start it and get other people to do it," he murmured, "like the shoot."

"We need to think," Mike said, "because it can't be too obvious. I thought we might get up money for a statue of Brother Edgar Bisset, but of course that would look like family pride. Besides, the town isn't all Apostle."

"We'll meet next week," Glover said, "and we need to find

whatever it is before then." In the golden-moted, hay-scented heat of the barn loft, they opened their cram books and began their week's work.

"It was good to have you guys back again at Willow Springs."

"I think your relief may have been a little obvious—"

"You mean what I said in Witness, praising the Spirit for my friends?"

"It went over all right, but it's a little dangerous—calling attention to the friendship a little too hard," Mike said. "I felt funny."

"Well," Glover said, "Mike is a very modest feller. Deservedly, I'd say, justifiably modest. The most deservedly modest person I know." They laughed. The Sunday leisure was healing them. It was one of the hottest days of the year, too hot for the barn loft, so they lay in the great, comforting shadow of the barn, conjuring the hair-thin breeze from the east. The barn beetled over them and they remembered how frightened they had been as children, lying face up to the imminent fall of houses and barns upon them. The barn roof watered and ran in the heat. They watched until a cloud came before the sun and darkened the flowing air.

"Modest Mike has an idea," Mike said. "He has the project we need."

"What is it?" Glover asked, and came up on an elbow.

"I've been listening to people in different Praises," Mike said slowly, "and to the things they're afraid of. I could never understand what people here are more afraid of than drought or prices falling. Last week some Negro on TV called the white people devils and this Sunday I heard Mrs. Mundelein going on about how the Negroes hate us when there's not ten of them in the county. John Wingate talks about violence and crime as though there'd been a bank holdup every five minutes. What are our crimes anyway? Calf stealing and land swindles and water-rights fights, and we've always had those. . . ."

"What's your point?" Edgar asked.

"What I hear all the time is that there is no respect for the past," Mike said. "I think it's why the turkey shoot went off so well, although I didn't figure it at the time."

Edgar nodded. "I think you're right. What are you saying, then?"

"I'm saying that we should do something for the community but that it should have to do with the past, with history, with remembering something, not initiating something new."

"Maybe an idea about the war honor-rolls in Memorial Square?"

"No," Edgar said quickly, "not war. When that wall went up over there in Germany people got nervous about us having to go over there and fight another war for those people."

"What then?"

"I don't know—that's what I'm not sure of," Mike said, "but I think it should include Memorial Square, a special way of fixing up Memorial Square."

"That doesn't sound 'historical' to me."

"No, but it has to do with people's pride in the way we held on here even in bad times. Now times are good and the older people are scared we'll forget things, important, spiritual things."

"You think we should plant more trees there or what?"

"No, not that. I'm not sure what I mean yet, only that we should look back and not ahead."

"I'd say you were crazy," Glover said, "except that your turkey-shoot idea was so good. Whatever gave you that idea in the first place?"

"I think I was a little down that day. Dad hadn't been making any new noises, no big new ideas. I hate those big-idea times, but when he's in one I forget how bad things are when he has no ideas at all and just goes wandering around the house in his bathrobe, not shaving or eating and halfway not caring who we are. When the three of us were talking about what to do for a project, I was thinking that my dad reminded me of a carnival, a one-man carnival. He comes to some dark, deserted place, he sets up a festival city there overnight—tents, magic, music. It's a wonder. It lights up the field and the sky over it and the whole town is caught up in it. Just as the town gets used to the festival, and just when the field begins to look natural with the magic carnival on it, he hears the call of another city, a city whose name he doesn't even know yet, a field that's still dark to him and far away. Suddenly the magic is all drudgery and the music all work. The tents come down and everything folds up and pulls away. The wagons groan on the washed-out roads. Everything is dark—no lights show anywhere. I thought of a carnival and I guess I was mad enough about those damn turkeys to think of a turkey shoot. There's your genius for you."

" 'To believe what is true for you in your private heart is true for all men; that is genius,' Emerson, 'Self-Reliance.' "

"Glover, you are the inside of a tin-roof turkey coop in August."

"I must be," Glover said, and lay back again. "I'm too hot to argue. What about this new thing, this history idea?"

"It feels right," Edgar said. "Let's give it a week and see what comes."

"We're losing time," Glover said. "We'll need to plan."

"We have to have something to plan," Mike objected.

"Yes, but you talk as though we have all the time in the world. We haven't. We have to get started—"

Edgar had suddenly jumped up as though he'd been bitten. "Oh, damn!" he cried at them, and then sat down again weakly. "Damn!"

"What is it?" they cried together. "What's happened?"

"Oh, it's Corella. I forgot. Dad wanted me to talk to her. He seemed to think it was important. I got so busy I let it slide and now it's been three weeks—"

"Why was it important?" Mike asked.

"The folks seem to think she's more unhappy than usual or something is bothering her. She does come out with funny things that make people upset, but then I remember her doing that for a long time. Still, she's been standing off at Praises."

"Yes, I've seen that," Mike said. "I wondered about it a little."

Glover lay back again. "It isn't likely that it will come out, is it, I mean your not talking to her? Your dad won't ask her about it and because he won't, you can tell him you talked to her and still be covered." He popped his fist into an imaginary glove, "Safe on second." Edgar was embarrassed for Glover and didn't say anything.

Mike mumbled, "That's not the point, Glo."

Glover shrugged. "The point is that Ed's dad had no right to ask him to do all that. If Corella is acting funny that's his headache, not Ed's. I hate those things, anyway. 'Talk to him,' 'talk to her.' Do you know how many kids come to me and say, 'Fix it with Ed to take my sister out,' or, 'Get Mike to join the French club.' I always say I will and I never do. It would make me look bad in front of you guys, and for what?" He rolled over onto his stomach.

"But families are different," Edgar said.

"They sure are. Worse. I'd stay away from it, if I were you. If Corella has a problem, she's not going to be happy with you tramping into it with your big feet."

"Oh," Mike groaned, "it's too hot to argue. I'm glad they Praised inside today. Everyone was melting and running together like gingerbread cookies."

"She'll probably be down helping at Grandma's," Ed said. "I'd better get down and talk to her before supper is on." Glover had opened his mouth to say something but Mike caught his eye and he closed it again. "When can we meet next, Wednesday?"

"Okay, Wednesday morning up in Memorial Square."

"And look, you guys think about what I said, will you? History, tradition. I think that's what we'll need."

"Whatever it is, we'll need it soon," Glover added, "to sew things up."

Corella was outside on Joe and Arla's back porch. She was sitting in Charlie's old rump-sprung chair, shelling peas, and they made a comfortable pinging sound in the aluminum pot. She was working slowly and did not look up when Edgar came through the back door.

"Hi," he said uncomfortably, "mind if I sit down here?" She shrugged and went on with her shelling a little faster. He did not know how to begin. He knew there should be a way, there always had been with him, an easy entrance. Talk about some shared feeling or experience, some general chitchat, and then a little closer to talk about the family, and still closer to talk about herself. The trouble was that he knew her so little, had so little in common with her, that there was no starting point. Some obsolete memories and nothing else.

Finally he said, "I suppose I ought to thank you for burning a hole in that blanket last fall. I got a lot of wear out of the jacket Ma made."

"So did everyone else in the school," she said flatly, "in the county, practically. I thought it was great—it made me give up smoking."

"Why do you always talk like that, as though somebody had just kicked you in the butt?" He wanted to kick himself for not controlling his impatience.

"I guess it must sound that way to you, but it isn't that way, really. I did see the whole world go red and gold last Thanksgiving. I saw all the feathers. I thought it was a good idea, so I gave up smoking. I thought when I did everybody would." He thought for a moment that he could dissemble about the feathers and had begun to say, "What do you mean?" but her tone was too flat and too knowing.

"I don't think the feathers hurt anyone. It was about town spirit and school spirit, and it made people feel involved in something they could belong to."

"Bull," she said. "It was you flexing your muscles and showing your power. It was you being the ever-popular wonderful fellow, you and Mike and Glover."

"Hey," he said, "I'm here to talk about you."

"Okay," she answered. "Go on, it's my favorite subject."

"That's why you don't get along with people, that smart-aleck way you have of putting them off. You stand aside at Praises now and you're not part of the group. At school you don't fit in and you don't seem to want to fit in, and all it is is being happy and belonging."

"I stand aside at Praises because I don't have the Apostles' curse."

"Which is?"

"You don't really want to know, do you? I mean, you don't want me to go into all this right now—"

"Yes, I do. I want to know. Tell me."

"The Apostles' curse—"

"Yes."

"Harmony at the cost of honesty, all-purpose cheerfulness, the kind that never looks beyond 'God Is Love' or imagines his 'no' to be as powerful as his 'yes,' his punishment as true as his blessing."

"God never punishes people—that's medieval."

"Then God is Santy Claus."

"You're playing with words."

"Yes, but not with people, which is what you do, you and the Apostles."

"What have we ever done but cure, help, bring people together?"

"You do it with all feeling and no thought, all need and no intellect. Every week I hear Ma Praise—three meaningless messages. The truth is something she can never state aloud or think to herself."

"And what truth is that?"

"That we're not all generous, happy, loving children. That she hates the responsibility of being Mrs. St. Anne the Apostle. That I hate being pointed at as an example of freedom and the beauty of sharing all thoughts with all neighbors and all feelings, feelings, feelings with each other and the Spirit. It's all high noon at Praise—no shadows, no difficult questions, nothing that looks like something else, no one that isn't what he is announced to be, no fears, no hopes turning downward. Why do I go on? You know it all, you love it, the whole playpen, the whole sandbox of it!" He was shocked beyond speech. While his mind spun it caught a little of what Glover had said before, that he would get no advantage from talking to Corella at his father's request. He had gone against Glover's advice and now it was making him unhappy and more confused than he had ever been.

"Just simply," he said, trying to keep the anger out of his voice, "just simply say what you don't like about the Apostles."

"They never made a law," she said, "prohibiting the wearing of pocket feathers for no reason. They never showed that it was bad to start a town wearing pocket feathers. They never said that there was evil in the world and that they were against it. They never said that cheerfulness can kill the spirit and that your mother was killed by it and you don't even know it, since your clothes are still ironed and your cookies still made. Other than that I think it's a swell religion."

"You're sick in the head," he said. "You're just plain sick in the head!" He went back inside and banged the screen door behind him. Arla had been setting the table in the dining room—there had been no one in the kitchen to hear them. On the other side of the screen door the peas had begun to fall again, plink, plink, plink, into the pot.

At dinner he avoided her eyes and did not take any peas when the bowl came around. Later in the evening he reported to Andy that he had spoken to Corella and had been unable to find out anything about what was upsetting her.

There had been a summer of pleasant days. Now that he was old, the heat never bothered Charlie and he liked to take his chair out on the back porch, where he tilted it against the wall and let the sun have him and the hot breeze off Kornarenses' south fields blow at the lapels of his ancient black jacket. His feet hung six inches off the floor so that he did not feel earthbound. Less of him ached. He had a closed look at these times, and people going in or out the back door did not speak to him and sometimes didn't even notice him. When he first heard the voice it was hard to place but he didn't want to open his eyes or tip up his chair.

"Charlie, you asleep?"

"Nope."

"Do you mind if I sit down here?"

"Free country."

"Charlie, tell me something about the old days." It was Edgar's voice. He knew it now. Sometimes it was hard to remember that Edgar was almost grown and had almost a man's voice.

He sighed. "The old days. I'm all told out. All the stories, all the things I remember, I've told a thousand times. If you're doin' a article for school about Edgar Bisset or the dust-bowl times, there's a dozen books in the library with good grammar and a fund of inspirin' wisdom. . . ." He began to drift inward again, toward a sun-drugged doze.

"I don't want to ask you about Brother Edgar or the dust,

but just the old days—how it was here then, back before the dust."

"Well, things looked pretty much the same as they do now. The land that's in soil bank now was scrub then anyway, when people was usin' mules to plow it up." He thought for a moment. "I guess people worked harder then. First they had to, or starve, but then they did it 'cause there was nothin' else to do. It was a long way into town back then, and folks had no radio or TV. Family'd get sick of lookin' at one another and the only thing to get away from 'em was more work. Women 'specially. A winter or two in one of them soddies and some of 'em would go off their heads. It's so, though you don't hear about it none in the history books. Bissets lived in a soddy at first. Edgar, he didn't live in a house until he was nine or so—"

"Soddy?"

"A sod house. You know about them, don't you? People didn't have no money to buy lumber then and it sure didn't come with the ground. They sort of dug themselves into the turf and pulled it up over their heads. It was warm in the winter and cool in summer, but it had a way of bein' dark and close, awful close with five or six people, a wet dog, and a soggy baby all breathin' one another's air in the one or two rooms of it. But the soddy was the first building out here. The soddy always come first."

"But Brother Edgar . . . they had that house—"

"Edgar and Tempe was born in the soddy, I tell you, and when they moved out of it it saved what was left of Cora's wits." Charlie's feet were off the floor, his eyes still closed against the sun. He barely perceived that Edgar was no longer listening to him. Then he ceased listening to himself and fell into a light sleep.

"It's perfect! Don't you see, a soddy is the perfect thing," Edgar said. "We could furnish it with old things people donate and it would stand in back of the memorial park. Tourists come to see Bent's Fort although there isn't anything standing except the outline of the place."

"Where would we find a sod house?"

"If none are left we can get folks to build one the way the settlers did."

"Pocket feathers!" Mike said, and they laughed.

"By senior year it's going to be all hard-sell," Glover said. "This is going to have to be our masterpiece."

They built their idea like a house, room by room, floor by floor. There would be a debate: Is History Meaningful in Modern Life? Glover and Edgar would do their senior papers on the county's local men in the Colorado Volunteers, on settlers and place names. Farmer versus cow-man. When school started they geared up their splendid system again and began turning out the papers and planning the football plays like people pursued. The historical angle was a great success. Mike won his debate handily, but what was interesting to the three of them was the number of middle-aged and older people who came to hear that debate. Attendance at the school functions had been falling off in recent years and the principal and the English department were gratified at the unexpected turnout. When the boys professed an interest in local history their teachers got them an invitation to the winter meeting of the county historical society. It was an aged group, and it set upon the three of them with an eagerness that was almost embarrassing.

"Don't you think everyone should know about his family and past?"

"Yes, ma'am, I do."

"You ain't one of those kids that goes around callin' this a dead town and a dead county, are you?"

"Oh, no, sir."

"What would you say if I told you I knew the exact spot where the first grain mill was set up in the county?"

"I'd say that was really interesting."

"Then, by hang, I'll take you there, you and your friends. It ain't but one mile out of town on the old wagon road!"

After the meeting the three boys and their sponsor were invited to tea and cookies and after a while Edgar mentioned their interest in sod houses as the first shelters of the plains. Her head trembling on a delicately wrought neck, old Mrs. Marsh looked up at them.

"You're so right to say how well suited they were to conditions here. It's a shame people don't keep the soddies on their places the way they should."

"Do you mean there are sod houses still standing?"

"Why, of course!" she cried. "People didn't tear down the soddy when they moved into the house. They used it for a root cellar or a storage room." Then her brow furrowed. "Of course, there are very few left as they were. Over the years a man will put in windows or a factory-made door. People never see the history in their own backyards. People bring with them what they can use." She smiled at them and then turned toward Mr. White, the head of the historical society, her pink scalp showing clearly under the sparse white hair. He began, in his high, tremulous voice, to describe a sod house he had seen in good shape in 1940.

"You say you're interested in visiting some soddies?" Mr. White asked. When the boys said yes, the old people, all the whitened old ladies and the weathered old men, perked up and began to smile and laugh and talk at once. Their eyes sparkled as they coaxed their memories for places not blown in or plowed under, people not dead. When the evening was over the old people were loath to leave.

The soddy hunt was on. Meeting in extraordinary session, the historical society combed its combined recollection, and, as some of its members were also on the school board, the library committee, a dozen altar boards, vestries, Moose and Elks and Kiwanis, there was no record, public or private, that was unknown to them.

Considering their hard use and age and the cataclysm of the dust-bowl days, the soddies had done remarkably well. At first the boys got calls once or twice a week from Mrs. Marsh or Mr. White, and then someone decided to make a map and locate all the soddies still in existence, and others went to view them. As more and more of the map was filled in, people began to take renewed interest in the first structures on their own places and Marvel Johns, who two months ago had been kidded for his lack of progress and his closeness with a dollar, was suddenly seen as a preserver of the "natural relationships of the land." Actually, he held that aluminum gave forth

247

malevolent vibrations and was the cause of the national decline in health and morals.

In October, before the real cold came, the society made a tour of the eight sod houses in the county in best repair. The mayor had said that he was afraid of the cost of moving any one of them; it might have to be carefully excavated, and the owner might ask a high price. But three society members on the town council raised many compelling arguments in favor of the project. Nearby counties had gotten tourists on their way elsewhere to stop and look at lesser sights. The tourist dollar did not leech the land or pull away the water, and its spender went home again without affecting the soil allotments or the irrigation systems. The house might give the community a little more pride—especially the young people, pride enough to look for work closer than Denver.

In November the mayor, Mr. White, and the three boys were assigned to ride out and see the oldest and best-preserved unremodeled sod house in the county. It was on Odel Hemingway's farm, some forty miles from town in what was now bone-bare scrubland. He ran some sheep and cattle but did no farming.

During the drive the boys were careful not to refer to the soddy as theirs. They made respectful conversation with Mr. White and the mayor and showed interest in but little knowledge of local politics, about which the men spoke now and then during the trip. Edgar felt strangely tired. He sat staring out the window, held by the hypnotic perspective of the straight road and the flat plain on either side. Over to the east, a distant cloud was darkening 150 acres of thin sod covering the smooth, dry bones of the prairie. Where the sod was broken by erosion or the wheels of trucks, the ground glowed blue in the shadow as though it were water. Although Edgar's father never spoke of his years of imprisonment he had often mentioned his short time at sea. He spoke of it with awe and delight. Edgar had once asked him why so many local men chose the Navy for their service.

"City men and mountain men—I guess they can't take too much sky. The bigness of it weighs on them till they feel sat on. Sky and wind are home to a plains man—a home without dust. He rides high on his tractor and harrows the land and threshes the wheat out behind him. The sky is your 'landscape' on the ocean just as it is on the plains, and for once there's enough water and the rain falls sweet as wine." So they rode over the long, flat surges of wintering land, on the only paved highway on this side of the county, and Edgar smelled the ocean and listened for the calling of seabirds.

The sod house stood in a shambles of other outbuildings, mixed wood and adobe, crumbling clapboard, tarpaper and tin, a history, in brief, of poverty architecture in the American Southwest. The house the Hemingways lived in was different from the outbuildings only in that it had a TV antenna growing from its rusting roof.

"This is Odel's place," Mr. White said. He got out and waited for the mayor and the boys. "This is the back of the property. Odel's boy Sam and his wife live in the house here. Odel lives about a mile west where there's a break in the land, so you can't see his place." A woman walked heavily out of the antenna house with a dirty pink shag rug which she began to shake. The dust flew downwind toward the car, and the mayor and Mr. White and the boys watched dumbly as the woman followed the dust with her eyes until it came at last to the car and she stopped her shaking for a moment, facing them with a heavy expressionless stare. Then she began again. When she was done, she went back into the house and a moment later two people came out followed by the woman. The mayor walked forward.

"Hello, Odel, Sam," he said. "How ya been?" The men nodded. Edgar looked at the younger one, Sam, and tried to keep his expression as flat as the one he was facing. Sam Hemingway had only been two years ahead of Edgar in high school and now he was married and a father. He stood a little apart with a vague, watery stare like something newborn, unlicked, trying to bear his awful ordinariness with dignity. His embarrassment made him grin when his father or the mayor spoke a word to him. Behind him stood the expressionless woman, his wife, Clara, whom Edgar had not recognized at first. Two years ago at school she had been a richly sensuous dark-haired girl, the naked-longing, love-specter fantasy of an entire school's adolescent boys. Now, she stood in flatfooted heaviness, her skin gone bad, her dress torn at the collar and patterned by the greasy fingers of a baby.

They were talking about the soddy. Odel was being asked to donate it to the county. Edgar had never seen the mayor at his persuasive best, and was impressed, but Odel stood fast.

"I ain't makin' no free donations," he said. "This ain't no free operation." They tried to tell him how he could take the cost of the soddy off his income tax, but it was no good. At last they settled on thirty-five dollars. Odel became animated, almost lively, going into the problem of moving the half-buried structure as though it were his own.

"Escavate!" he said emphatically. "You'll have to escavate the thing, I'd say with dozers first, and how are you gonna get it all onto a truck?" He took a quick walk around the sod house, checking the walls which could not be seen.

The historical society had done its work well. The structure inside and out had held up remarkably well. The straw bricks were still perfect, the timbers were thick and had been kept from rotting by clay of some kind put between them and the clothing sod. Mr. White took measurements and Glover helped. The soddy would go easily onto one of the big flatbeds owned by one of the ranchers in the area.

"It'll be a point of pride in the community," the mayor was telling the Hemingways, ". . . and of course your name . . . over the door . . . a plaque . . . something to show your grandchildren . . ."

They were away before noon, the mayor and Mr. White serene and contented with a job well done. The three boys were silent in the back. Edgar wondered if Mike and Glo had been as stricken as he was by what he had seen. Sam Hemingway had never been a great brain or what people called a winner, but to see him blinking and grinning in his litter-strewn front yard had brought a shadow across the flat scrubland to darken Edgar's afternoon. Sam had had dreams, surely. He must have planned, hoped, wanted something beyond the place where he saw himself standing on his high-school-graduation day. Somehow it had ended ruined and wrong, the dream bent shapeless. Maybe it was even something beyond him—an egg in the ovary too soon or too late, the price of heifer too high, a stud bull developing symptoms and having to be destroyed—things of which the high-school boy was innocent, but which could beat down the man and turn the ripe girl stolid and old. And it could happen to him, to him and Mike and Glover. Unless they went on and triumphed over time and forced these gifts from the town, it could happen, all of it, to them. Let Corella go on about his blindness to other people's needs and to the Apostles' problems. Her talk had worried and upset him, but what did she know about the things that could happen to a person who turned his eyes away from the goal for a single minute, who thought about the egg or the bull as other than *things?* That was why Sam blinked and grinned and couldn't move and let his horror overtake him without even the strength to fight it. For a moment he felt himself trembling in anger at the sister whose life he had, until last week, ignored.

By December the sod house was mounded up and backed in against the far end of the memorial park. It had Odel Hemingway's name on a plaque outside, but it was also known as the Historical House. Most people called it "the boys' house."

22

They heard it on the TV news and at first they thought it couldn't be true, that there was some mistake in the wording, or that the announcers didn't mean what they had said. Someone back East had objected to her child saying a prayer in school and had taken her argument to the law. The case had gone to one court and another, a thing confusing enough in itself, and suddenly there was an issue about all prayers in all schools everywhere. There were no regular prayers said in the local county schools, but Mrs. Madison, who taught second grade, always started the year with a prayer, and on December 7 and national holidays when school did not close there was a moment of silence in which all the students in all the schools were told to pray for the dead and for the country. What could the government be thinking of? People began to follow the case through this court and that and when the School Prayer Case came to the Supreme Court, perhaps to be made into law, the Praises rang with denunciations. To be neutral about prayers was one thing. The forbidding of them seemed to strike down basic freedoms—of speech, religion, or both. At the grade school, teachers who had never said prayers began to say them and on opening day at the high school a prayer was said for the first time since December 8, 1941. The mayor began to pray at the opening of the town-council meetings. The Reverend Withrow was asked to come to the historical society's first gathering of the season to express his trust that the Lord looked upon the county with favor.

People from all the churches in the county got up petitions and mailed them off to the Senate and the Court. People who hadn't agreed on anything in twenty years signed heartfelt letters together because to forbid prayer was like forbidding God. It struck at something deep and personal in the kinds of freedom people did not use but honored all the same. Not to decide about praying, but to be forbidden to pray. How could that be, people said, when "In God We Trust" was on the money and every patriotic speech had its references to the Almighty? The city people on the TV looked piously back out of the sets and said, Did the word *God* on the money make anyone handle it more honestly, cheat for it less enthusiastically, covet it less wholeheartedly? Then it seemed, to the people watching, that it did, that the godly words and the reverent moments could make people better, did make them better, and that to take the words away was in some measure to take the Lord away, and to take Him away from the children was worst of all.

Prominent senators and congressmen spoke out for the prayers or at least for compromises that would, or should, suit anyone, even people who had no religion at all. Just when the battle seemed won for sure, when everyone was certain that a proper balance had been reached, the Court handed down its decision. No prayer in the schools. The decision was a law.

There was a terrible feeling of loneliness, of being set aside in a colder, drier climate, separated from something valuable and nourishing. It gave a chilly feeling to know that Mrs. Madison was no longer able to utter the traditional words.

It was a law meant to be broken in a dozen ways. Mr. Frischer told the senior class, "I *pray* we may have a fruitful year," which he said with his head up, his eyes closed. Mrs. Carlson, the art teacher, began the first class in a completely unprecedented way, announcing, "May Whoever it concern send blessings upon us all from wherever it is. Amen." She had the look of a martyred queen.

At Willow Springs, the anger at the decision seemed to close the gap slightly between the older and younger Apostles. They shared their anger at the rule and their confusion at why it had been forced upon them.

"Bad things are forbidden," Martha Wyer said during a Witnessing. "Liquor is not allowed in the schools, or cigarettes because they are harmful things. Now God. It makes the Spirit of the Lord seem like a kind of plague." The whole Praise moaned in agreement. When Edgar took her home, Martha said to him, "Praise means more to all of us now— have you noticed the younger kids don't play around at all? They know that the Spirit is under attack."

He had been taking her home for some time now. She lived in the town of Willow Springs, where her people had the dry-goods store on the main street. They lived one block north, on a sidestreet which had been replanted with cottonwoods after the thirties. She had told him how the first settlers had mistaken the bare cottonwoods for a kind of willow and had called the place Willow Springs.

He thought back now, remembering how formal and reserved she had been at first. He realized that his interest in her had launched her as a popular and sought-after girl in school, and that this had opened her up, made her bloom, and given her a new but still gentle glow. In a quieter, more decent way, she was a pocket feather. Without his interest, she would have been too shy to be popular; her looks and ways were all harmony and stillness. There was, or had been, little vivacity in her. He still cherished that quietness. In the intensity of his life he needed it. The fourth time he drove her home from Praise she asked him to stay to lunch.

Her people were quieter even than she and a little grayed with work. They were apologetic that they seldom came to Praise.

"Workin' the hours we do, both of us in the store, Sunday's the only day, you see—" It embarrassed Edgar that he should have to be Founder's kin in their eyes. He had wanted to meet Mike and Glo before Praise at Founder's but the Wyers were so eager that he stay, had planned the "spontaneous" idea in advance with such fussiness, that he had no choice. The meal was a townwoman's meal. Charlie would have said,

"Not enough to make a cat belch." Edgar heard Charlie saying it and had to bite his lip as the plate was passed. The talk was careful and friendly, but there was nothing of Martha's serenity. Even to look at her made his soul go quiet.

He was very late driving home and felt the pressure of it, so he found himself racing a little beyond his natural control of the car. It was stimulating, even fearful, to go beyond the limits. For plains-raised boys, the straight, flat road, narrowing to end at the edge of the world, was an almost overwhelming temptation. His father had warned him often enough of stock that had been killed, drivers, too, firing the fields with their deaths in explosion. It was an old struggle between the generations. All his friends sped in their cars, but Edgar had seldom succumbed to the urge so consciously before. After all, he was already late to see Glo and Mike. They were waiting for him; it was only reasonable to hurry a little. It occurred to him that lateness was rare for him. His life had been so minutely planned, so choreographed, that the unusual event, the sudden enthusiasm, the winding out of a pleasant conversation, none of these things had had any place in it for quite a long time. Why had he never seen it before? Why had it never disturbed him before? It was being busy, he thought as he shot thrillingly past sideroads that gaped with shock as he passed them, blurring the land until it ran like gray-brown water on either side. He found himself going still faster. Any mistake now could be death—a calf in the road or a rut or a patch of oil—and yet he couldn't stop, even though his mind saw the car turned over and in flames. At last he recognized the beginning of town. Two cars passed him, and far ahead he saw another car pulling out of a sideroad, and he slowed. By the time he was on Main Street, the ordinary laws and habits had claimed him again. On Sunday afternoons the town was almost deserted, but there were young people walking around waiting for something to do, and they waved and called out to him, and he greeted them smiling and waving through the now-dusty window. He was aware again of the specialness he had—so much popularity and so much envy. He knew now that it wasn't his looks, although he was good-looking enough, or the self-feeding nature of popularity. Part of the secret was the very thing that had come to be so oppressive. The busyness. He had never had to walk on a Sunday up one side of the street and down the other, looking for something or someone to change the day or, in the end, for the day to change. It was always he who was waited for, needed, his plans, from morning to evening, one after the other, that filled the day without boredom or the kind of restlessness that he saw in the streets now, the wanderings, groupings, and regroupings of his schoolmates. A dozen plans and the Plan, Glover's, Mike's, and his. It would work. Was working.

"Think about that," he said to the invisible, quiet, soul-stilling image of Martha beside him. "Think about that," he said to the bitter image of Corella.

When he came late to the Praise, Glover and Mike acknowledged him with glances and he ducked into the circle apart from them, according to the plan. The Praise was almost over. Mrs. Owsley was putting forth a petition to the group to cry to the Lord for her brother, who was dying of a bone disease in a hospital up in Denver. Some people were annoyed because she had put the petition in after most of the petitions were finished. Hers had become a weekly one and the group took it up dutifully but without excitement. It didn't seem fitting that a God who could hail-kill a thousand-acre field of grain in half an hour should have to be so nagged at for the easy death of one old man.

Around went the dance, hands linked or held to the heart. Some old people liked to hold their hands up, as though to let the late sun warm them. After it was over, Edgar went unobtrusively into the barn, where Mike and Glover joined him. They went up to the hay mow and sat in its fragrance and talked.

"The county gives the scholarships, but who votes on them," Mike asked, "besides the teachers and the principal?"

"No one really. There's someone from the family but that's mostly for form and to break any ties."

Mike turned to Glover. "How did you know," he asked quietly, "that there wouldn't be any winner this year?"

"Yes," Edgar said, "you were so sure. I thought Mary Alice

256

would get it this year. They always give one, even in years when there's no one outstanding."

"Mary Alice is a girl. They only give it to a girl when she is really exceptional—only four of them since 1919. They were saving the award. They are saving it for us."

They looked out silently into the cloudless autumn sky. Now and then a bird would dissect it with a straight, sudden flight line, east and west, and then the bird would disappear and the sky close over. Edgar noticed that the sounds had changed. In summer there was the fat buzz of flies and birds twittering. The chittering of grasshoppers was muffled by the long wheat of late spring. Now, with much of the land plowed for winter planting, the ground sounds were fewer but sharper, as though with the beginning cold. He had a strange, dizzying feeling; the height of more than the hayloft was making him giddy. He knew in his bones it was true. "A dedicated student also exemplifying qualities of leadership and service."

"Three of them," Glover said, "and the money has to be gotten from somewhere. Tough luck, Mary Alice."

Edgar was a little embarrassed. "When did you first know?" he asked Glover.

"Back last winter. The kids had written away and been accepted or not accepted at different schools—six of them last year. I saw the teachers looking at those kids now and then with a kind of measuring look. There was a sort of dance they were all in, the teachers and the kids who were accepted somewhere. It wasn't like the year before, when everybody knew and was relaxed about the whole thing."

"A feeling," Edgar said.

"That's not all. One day in December I was in the art room helping Miss Feeley. Miss Feeley said, 'There are so many bright, cooperative people in the senior class this year, don't you think so?' I said I thought there were. Then she asked, 'If a person had to pick one special one, who would it be?' I thought awhile and said I didn't know. I didn't want to make it sound so bald, so I said there were too many to choose from. She wanted my opinion, because popularity is part of the thing they look for. The year before last the right kid was there to be picked. Last year there was no top kid. And next year there's us coming. They can feel it. They must have felt it then."

The three of them lay quietly in the hay for a time, saying nothing. It felt still warm from the day. Below them on the barn floor they saw the cat move with its efficient silence, no motion wasted, with the sun.

"We'd better make the week's plan," Mike said. "I've got a lot of homework to do." They got the little coded assignment books out of their pockets.

"Two games away this month," Glover said. "Say, listen, do we have to go in the bus?"

"What about this English paper that's coming up? Do you think we can fit it in?" Edgar asked.

"I don't have an idea in my head."

"I do," Mike said. "I've been thinking it out for a long time. The school-prayer thing has got everybody upset. This composition should let people know that we're not only strong in Praises but that we are upset too by having religion taken out of school. Jesus was a teacher. His words are literature. The point I'll make is that Jesus would be at home here in this county, in 1962, in spite of combines, cars, and TV. I've been reading up on Nazareth and Jerusalem and you wouldn't believe how close the climate is to what we have here—it's hillier over there, but they have the same kind of climate, the same problems with getting and keeping water, the same need for care and thought, the same struggle to grow things, and the same—well, competition between cattle, farming, and sheep."

"Well, what would you want *us* to do? Wouldn't it give us away—the three of us hitting 'independently' on a subject like that?"

"No, I wanted you to hear my idea and see if it would work, and maybe to see if you could use any of it in your things—a paper on old-time school prayers, or the Bible as literature—"

"The people who settled this area were a strange mixture," Edgar said. "Churchy people but they never put biblical quotes on the tombstones, not often anyway. My paper was going to be on old tombstone epitaphs in the county."

"I think Mike's idea is good, but it's going to have to be done carefully," Glover said, "not overstated. If you come off sounding *really* religious, you'll sound fanatical, and people are scared of that."

"I'll get you something, Glo, never fear."

There was a sound below them. Linton Jones and his girl, Kathy, had come to the barn to be alone together after the Praise. Linton's love life was cutting into their meeting times. Edgar went noisily, cheerily down the ladder from the loft to distract the couple while Mike and Glover slipped away from opposite places in the barn. They had planned this maneuver in the first days of their meetings. From the beginning it had been important to establish habits of caution. Not secrecy, they said, but caution. They were to be thought of as always together but they must not be seen always alone together.

Two years of the secret, two years and upward of the careful appearances and disappearances, the calculated time, the measured camaraderie, the orchestrated life and destiny, and he told it all to Martha two months after they began going together. Martha was a serious girl, studious and still shy. Glo and Mike did not like her. They all took girls to dances and Praise picnics and Youth Nights, trading dates back and forth as the whim took them, settling now on one, now on another. By this time there was a steady, congenial group of girls who got along well with the three boys and with each other. Martha was different, less adaptable—because she cared more. Her interests were real.

He told her about the plan in response to an almost-idle question she asked, something that stung him because it hinted that he was too casual about his life, too careless about friends and studies, always affable, never deeply concerned. After telling her, he was horrified at what he had done. He had thought it would relieve the tension he felt with Martha, ease the strain of his years of careful duplicity, but all he had when he was finished was the fear of her letting the secret loose, telling her friends out of defensiveness or jealousy, or simply giving in to the need to be an insider, someone who "really knew." Maybe she would blackmail him without really meaning to.

She had listened in silence and then said very quietly, "I never guessed it. It seemed so natural for you and Mike and Glo to be always waving good-bye, always just leaving for someplace more interesting and lively than where we were."

"You won't tell anybody—"

"It's going to be in your way now," she said, "that you told me. You won't be able to act natural when I'm in the group, will you, because you'll be watching me watching you, saying to yourself that I know what the busyness is really for—"

"Maybe I told you because I needed a place to rest, to be myself, and you're so—so—"

"Plain?"

"So still. You don't jabber or giggle or clink or clatter. You're like the fields during wheat harvest when all the machines are turned off for the night. A person hears the natural sounds but they seem so quiet and so special after the noise of the combines that he thinks, Where have these sounds been all this time?"

She smiled. "You're sorry you told me," she said, "but you're safe. Really safe. From me, anyway."

However he tried not to, he felt his telling Martha had something to do with the terrible cold he got two days later. It was ridiculous to think this, but he couldn't help the feeling that his letting down, the breaking of those elaborate defenses, had opened a path inward in him and allowed all the outer world to come flooding in, sickness, doubt, exhaustion, everything he had held off for so long with perfect affability and graciousness, the incontrovertible proof of his specialness, the fact of his superiority, his, Glover's, and Mike's. "No one should be sick," he muttered to Anne as she rubbed him with Vicks and put the warmed flannel on his back and chest. He went to school on Thursday barely able to stay on his feet. Friday was hopeless, and against his protests Anne and Arla kept him home, drugged with fluids and heat. On Saturday he was much better, but they talked him out of going to Willow Springs on Sunday. The air was deceptively warm and balmy.

"You'll run, you'll have to," Anne said with what sounded almost like bitterness, "and you'll overheat and get a fever again. Stay home here and open the window and listen to the Praise here."

He slept through the afternoon Praise and woke in near-dark feeling almost himself. Someone was knocking at his door and he thought it might be Anne with a hot drink for him. He was surprised to see his father, more particularly that his father was standing irresolutely and uncertainly in the doorway even after Edgar said, "Come in."

"I didn't want to disturb you if you were sleeping—" Andy said.

"No—I'm awake," Edgar said stiltedly, "I'm fine." Andy came in and sat on the bed and Edgar waited.

"Something happened at the Springs this morning," Andy said from the twilight place at the end of the bed. "Actually it's been happening for months and it's only come out this morning. Some people came and told us before the Praise started here, and there were others telling about it afterward. People are upset, very upset."

"What is it?"

"You know Annie Kinbote?"

"Sure, she's Shirley Kinbote's younger sister who Praises at the Springs—she's thirteen or fourteen, a cheerleader in the junior high, I think. What's happened?"

"Annie told the Praise that last year the Spirit of the Lord came to her and asked her to do what she called a bodily offering. She did this by whipping herself with a harness strap once or twice a week, and then three or four times a week, and then every day. Two of her friends found out about it and asked the Spirit of the Lord in a private Witness if it was pleasing to Him and the Spirit—they *said* the Spirit of the Lord told them yes, it was. The three of them have been using harness straps on one another for three or four months now, singly and together—" Edgar could tell that Andy was deeply embarrassed. Had the light been on he would have seen his father blush. "They say—they say the girls can't take their blouses off it looks so bad."

"Why did they do it?"

"The girls said they had special visions because of it. Special revelations. I don't want to burden your mother or

Corella with any of this just yet. After dinner you and Grandpa and I will go over to the church and we'll sit down and talk about it."

How tired his father sounded, and how sad. He felt a momentary rage at Annie and the whole Willow Springs Praise for all its troublemaking. Whippings, he thought, I'd like to whip her good.

"Son, I wish you could tell me what's been going on at Willow Springs. How could a thing like that have happened?"

"I don't know, Dad. I told you about the split that's there between the young people and the older ones—how they don't listen to each other—"

"But there must be more, something behind it all."

Hopelessly, Edgar shook his head, and then, aware that his father couldn't see his action in the dark, murmured, "I don't know, I really don't."

"What's the Kinbote girl like?"

"That's what's so confusing. If you were going to choose a cute, good-natured, lively kid, you'd choose Annie. Everyone likes her. She's the last girl you'd think would do a thing like that."

It took Joe a long time to believe what Andy told him. "I've known Russell Kinbote since he was a kid. I've known his dad and his dad before him. They're solid people, ranchers. Always had that place over by the Springs—always been dependable and level-headed . . ."

"What's Annie like in the Praises?" Andy asked Edgar.

"Full of spirit—she seemed happy to me, always happy," Edgar answered, feeling at a loss. He tried to see her apart from the general joy of the Praise, and couldn't. He had no memory of anything special she had said or done, and it made him feel caught out again like a soldier fallen asleep on guard duty. "She used to run a lot. Her Witnessing was always happy—like cheerleading."

Andy shook his head. "Funny you should mention cheerleading. Martin Winder, who came and told me about this, he said that what finally got Annie to speak out in Praise about—about what they had been doing was because of it, because of her cheerleading."

"How's that?" Joe said.

"Apparently she started to worry about what she'd look like in May when the cheerleaders go to practicing in shorts and those little tops they wear without any backs to them."

"You mean *that's* what got her speaking out?" Joe said. "How she would look in *summer clothes?*" Edgar laughed.

"I guess all the girls were worried about it," Andy said. "I heard someone say that Mary Nell, the youngest of them, started to have dreams about suicide because of it. Russell called me before supper. He wants to bring Annie over and for all of us to have a talk. He said he'd talked to the doctor first, and the doctor had said that it wasn't a medical matter. The whole family is confused and upset. Russell wanted to know if he should whip her. I almost said she'd already done worse than he ever would. I told him no. I'd want you there, son, only I think it would embarrass them all too much. Dad, do you think Russell could face you? I'd just as soon not do this alone."

"I'll stay for a while and leave if I see it would be better."

The next afternoon Edgar saw the Kinbotes driving up. Joe and Andy met them at the door and together they went out across the road to the church, Annie hanging back, pushing the sun-streaked blond hair away from her face as she walked. They spent over an hour talking. Edgar had been at his grandparents', helping Arla get food ready for a sick neighbor. As he worked, he kept thinking about Annie and her two friends. How awful it must be to know that everyone who looked at you was looking not at the surface of you but wondering about the body beneath the clothes. What did her back look like? What did the welts look like? How far down did they go? As he spooned potato salad into a bowl he found himself blushing furiously and unable to stop. Did the girls cry out or were they silent? Did they stop their mouths or pray to be released from so awful a command? Why was he feeling something sexual about this and blushing so badly? He tried to think about something else and couldn't. He tried to think about another part of it. How could anyone know if they were telling the truth, those girls? Would the Lord desire anyone to cut himself with horse-sweaty harness ends—in the presence of anyone else? Why would He wish it? Edgar remembered having seen a man's back all white-scarred and ridged, but he couldn't remember where. Why couldn't he stop thinking about it! Could the Lord wish such a terrible thing? If it wasn't the Lord who wished it, who then? Annie herself? How could that be? That people did such things Edgar knew. The TV news was full of stories of violence and horror, but it was people doing things to others, not to themselves; children killing their parents, a group of ghetto boys setting an old man on fire, a crowd killing a victim. The TV showed pictures of such young people, snapshots from family albums; they all looked normal enough, but they came from hate and horror, these people, from crowded ghettos, violent homes. They were friendless, aimless people. They did not come from this county, from Apostles. Or could they? If they did, how could anyone separate the messages of his own will-fulness from those the Spirit of the Lord sends in His love for the pleading soul? There must be a way—some truth a man might use to separate himself from secret floggings and ugly fantasies of blood and pain . . . or from a mistrusting of everything and everybody.

The late light was leaving the kitchen window. Edgar finished what he had been told to do and went into the front room where the light still hung golden in the last few dust-mote shafts. He saw his father and grandfather coming up the road together from the church. They walked close to each other, and as Edgar watched the last rays were quenched and their shadows killed instantly. The westering light was mellow, the sky subduing the harrowed fields was a rich and luminescent blue. The two men walked on, making the gracious gestures of good conversation.

Edgar did not often have the luxury of time enough to watch a thing for no other reason than the beauty of it. Now he saw the colors in his father's plaid work jacket glow warmly in the sunless afterlight. As the darkness moved forward, the singular clarity of the figures began to melt together with each other and all the space around them. Had they joined hands or not? Was there a slight wind against them that made their bodies seem to ripple? He felt it must have gotten much colder since the sun had set and he perceived his own warmth and the pleasurable health and strength of his body. His own house was dark, his mother and sister were in the kitchen with Arla; they had turned on the lights and were talking in comfortable voices. Edgar didn't want Arla coming into the front room to find him standing at the darkening window watching the night come on. He wanted even less to turn on the light himself and be blinded to the gentling dark outside. In a moment, he saw his father and grandfather go past the window and heard their sounds—feet on the gravel, the low murmur of their voices, a door opening. He turned away and left the night to itself.

Supper was half over when the men began to talk. In tone, it was like the usual supper talk, slow, low, and resonant, with long silences.

"It's sad, really, a girl so confused."

"Family's bad upset."

"Yes, I feel sorry for Russ Kinbote."

"Yes."

"What did you tell them?" Edgar asked, trying to keep his voice in the low, slow rhythm of theirs.

"Well, the main thing," Joe said after a time, "was not to sound like a preacher poundin' hell into someone. We talked to Russ, told him not to blame Annie, that it was in wantin' to please the Lord so much she had blundered into a mistake. Andy talked to the girl and he just explained that the Lord means for us to love each other and be happy. The Lord had made her a beautiful little girl—how could He want her to be cut and bleeding?"

"Did they ask any questions?"

"Some—about leavin' the Apostles or leavin' the Willow Springs Praise."

"We urged them to stay, told them that the Praise needed them more than ever now," Andy said. "I can't help feeling that there's something wrong going on at Willow Springs. The special baptism and then this business with Annie and her friends. I think, and we told them this, too, that what Annie was doing was a kind of reflection of something strange creeping into the Praise up there."

"I don't know what it could be," Edgar said, and shook his head. "I haven't seen any real problems in it, any fits or falling down, or tongues, the way it starts to go in some places. I've looked at the people and the Praise, and except for what I told you I don't see anything else." He felt their eyes on him. Down the table Charlie sat, silent but intent, his eyes studying him hard. Even Corella, who usually tried to seem as if she were somewhere else, was watching. Only Anne rustled in and out, collecting dishes, murmuring small peacemaking phrases, in case there should be some smallest note of disagreement among them.

"You did say it was a younger Praise," Andy said, "that there was a kind of split between the old and the young there."

"A Praise needs balance," Joe said, "the Praises that have trouble are just the ones that don't have balance." He and Andy began to talk about what that balance was and how it might be restored to the Springs. When Edgar looked down the table again he saw that Charlie had withdrawn and was rolling bread into little pills, which he ate when he had three or four of them. Corella was staring into space. He, too, felt that some necessary question had been let go of when the talk had left Annie and gone on to the Willow Springs Praise without including her. If those floggings were not the word of the Lord for her, why did she do them, and what was the Praise to say to her? For no reason that he could tell, he thought of Corella saying angrily, "It's always what everyone *feels*. The most important thing about an Apostle is what he *feels!*" If only he could get his mind off Annie's having *done* that.

"Charlie, why would someone go and hurt herself on purpose day after day like that?" They were unloading drums of chemicals that the crop duster would use. It was a new kind and had to be handled very carefully.

"I don't know nothin' about women, and any pains I ever had in my life was give to me by other people against my will."

"Why would anybody do that to herself?"

"If she really is religious, maybe she was tryin' to find the other side of God, the side that ain't easy and good."

"But God is good—all good. Everybody knows that!"

"To the Apostles He is all good. That limits Him, don't it? Where's the line where He stops bein' only good? Where's the line where good ends?"

"I don't understand that kind of talk," Edgar said impatiently, "but I know that Apostles don't want hellfire talk and all the stuff the ordinary churches give, things that scare people into fighting wars and burning witches."

"Maybe we're talkin' about sacrifice. It's a thing Apostles have no taste for, and I don't either. Me, well, I always had things sacrificed *for* me without no choice on my part, but you take a girl like that, maybe she was lookin' for somethin' more to give. Maybe she had so much freedom it got her scared because she knew it ain't the way the world really is. Showin' God how happy you are all the time is a hell of a strain, anyway. Edgar, he told me that."

"You mean Founder talked to you about things like that?"

"Not Founder. I never heard no words from Founder, but my friend Edgar Bisset, he was always pickin' at the places where justice ended and anger began—what was kind and what was only lazy."

"You think we're run by feelings too much?"

"Maybe people don't feel enough because they don't think enough."

The drums had been stacked carefully against the wall of the barn. They had a pleasing geometrical pattern, curves and circles in a pyramid. Edgar loved the simple, strong forms they made. Clear and simple things were best, strongest in the end. Many Apostles said this in Praise, that the simple faith was the best, that working everything around was dangerous and wearing, and death to a true, spontaneous, joyful faith.

"You know, Charlie," Edgar said, "religion is *for* feeling, not thinking."

"For feeling good," Charlie said, "only good."

"Well, yes. When tragedy comes, religion makes a person feel better, and when he feels good he goes to Praise and feels better still."

"I get that from cigarettes," Charlie said.

"You get that from booze."

"You're right, I was just tryin' to be delicate."

"Annie Kinbote whipped herself because she was crazy."

"A good Apostle—maybe she went crazy from all that good feelin'."

"Charlie—"

"Oh, hell, I'm sorry. I got a terrible yearnin' in me for the last word."

"Yes, but this time it's the wrong word. All wrong." Charlie opened his mouth, then closed it again. Edgar could see him clamping his jaw, the muscles moving under the stubble-hazed skin. He felt a perverse glee in the struggle. "You'd better finish up here while I pull the truck in," Edgar said. Charlie nodded shortly and turned away. Edgar left him in the barn, finishing the chores and muttering quietly to himself.

It was a luminous blue night. The moon was full, the air ringing-cold, and the sky so clear that stars lay massed in millions and it was possible to see the blue of some planets and the red of others with the naked eye. He had been at a basketball game that his team had won, and he was still elated from the game, too high to let himself fall asleep. After tossing for an hour he decided to go down to the kitchen for a snack. He seldom did this. Anne didn't like coming down to dirty dishes in the morning and the table full of greasy crumbs. He rooted here and there, refrigerator, pantry shelves, and at last got himself a plateful of leftover odds and ends. He was sitting down with it when he heard someone coming. He hoped it wasn't his mother. She would dutifully make him something, and there would be fussing and worry and the insistent hovering she did when they were alone together, as though she were performing for him as she did for strangers, and failing in the performance. It was Corella. He almost sighed with relief.

She was wearing one of Andy's old flannel shirts over her pajamas, and it made her look dumpy. She had a perfectly decent bathrobe, why didn't she wear it? She looked at his stacked plate.

"All that's missing from that is pig's knuckle and fried tripe."

"It's all there was," he said defensively.

"C'mere," and she motioned him toward the pantry. Then she made her voice heavy and seductive, batting her eyes and swinging her hips. "Velcome to my vurld, voman's vurld. A voman knows vere is hidden de trazure. No, hide your ice. Do not look upon my forrrrm or you vill be blinded. Follow me." He hid his eyes and followed her into the pantry. When he opened his eyes there was a large chocolate layer cake and two jars of Arla's cookies.

"Where did that come from?"

"It's for the Memorial Square Cake Sale. The Ladies' Aid wants to buy a fountain and benches and stuff."

"But the cake hasn't been cut—we can't just take a piece out of it."

"Nothing of the sort," Corella said. She cut the ends off at all four sides and smoothed the icing over, taking some from the cut pieces. "Just make a square cake," she said. They drank milk from the pitcher and used paper towels for plates.

"You're quite a faker." He laughed. "You know all the tricks."

"It's a family for faking and tricks," she said.

"Oh, come on, don't start that again!"

"The worst thing we do is think that no one can criticize us and love us, too. I'm going to tell you something that no one else knows. Maybe you can help me make it so it doesn't seem like criticism of anybody else, but like what I need to do, me, myself."

"What's that?" he said, wishing she wouldn't tell him, would tell a joke instead, eat her cake, and go to bed.

"I've talked it over with Mr. Withrow and Mr. Dodge, the new minister. I'm going to join the Methodist church."

"What!" The cake he had been eating fell out of his mouth.

"I've made arrangements to be baptized," Corella said. "I'm serious and the decision is serious and it's one I've spent a long time making."

"But you *can't.*"

"Why not? It's been years since I've felt at home as an Apostle, years since I went and talked with Pastor Withrow. Wait, he said, wait and pray, and I did. I've been taking religious instruction for almost a year, reading and studying and thinking, and now it's time to go. There's one more thing, though. Because of my age my parents have to consent. I want you to help me tell them."

"You can't do this, Corella!"

"I think in the end they'll consent."

"That's not the point. Think of who we are—Founder's closest kin, the leaders of the most influential Praise in the country—"

"*You* are all those things—I'm not and never was."

"Is that it—some kind of jealousy that's making you do this?"

"Maybe it was, long ago, when I looked around and saw how sufficient you were, you and Dad, with all the work and the visitors and the important questions to be solved, while Ma died slowly in the background. Later, I realized I didn't fit into the picture either, so I pulled back until I was invisible. I have questions, Edgar, and Praise wants only answers, big, happy answers. 'Yes' to life has turned into 'yes' to everything. What hope is there for questions in all that happy sureness?"

"Come to Praise again, pray, really pray for an answer—"

"I don't want it!" she cried. "I want a creed, a law, a vision of what life should be, not what God is! Pastor Withrow asked me why I wanted to leave so joyous a faith. Once upon a time we all had maps. We heard that God was riding by in a big parade and we would see Him and wouldn't need our maps anymore. So we cut all the maps up into confetti to shower on Him when He passed. I heard the cheering some street over, somewhere near, but I had cut up my map and couldn't find the way, and now the cheering is getting fainter and further away and what use is a little bag full of confetti, as happy and joyful and jubilant as confetti is?"

"But think of how everyone will feel, Dad and Grandpa and everyone—"

"I'm not going off to a whorehouse in Trinidad, or the jail in Canyon City, or the asylum in Pueblo. I'm going to the most conservative church we have here, right *here*, where I've always been. Or is that what bothers you, that I'll be a bother *here*, and not somewhere else?"

"You're too young for a big decision like this."

"Yes, probably, but when I'm eighteen I won't be able to go away either, not until Ma has something or somebody else, and the way this family is going, that's not likely."

"If you were considering Ma, you'd stay Apostle. You know how people are going to talk, all the gossip and phony sympathy they'll give her. Is that going to help?"

"No," Corella said gravely, "and that hurts me. Being a hypocrite hurts me more. My standing around the Praises makes gossip and so does my missing them. . . . I—"

There was a cry, a terrible cry, and for a moment they didn't know where it was coming from. At first Edgar thought it must be some scavenging animal caught by another and screaming in pain and anger, but the sounds were too loud, too racking, for anything but a wolf or a mountain lion. They both jumped up and Edgar started for the door, but as he left the kitchen he realized the sound was coming from above them, in the house. Corella ran past him and up the stairs. He followed her, taking them two at a time. There was a light on in his parents' room and the sounds, now softened and broken, were coming from there. The two of them hesitated at the door. Edgar knocked and they went in.

Andy was sitting up in bed, pale and shaking. Beside him, Anne sat trying to murmur comforting things as she alternately plumped his pillow and fussed with the lace on the front of her robe.

"Dad—"

Andy turned toward Edgar as if with only dim recognition. His look was one of awful sickness and his face was beaded with sweat. "Dad—?" Edgar crossed the room to the bathroom, where he wrung out a washcloth in warm water and brought it to his father. Andy took it and began wiping his face with it.

"Just a dream," he muttered and looked up at Edgar. He began to look more himself. "Thank you, son. It was a bad dream, that's all. I'm sorry I woke you." He looked at their shocked, frightened faces. "Really, it's nothing serious, just a dream. I'm sorry."

"We weren't sleeping," Corella said, "so you didn't wake us up." They were simple words, meant to reassure, but they came out sounding flat, almost like an accusation. Anne began to fuss again.

"Not sleeping—what's the matter? It's two o'clock, why weren't you sleeping? Are you feeling all right? Do you need anything?"

"No, Ma, really. Ed was replaying tonight's game for me." Again, they were words meant to comfort, but they were said in so dead a voice that they sounded sarcastic and demeaning. Edgar realized with a start that Corella must have trained herself to speak that way so as not to sound bright or eager or sincere. So as not to sound like an Apostle.

23

They were sitting in one of the derelict turkey coops at Mike's one afternoon, planning. They had gotten their college applications from the state agricultural school and were filling them out, joking and at ease, with success moving toward them as quietly and clearly as the days were moving over the long shoulder of winter. Mike was saying, "With a scholarship I can work summers and have a little set aside. No need to decide right away if it's to be agriculture or the veterinary school—as farmers or vets we'll be together anyway."

Glover nodded. "I've got some acreage picked out that Dad's boss will let me run a few cows on. I really want the veterinary program; I guess I always have." He turned to Edgar. "Of course, you have your dad's farm, but you might want to let me run some cows on any little acreage he's not using."

Sitting in the companionable closeness of the coop with his two best friends, Edgar had a jolt of cold panic so sudden and so intense that it took his breath away. He knew his face must have drained, he felt so faint. He put his knees up and leaned his arms on them, putting his face between his arms as though he were studying the pattern of the floorboards. The panic slowly receded, but a numbing dread, a fearsome sense of emptiness and loss, remained, blotting out the simplest thoughts, the most ordinary sensations. Mike and

Glover talked on, Edgar desperately feigning casualness and even gaiety for them, laughing when he needed to, putting his whole attention into the lie. Even so, as time passed the other two went silent, and at last Mike said, "What's the matter, Ed? You seem far away today." Edgar told them he was tired and probably coming down with something and needed to leave early. "Well, okay, but we'll have to meet before school tomorrow so we can finish these applications." Another bolt of terror broke in him, arms, legs, brain, belly, like webs of lightning stitching the sky with sudden, white-hot scars. He felt himself cramping with panic so that he had to sit down again.

"Got a little dizzy," he murmured, "a little stomach flu, I guess." The web loosened after a few minutes, enough to let him get up and go. He knew he must look awful, that he must be making them anxious. His mind kept repeating over and over, It was what we always wanted. It was the thing we always planned. He went home and took a long, hot bath, and the panic eased until he turned again to the application. He couldn't even write, his hands were shaking so badly. His head was full of meaningless words, words without thoughts, endlessly repeating themselves. He put down the pen and the panic eased a little; he got up from the desk and stepped away from the neatly printed sheets. It lightened a little more. He watched himself, mesmerized, as he stepped toward the desk and then away from it and felt the fear tighten and loosen in degrees as nicely calibrated as the lines on a ruler. He did his homework that evening on the dining-room table, and when he went to bed he had to put the application out of sight, back in its envelope in his loose-leaf, before he could sleep.

The next day, when he saw Martha going by him in the hall, he headed her off, saying quickly and softly, "Marty, I have to see you about something. Wait for me after school. . . ."

"I have to get home early today. I'm working at the store."

"I'll drive you home—please wait."

"But don't you have a club meeting this afternoon?"

"*Please*, Marty—"

"Okay, I'll be in your truck. I'll get down so nobody can see me." He gave her a quick, unsmiling look, from which he turned with practiced smiling ease to say hello to somebody who was passing.

That afternoon he was in the truck and away before most of the other students had left the school. Martha was lying down in the front seat. She kept down until they were away from the school grounds and on the road going out of town.

"I said I had some work to do for Dad," he said quickly, "so we're going to circle around and take the old cemetery road out to the highway."

"Edgar, what's this all about?"

"I'll tell you when we are out a ways and I can think," he said.

"I know, in a minute you'll slip me the secret plans in a microfilm pill."

"You may be right." They headed up the long sweep to the cemetery, turned past it, and went on. The land and the roads were held in afternoon stillness and the dust they made hazed the light behind them.

"I don't want it, Marty. I don't know if I ever did. We talked about scholarships, but I never questioned that we would each go where we needed or wanted to go. They were laughing and happy all day today, kidding at lunch about us going to Ags together. I sat there all cold and feeling like I was drowning. I couldn't tell them I didn't want it—don't want it. I want to go to a university. I want to go to a place where they teach ancient languages, nuclear physics, oceanography, everything I don't know and never heard of. Maybe being a farmer is really what I want, but not—not till I know!" In his excitement he was driving too fast and swinging back and forth on the empty road. She pointed to the highway and he slowed down and went back into his lane.

"I feel so caught in it," he said, "it's all been set for so long. Mike and Glover have it fixed in their minds now, the three of us in school together. Dad and Grandpa are happy with me as a farmer and Praise leader. How can it make sense to them that I want to go off and study French or fossil fishes?"

"It hasn't happened yet," she said. "You don't know if the university will accept you or not."

"That's true—that's very true." He was surprised because this had not occurred to him before. "Maybe I could just apply—it doesn't mean they would accept me, does it? Maybe they won't. The university is crowded and the competition is terrific. If they didn't accept me, of course, the problem would be solved." He smiled at her, full of relief as though she had said something of great wisdom. "I knew things would be better if I talked to you. I knew you would have the answer. I could write away for an application. If they sent it to your house nobody would know." She nodded, and he pulled her over so that they were sitting close. Neither of them mentioned the possibility of success.

In a life as circumscribed as Edgar's, any deception had to be planned with farmer's forethought. Edgar made plans to be in school before the bus. He did his chores, bolted his breakfast, and left for town in the foredawn. When the sky began to pour light on the east-facing walls of the houses, Edgar was crossing the town square. He stopped in front of the drugstore. It was still closed. Looking to the right and left, he ducked down a sidestreet to the post office, where he mailed the letter. When he came back he waited in the truck until Mr. Tovey opened the drugstore. There, he bought a box of cigars for Charlie. He was at school and hard at work when the first buses pulled up and the official day began, and there was only a passing heaviness from his too-quickly eaten meal.

They argued that week, Edgar, Mike, and Glover. It was the bitterest argument they had ever had. Mike and Glover wanted to work the cause a little, to put themselves forward, suggesting here and there that a subscription might be taken up for the money needed for a third scholarship. Edgar saw that it would be pushing and that it would be resented.

"What would you tell them? We're not supposed to know, to *dream*, that last year's money was saved for us. The strongest thing weighing for us now is that we're not competing with each other, that we're so close and so closely identified that we *can't* be separated. That's why they'll have to give us three scholarships instead of one."

"They won't make the leap, Ed," Mike said. "People don't. Just because our closeness is obvious is no reason why the committee won't operate on its own weird logic—one of us and Ivy Dann or even Martha Wyer."

"We can't pressure them," Edgar said, "it would give away our case. The teachers would feel used and people don't take to that. We have to wait. Excel and wait."

In the end they waited, not because Edgar had convinced Mike and Glover, but because neither of them could think of any way to raise the question to the principal or their teachers, no less the people at the bank who oversaw the funds. Waiting made their sports performance better. They pounded around the track and did push-ups with a new kind of fury, the frustration of their waiting a goad.

And they were always together, always full of pride and delight in each other. If their bodies seemed charged, their smiles brittle, their comradeship a little forced, no one seemed to notice it. Walking down the halls or sharing lunch with the eager group of acquaintances, they seemed to give off the same light they had always given off together. It was not easy to perceive whether it was a light with any warmth.

"You're in another gear," Martha said to him. "If you stop for me, you'll stall out, and then you won't be able to start up as fast again." Once she said, "I love to watch it, the professionalism of what you do, you and Mike and Glo. You're like the gymnasts on TV or a high-wire act at the circus, when you're together."

But there were other times, too, at Praises, Seeking out of the circle, when he would catch a glimpse of her watching him and his body would ache for her so much that he thought he would fall to the ground. Once they missed half a Praise, arriving early and wandering away together, losing track of time. They walked across John Hendry's unplanted back section, talking quietly, not even looking at each other. They did not kiss. Anyone looking out from the circle of Praise could see them two miles away over the flat fields. Once or twice he said loving things to her. The words had a flavor of anguish.

"I wish it was spring. When it's spring and the wheat is still green and high, we'll both creep away into old man Hegethorn's field, and we'll make ourselves all small, and we'll sink down into that green wheat and be hidden, and then we'll just rest there, and there'll be nothing to do but look at each other and touch and listen to each other until the wheat darkens and the combines come to harvest it." Most of the time they didn't say such things. There was a release in saying them and a tremulous joy in hearing them, but later, alone and trying to do homework or chores or plan the next day, the words would anchor in the mind, dragging along its bottom, catching on memories and hungers. Then there would be a terrible wrench before the work was started again or the chores done.

And sometimes he would see his father or Charlie watching him, and he would feel a sudden start of fear or anger because everything was now so opened in him that he felt anyone who looked at him could see his hungers and their war in him.

The application from the university came to Martha's house. Edgar filled it out there and Martha mailed it. The references he sent were not from Apostles and not from teachers long in the community. The weeks passed in a strange kind of silence. The time was filled with football, tests, basketball, tests, debate, more tests, study, reports. The more intensely he pushed himself into his public place with Mike and Glover, the more sealed off and silent he felt, in a loneliness wider than his father's widest field. The Praises that had held him so long were empty exercises now in which he spoke with one kind of duplicity to the eager faces of the dancers, and with another, deeper duplicity to Mike and Glover. There were times when his yearning for Martha made him weep at night and go sleepless into the gray morning and his chores.

The weather changed. It got wet and slushy, a gnawing cold that burdened the fields and weighed down the sky and ran gray-brown mud down Main Street. The light was grudging. For days the sun did not appear. The landscape was bare and starved. Edgar did not dare ask if this grimness had ever happened before or if it was common in these months before spring and he had been so happy and busy in the past that he had not seen it. He only spoke of it to Charlie when they were out laying new wire for Arla's chicken run.

"There ain't been no break, that's what it is," Charlie said. "Usually about the middle of the month you get a couple of days or a week of the chinook winds, the warm winds. This year, though, they don't seem to have come. Heartbreak warmth is what it is. It lies to you that it's spring, and when you're ready to believe it the wind turns again and you get the frosts and the bitter-cold rains. Me, I like my springtime honest."

And then in two single hours of a late morning, a Tuesday at the end of March, when Edgar was sitting in school under the discipline he now commanded by force alone, the winter's doors were opened. Under the dark ice at the roadside bright water was running, and when he came out into the day a warm wind met him and the earth was steaming under the wide-open benison of the sun. He stood and stared about him like a sick man whose crisis has passed, but to whom the world is not yet real. The trees in the courthouse square were still bare, but now their branches looked pliant and alive. That morning they had seemed twisted and as brittle as old-men's bones. The light—a summer light—was pouring like honey. Beside him, other students were passing, taking off their overcoats and scarves, laughing. Wishing he could get away, but remembering his mandatory half hour in Burkett's and his meeting with Mike and Glover, he walked slowly down the school steps. Then he saw Martha.

She was standing to the side, her books and coat on the railing. It was still too cool for the simple blouse and skirt she was wearing, and she was hugging herself for warmth. Her eyes were closed and her face was lifted to the sun. At that moment he knew that he couldn't go to Burkett's or to meet

Mike and Glover. He couldn't study or scheme or lie or laugh at one of their secret jokes. He went to her and said very quietly, "Don't take the bus—let me take you home."

"You're supposed to . . ."

"I know."

"It's so far out of your way."

"I know."

"All right," she said.

Then he turned and saw Mike coming out the door, and to his own astonishment called out, "Hey, Mike, I'm going to take Marty home, so don't wait, okay?" Mike's head came up, surprised, and he looked hard at Edgar for a moment, wanting to remind him, and unable to in public, of their plans. All he could do was go on with the act and yell back, "Okay, Ed, sure!"

Then Martha gathered her things in her arms and they went out to the parking lot where Edgar had the truck.

They lay on their coats in the bed of the truck in a grown-over field. The highway was a mile to the east, and no one was on it. There was not a sound, not a muscle to move or a thought to force to yield up words. They had meant at first only to lie close, to be as silent and mindless as they were now, to be happy together that the numbness, the awful dailiness of winter, and their isolation from themselves and each other seemed to be over. They had tried to keep from imagining the power of their desires.

When he began to kiss and stroke her, he was afraid for a fleeting moment of the simple mechanics of going on, as he had once wondered where, in kissing, the lips and noses fit. He found that although they were both urgent, they were not frantic. They were not crowded into a car seat or the cab of the truck, where Edgar's earlier and more furtive gropings with other girls had taken place. There was light, space, time, and peace, and they found their way. Afterward they lay side by side, hand in hand, and Edgar wondered if death could have such a resonant peace. This thought seemed to him for a moment to be one of the most profound he had ever had, but he realized it was only a common thought bathed in uncommon joy. On Martha's bare stomach the fine down shone in the golden light and wherever the sun struck her she glowed.

"We'd better get up," she said, "the sun will go soon and somebody may see us." But for a while longer they did not move.

"My mind is so quiet," he said in wonder, "so still." After a while they got up and dressed. Martha, to his astonishment, took her clothes and disappeared around to the front of the truck where he couldn't see her.

On the way to Willow Springs they both were quiet. The mellow day was cooling down. The girl he said good-bye to in front of her house seemed bundled in clothes, and he could hardly see her hair under the scarf she wore. He rode home formulating excuses.

He lay in bed that night reliving the warmth of the afternoon sun, the silence of the field, his own inner stillness, the clarity of everything in those moments of golden light. Old people have "memories." Do they choose them, build a kind of wall around them to keep them just as they were? Could he, he wondered, choose this, stop it from drifting away or diffusing any of its warmth and sweetness? This is what he wanted to save, every shadow, every bit of the clean warmth on his back, every moment of his consciousness of her. . . .

There came the terrible, wrenching cry, drawn out into a howl and cut off suddenly to silence. In the instant before he knew it was his father dreaming again, the parade of horrors ran wordlessly across his mind, rattling like panicking cattle at the sides of the chute. Then he got up and shook himself free.

He knew the dreaming embarrassed his father. Now when he heard that cry, Edgar stayed in his room, the door closed discreetly in the lie that he slept right through the nightmares, heard nothing, knew nothing. Corella always left her room or else mentioned it the next day, rubbing her eyes and yawning. No wonder she was unhappy. She deserved to be unhappy, making everyone miserable with her selfishness. There. He heard her door open and the sound of her going down the hall. Then there was a soft stir by his door. He bolted for his bed, and before his door opened he was lying stiffly in an attitude of sleep, breathing deeply and evenly. It was Anne, looking in. She paused for a moment, while he wondered if he would get a cramp in his leg, and then she closed the door softly and he could hear her going back to bed.

Whatever was happening to his father, it was a contained torment, carefully kept from impinging on Andy's busy daylight life. The terror had power only at night. In the daytime Andy was the same as he had always been. There were times when Edgar wanted very much to ask his father what had happened, what had gone wrong, that out of nowhere these terrible dreams should come to claw at him one or two nights a week, and one time twice in a single night. When he thought of what he could say he was confounded. He had already made up his mind to spare his father's feelings by pretending to be asleep. It was the kindest way, really. Everyone seemed to appreciate not having to face Edgar's fears or answer his questions. Yet, as much as he realized the advantages of his choice, he didn't like being frozen in it, unable even to look up at his father from his seat at the breakfast table the next day and say, "I'm sorry you had a bad night again, Dad." A bad night! The cries sounded like the shrieks of a man being tortured to death. Once or twice, on nights of high winds or a full moon, Edgar found himself lying awake waiting for the awful sounds, his own fantasies brewing horror out of the silence.

On Sunday at Praise, Martha gave him a letter from the university. She was with her cousin and would not be riding home with him. There was only time to slip the envelope to him quickly and give him a penetrating look before turning away into the dance again. He put the envelope inside his jacket and did not open it until he was in his room at home. He had been conditionally accepted. He could get full acceptance by passing an examination at the university or one given through his own school on or before the tenth of June. It struck him then how he had been fooling himself. He had never had any intention of going to agricultural

282

school if there was the slightest chance for him at the university. Everyone would have to know, there was no way around it—his parents, Joe and Arla, Mike and Glover.

Why had he formed these plans without his friends? Why was he so guilty and afraid about telling them? It had been taken for granted that they would use the scholarships together, go to State Ag together, but there had never been promises made, oaths sworn. Perhaps he was putting off telling Mike and Glover because that would make it real and decided after all, and there was still a part of him that loved the thought of the three of them in a comfortable, familiar place, studying comfortable and familiar things. The family would have to be told first. He spent the next days preoccupied with how he would break the news, still cursing himself for worrying about it, fearing the moment when he would have to face his family and then his friends.

Busyness saved him only so long. For almost a week he was able to slip in late for meals, avoiding the times alone with Andy. On Sunday night after Praise he found himself seated at a silent table, the family waiting. It had been a hearty, exuberant Praise, a Praise reaffirming everyone's anger at the Supreme Court for its false and immoral school decision. Everyone was tired, even Corella, who had pointedly come home from church in town and gone up to her room for the afternoon. Edgar found nothing to do but begin.

"I've applied to the university. I applied to Ags, too, as you know, but I also wanted to try and see if I could get into State, and I've been accepted. I've been accepted and I want to go."

Anne was first to react, saying, "Oh!" in simple surprise, looking quickly at Andy to see whether she should make it a cry of joy or of anger.

Andy looked across at Edgar. "Have you thought it out, and do you really want to go up there, all the way up there to Boulder?"

"I've thought a lot about it," Edgar said, "and it's really what I want."

"Then I'm happy for you, son," and Andy smiled a little,

rose, and leaned over the table to shake Edgar's hand. The table relaxed into congratulations. Arla remarked that Edgar would be the first college man in the family, and there was pride to be found in that. Joe was more careful, saying he hoped the university was going to be what Edgar wanted, but that he should remember he had the life and ways of a farmer in his blood, and even if farming these days was more accounting and management than plowing and planting, there was a great future in it for him here where Christian Kornarens had homesteaded back in 1904. Edgar would be the fourth generation. It bore remembering.

"Well," Edgar said, "I've only been accepted conditionally. I've never seen the place and I also need to take their entrance exam. I'd like to go up there for a day or two, take the test, and look over the school, talk to people, and see what things are going to be like if I go."

"It's a good idea," Andy agreed. "Do you want one of us to come along, or do you prefer to go by yourself?"

"Herman Janes from Forks has been accepted too. I haven't asked him yet, but I thought we'd go together. I could drive up to Forks or catch the bus at the junction and we could ride up together."

"You told Mike and Glover yet—about this school thing?" Charlie asked.

"Well, I just got the acceptance," he lied. "I was planning to tell them the next time I see them."

"I'm sure they'll be pleased for you," Anne said. "After all, they're your best friends. You three have been so close. . . ." Corella sighed and shook her head. Edgar looked away from her.

He knew his mother's evaluation was wrong, but the rightness in it, the simple conventionality of it, lifted his mood. Anne always saw reality as what it *should* be. People *should* act for the highest motives, and therefore they assuredly did. Friends *should* be pleased and proud of an independent, courageous decision, and therefore they surely would be. It made him smile, but it also gave him the strength to go ahead. On Monday, when he saw Mike and Glover at lunch in the crowded cafeteria, he thought he might introduce it then, say it in the crowd of friends and acquaintances that were always around them, and thus stop any extreme reaction they might have. They would have to remember where they were. Then he realized it was a cowardly way, beneath him, and besides, it would add to their anger later, the unfairness of what he had done. Instead, he and Glo and Mike talked and kidded and played their game, casual, self-assured, and popular, keeping things light but not silly, acting confident but not smug, bright but not sophisticated. He found himself barely able to conceal his annoyance at having to give and take the banter in the deadening ritual, to watch, to listen to Mike and Glover doing the same.

They couldn't have been doing this all year, playing this silly game—unless he was just so impatient that it seemed worse today then it really was. Didn't everyone see through it—teachers, other students, even the clustering friends who kept coming around to share in the game and take duller, smaller imitations of it home for themselves? By the end of the meal he felt the strain, and Glover was looking at him clinically. Always before, the lunch break had been something he waited for eagerly. Today he was glad when it was over and he was back in class.

The afternoon was science, music, and math, an hour in the gym, and then Burkett's, now the hardest part of his day. Martha never went to Burkett's. She had to take the bus home right after school. He took long and complicated detours from class to class to be able to see her and recuperate for a few moments in the serenity of her existence. They had met and been together only three times since the afternoon in the back of the truck, and as much as she had eased his soul, his body longed for her.

The day went on; he coasted on assignments already done, knowledge already crammed. Just before they left school together, in a push of others toward the gym for practice, he said quickly to Mike and Glover:

"Be at Burkett's, will you—I have to see you after."

"Something important?" Glover asked, and Edgar knew he

was putting together this need for a conference with the way Edgar had acted at lunch.

"No, not really—I need to see you guys, that's all."

It was five o'clock before the endless day was over and they left Burkett's one by one, ostensibly for home, circled around the back of the town, and converged on the bench in back of the soddy at the far end of the park.

"I didn't mean to sound melodramatic—it's three weeks until graduation, and something's happened to me—something I want you to know about before anyone else does—" He could see them saying "Martha" in their minds, and he went on, "It started when we were applying for Ags—a feeling I had, an awful feeling that it was all wrong for me, that if I went, it would be easy and pleasant and familiar, and that I'd never forgive myself for not trying a bigger change, a bigger world—"

"What are you talking about?" Glover asked. His voice wasn't cold, but only objective, interested.

"I put in an application to the university," Edgar said. "I thought, I'll see what happens, and if they deny it, that will be that. But they didn't deny it; they accepted it, and when they did, I knew it was really what I wanted. There's a college entrance test, of course, but Ags has that, too, and the folks said it was okay with them if I went up and saw what it was like—"

Something in their silence destroyed any hope he had of continuing. The words had gone on too long without being understood. They had just stood there and stared at him as though he had reverted to some older language completely foreign to them.

Mike was the first to speak. "Is this a paper you're doing—some kind of a test or something?"

"No, Mike, it's real, but it's nothing to get all upset about. I want to try to get into the university—"

"But that wasn't the plan. I mean we have a *plan*, the three of us. You know, we planned the whole thing, you and Glo and I, and the plan was for the scholarships for the three of us—you remember that, don't you?" He spoke as one does to an invalid or a child.

"Sure," Edgar said wearily, "but that was for the scholarships. We've got them, I know we have. All three of us, just like we planned, but we never promised we'd all go to Ags. We sort of thought we might, but we never promised we would—the idea was that we would all—would all be able to be—to be—"

"To be what?" Glover demanded coldly.

"To be free!" Edgar blurted. He had not dreamed he would say such a thing, but the word was out and could not be recalled, and he was more exhausted than he could ever remember being, and it was true, though he had not known it before, that he wanted to be free of them, Mike and Glover, free of the responsibility of them, and of the comradeship that had somehow degenerated into a cynical game. "Look," he went on, reddening, "it's nothing against you—let's all go to the university. There's still time to try out for it—it's only that right now I don't want to be limited the way Ags limits a person. Not when there are so many other things to study—" He couldn't plead anymore. He had blundered into a mistake, into hurting them, because he was too tired, and now he had to stop; there were simply no more words.

Glover got up quietly and came around to the side of the bench where Edgar was sitting. His face was gentle. "Ed." he said, "you look beat. We're all beat. This has been a long season; the waiting, the wondering if it's really going to happen, the work of it all. And Martha—oh yes, Martha, too, because you've been running back and forth taking her home all that way and then coming back to chores or homework or Praises—and we're all tired, we all feel like throwing the whole thing over and going fishing. Let's not talk about it now. Let's put it off till—well, till graduation. Then there'll be all the time we need and we won't be under all this tension—all of us." Glover sounded so reasonable and Edgar was so tired that he only nodded. Now he was between Glover and Mike, and for a minute he thought they might even help him up, as though he had been stricken as he sat there; they got up slowly with him, and the three of them walked through the closing town, in an ambling, comradely silence. They didn't pump each other; there was no game. They might have been walking as they had walked three years ago, just three good friends who, Edgar remembered, had once been able to hear each other.

Everywhere they looked it was before them. They felt it in the teachers' greetings, the principal's special look, the notations on their papers, the extra care the teachers took with reading and commenting on what they had written, most of all in the sudden silence that surrounded them when it came to any mention of the Mohlencamp Scholarship. The scholarship had been opened to three. The three of them had won. All three.

Suddenly everyone was busy with class rings and pictures, all the flurry of the end of school added to the extras of graduation—the last drama and debate, the yearbook, the finals. Then they had to prepare for the graduation ceremonies. They had waited all year, but it seemed sudden, all the rehearsals and traditions and speeches. In a county where few went on to college, the high-school graduation was the most important of all civic events. For some it would be the single public ceremony of their lives. Honors and recognition for most popular and best wit and most cheerful and most patriotic were voted, half in fun, half in the deadliest earnest. In the old days, the principal reminded them, everyone was voted best in something. Now with the school so big there weren't enough honors, but the spirit of that old way should stay the same—everyone should share in the great day. Because of the impossibility of choosing a single valedictorian this year, the tradition was being slightly altered to give Edgar, Mike, and Glover equal honors and a five-minute speech of farewell to the graduates. The three boys smiled when they heard this. It was the last proof of the reality of their winning.

"You were right not to press about the thing," Glover said. "I remember thinking we should ask the teachers or the principal about three awards."

"Yes," Mike said, "and he talked us out of it."

"Ed's usually right," Glover said, "and maybe that's what I should say in my five minutes something personal, about friendship."

"We'd better start figuring out who says what," Mike said. They began to do what they had done so often before. Edgar watched the old process, the picking of a subject, the division of it into three parts, something witty for each of them, something serious. Gratitude, respect, but not servility. Edgar wanted five minutes to himself. For once there should be something real, something honest, said. What might there be in that five-minute speech?

Mr. White, Dr. Slater, members of the faculty, honored guests, parents, and friends. On this auspicious and fragrant evening I wish to remind you of sex and love, and the power of passion. I am reminded as I look out at all your familiar faces that what I most wish to do is to float out of this hall and fly with Martha Wyer up to Cemetery Hill where there is a nice breeze. There we will take off our clothes and make love in the deep grass that the Elks have planted to keep down the dust. It is my fervent hope that each and every one of you will find some deep grass or some green wheat and do likewise. We must never forget to be grateful to our parents and teachers and to the night wind that blows across our bare bodies and to the little stars that glisten at the ends of our fingernails. As we leave the sheltering world of our childhood days, let us resolve to let our smiles flow out in the wind and combine with the smiles of the person we love, and our legs and arms intertwine with the legs and arms of the person we love in the nights sweet with grasses and grains and growing things—

"Hey, Edgar, snap out of it; we're wasting valuable time." He pulled himself back and looked at them. "Come on, man," Glover said, "we've got to get these speeches mapped out!"

"All right," Edgar said, "I was just wishing it all didn't have to be the same old stuff."

"It isn't—haven't you been listening?" Glover cried. "We're going to get one more play out of that old soddy. We're going to hark back one more time."

"Oh, I meant to ask you both," Mike interrupted, "what are we planning to do graduation night? There's the school party and Pam Dixon's midnight party, but some of the Young Apostles from Founder's and the Springs have been talking about a special Praise that night. . . ." Edgar had not heard about those plans, or maybe he had and they had slipped his mind.

"I'm afraid I'm going to be out of it," he said. "They give the university entrance tests on the ninth at the latest and I'll have to leave on the seventh to get up there by the afternoon of the eighth. The bus leaves so early I won't be able to stay out much after ten or eleven. I was figuring on dropping in on the school party for an hour or so and then going home to bed." They gazed at him blankly. Mike's face had a wounded look.

Glover said, "I thought we weren't going to talk about it, about that university stuff, until after graduation. You said you weren't going to mention it."

"But Mike asked about the parties and I know—"

"Okay," Glover said shortly, "it's not going to be talked about and that's all. Let's get back to the speeches." He said the words coldly, sounding very much like one of the teachers they all laughed at for his prissiness. Mike looked as though he was about to say something, but thought better of it. They went back to the speeches.

Edgar missed Praise at Willow Springs that Sunday. Andy had had two nightmares, ripping the night apart first with shrieks for help, and then toward morning crying out again in a long-drawn scream of agony. The first time Edgar managed to get back to sleep, although he had awakened with his heart pounding. The second time, after feigning sleep for Anne, he lay wide-eyed in the darkness to wait out the night. At about five he fell asleep, and Anne let him sleep until eleven. It was too late to get to the Springs. He realized that Anne must know about his faking and that she was collaborating with him in his deception out of tact or a desire to avoid conflict at all costs.

They had all been put off schedule, eating a pick-up meal at about noon and trying a little groggily to get back into the routine of the day. Edgar and Andy went down to help Joe set up for Founder's Praise. It was a day of sun and wind, a nice day for Praise. While Edgar and Charlie were setting up the water cask, Charlie looked levelly at Edgar and said, "Everything all right over there?" looking quickly at Andy's house. Charlie must know too, then. Edgar looked around to see if Andy was coming. He wanted to deny everything. He knew he could by just going dumb and asking Charlie what he meant, but Charlie himself was so vulnerable that Edgar simply couldn't keep up the pretense.

"You've been hearing—"

Charlie said, "Up there in the attic like I am, and in front of the house, I've been hearin' it now and then. Is it your ma?" It had never occurred to Edgar that Charlie would think so. He shook his head. "You ain't bein' disloyal, boy," he said, "and neither am I. I only want to help if I can and I ain't told anyone all this time—"

"No, it's not Ma, it's Dad. It's about the camp he was in, I think, that prison camp during the war. I think he dreams about that place."

"He ain't told you what it is?"

"No, only once or twice he yelled things that made me think so, and once he said some words that maybe were Japanese."

"Did you ever ask him?"

"No . . . I can't. He likes to think I sleep through them—after the first one, that is. Then he doesn't have to apologize to me all the time for something he can't help doing."

"Yeah, but it kind of gets you both stuck, don't it, so's you can't move, either of you?" Edgar nodded. He felt slow and tired, as though he had had no sleep at all. Charlie shook his head slowly and went on, half to himself, "Anne, I guess she don't say much—afraid she'll say the wrong thing. Corella's got off on the wrong foot with your dad, and anyway she's a daughter—he wouldn't want to be showin' her any weakness. It's a funny thing, the war memory, his war, after all this time. I wonder why it's come back on him again. When did it start, do you remember?" Edgar was half listening.

"Annie Kinbote," he said, scarcely knowing he said it.

"What?"

"I said it started around the time the Annie Kinbote thing came out."

Charlie pursed his lips and his eyebrow went up. "Hmm," he said. They finished filling the cask.

It was a happy Praise. Whatever combination of youth and age, energy and repose, weather and climate, petition and thanksgiving were necessary for the fulfillment of a good Praise, it was in Founder's that afternoon. Edgar had thought about going to his room for more sleep, but decided to stay to Praise. Mike and Glover would be there. He might be able to be with them, to run Seeking with them, to feel the old strength and warmth again. Perhaps he could show them in some way that he hadn't betrayed them or the friendship, that he would always be close to them no matter where he went to school or what happened to any of them later in life. That would be the way to seal the bond so that it would be strong enough to overcome any distance and all the time he would be away.

They were glad to see him, waving him into the group, holding hands out, and clapping him on the back as he came from the house and walked in between them. The other dancers smiled as the circle widened—here were the three friends, the three devoted friends Praising together in a simple, wholehearted way. The old people smiled at them. Anyone who remembered his youth knew how rare such friendship was in the years of fickle choices, school cliques, and the pressure of position and wealth, cars, clothes, girls. How fresh and engaging they looked together, and how alive.

For the first time in years there was more thanksgiving than petition. Surely the Lord would be pleased that people saw fit to remember his miracles more than they begged for others from Him. The Seeking and Bringing began.

This time as Edgar ran he watched Mike and Glover running also. They weren't far away. How good it was to be together, naturally, joyfully, without compulsion. Coming back he saw as his vision the three of them going out to claim their places in the great field alone, but bonded forever spiritually and in memory. Coming back into the circle, he gave his Witness full of happiness.

"I had a vision of a bird in a cage. No one knows where

that bird would fly if it were free. The Spirit of the Lord told me that only by freeing one another can we know that when the choice to come home is made it will be a real choice, a choice of real love, not fear or—" He couldn't finish. He had gotten a little tangled in his metaphor. "Real closeness—" he started again, "real closeness is the closeness of free people, people with all their choices—" He stopped again. The old people were nodding at him tolerantly. Sometimes it is hard to get a deep thought, a very personal vision, said in Praise. Everyone understood and sympathized, especially since Edgar's Praises and Witnessings were usually so clear and sensible. He heard one old woman murmuring to another, "What a dear boy!"

Mike's Witness was more confusing than Edgar's had been. He had run very far. Edgar had seen him running when he himself had turned and started back. Mike came back to the Praise pale and winded.

"The Spirit of the Lord," he sobbed for breath, "wants people to be friends. To stay and help their friends and not to run away! Other places look nice, but are the friends there so close and true as the ones here? It's right to be where we are needed. Where we are *needed* is where we belong!" Many people murmured with approval, but there was some stirring, as though some recognized the message as not for them, but pointed, more pointed than it should be. Perhaps they saw the Praise being used. It happened now and then. Often these private visions cleared with time and were presented later as the Lord wished. It was not good Apostle behavior to question any vision, especially the visions of the young. Mike had been looking directly at Edgar while he spoke and some people noticed it. Glover looked at a spot in the unoccupied middle of the circle. It was where Witnesses usually looked while they were giving Witness.

"The Spirit of the Lord came to me when I sought it," Glover said calmly. "He told me that loyalty is the greatest virtue of all. What's faith, really, but loyalty to God, even when the miracles don't shower down? A man's loyalty to his family and friends and the past, yes, even to the past, the old spirit, is a way of being loyal to the Spirit of the Lord. And the Spirit of the Lord told me that a man should try to be whole, to make himself loyal to all those things, his country and his family and friends and his beliefs, and then he'll be being loyal to himself."

The Praise hummed with approval. How good it was to listen to clear, true Witness so simply given. People murmured "Amen" and "Bless the Spirit" as he finished and smiled at him across the circle.

Then there was a stir as the circle moved slowly onward, waiting for more Witness. Someone was moving into the circle, trying to come in. People bunched up at one side and began to bump into one another and at the other side a big gap was left.

"Could you wait a minute—just a minute—" The voice was harsh, an old man's dried-out voice sounding nervous and defensive. People stopped and stood staring at the man. It was Charlie Dace.

"I know how you like to move while you're talkin', even if it's only a little, but see, I got to stay still; I guess I ain't got brains enough to walk and think at the same time." The Praise slowed. Some people stood still while others, used to the rhythm of Witness in motion, shuffled in place. Charlie's tone and made them all feel self-conscious. The harsh voice went on. It was higher than normal with his nervousness. "I got somethin' to say. I got to say it even if it don't please nobody and it ain't from no spirit, but only from me, so for Christ sake be still and let me get it said!" The Praise stopped. Edgar could feel the life go out of it.

They were more than surprised, they were affronted, and now they stood still in a resentful silence, utterly silent, and they listened. "This ain't easy for me," Charlie said. "I ain't no way goin' to dress this up in fancy talk. Like I said, I'm speakin' from me, and in a way, from Edgar, Edgar Bisset." The eyes of the Praise turned cold. Edgar could see the eyes freezing. He began to be afraid.

"Get on with it," a man said.

"Andy and Joe and me, maybe seventeen, eighteen years ago, we was talkin' about all of this—Praise Dancin' and the Apostles. They said it needed a law—laws, and I said it didn't; it needed Edgar's gift, and Edgar's gift died with him. I was wrong. Now, lookin' around, I think they was wrong, too. When they said laws, they meant customs, ceremonies, which God knows the Apostles have now—customs, but no laws. You don't have no *laws*. I see things happenin' here that don't seem right to me, and probably wouldn't seem right to old Edgar, and that's because there ain't no rules about it, no *laws*." They all stood still. Edgar saw men's faces working a little. He felt his heart beating up in his throat.

"People ask me sometimes about things Edgar said, Edgar Bisset. I'll tell you one thing he said, which come back to me sharp and plain. See, Edgar didn't love his ma very much, and he didn't *like* her none at all; and after she was dead he said to me, 'I forgot my ma, Charlie, and I lived to regret it. Forgettin' must be some kind of sin because it kills the gratitude along with the pain.' It seems to me that law is a kind of rememberin', and every law is a memory of somethin' bad that happened, maybe many times, until people said, 'We want to remember how this was and tell people about it so maybe it won't happen again.' Without no laws the Apostles have forgot somethin'—forgot it, and because there wasn't a law, they didn't even see themselves forgettin' and they don't even know what the thing is that's been slippin' away—and what it is—is—"

"Shut up, Charlie! Shut up!" a woman yelled.

Near Edgar, Mrs. Roscoe Ede turned incredulously to her neighbor. "What did he say about Founder not loving his mother? How could anyone say that about Founder?" Other people were whispering. There was a cold seethe of whispers in the circle:

"What's he doing, saying things like that?"

"What's he saying about Founder?"

Edgar looked around. Near him, Joe had his hand raised and was talking to Bill Linthicum, words meant to placate and calm, by the look of him. Andy was standing stock still in a kind of shock. Near him, Matty Andrews was hissing at Charlie. Edgar thought he might go into the middle of the destroyed circle and talk to them. Charlie was still standing in the place where he had broken into the ring. People had drawn away from him on both sides so that he was alone. The buzzing of the people and Charlie's standing there, his mouth still open, seemed to draw out before Edgar as though the people were trapped on flypaper. Then Andy regained himself and stepped into the circle.

"Now, friends," he cried gently to them, "we've never been rude to a Witness before. . . ."

"That ain't Witness!" Jack Empey cried. "It's craziness and blaspheming!"

"We've always listened," Andy persisted. "Maybe Charlie doesn't say things nicely, but we ought to let him say his piece."

"He's said it!" Roscoe Ede shouted. "He's insulted Founder and talked nonsense about makin' laws! Where does he come off? He ain't Apostle. All I ever seen him do was stand back and look down his nose at us, like we was on display for his amusement!"

Suddenly the wide part of the circle seemed to collapse toward the center. Some people thought the Praise was breaking up and others were moving in on Charlie to put him out of the group. Edgar did not know what was happening; there were too many people. Someone was saying, "He's crazy. It's just crazy talk." There was shoving somewhere and people started shoving back. Edgar stood up on his toes, craning forward toward the central knot of people to see what was happening. He couldn't see. Everywhere there was shoving and milling and Charlie's voice in the middle, cursing or defending, something about never lying to the Lord because He has no defense against the lie. Suddenly, Edgar was grabbed from behind and spun around. Someone had him by the arms. He wrenched around as far as he could go and saw that it was Glover. In front of him was Mike, his face red with anger, his lip quivering, and his eyes full of anguish and rage. Then Mike struck him hard in the face, and again, and then began to weep, shaking Edgar back and forth so that his arms ground in their sockets where Glover still held him.

"You aren't going away!" Mike was yelling into his face. "You won't go away! It's not right! You can't break us up!"

24

Waking the next morning, they scarcely believed they were physically unchanged. All evening and into the night they had been concerned with practical things. They hadn't eaten. Joe had been too busy with the old people, Andy and Anne and Arla helping to mend a torn shirt here and there, comforting anxious Apostles and pressing cold cloths to bruised places. Four or five Apostles had had clothing torn, two or three were bruised, but a far greater number was upset and frightened and needed reassurance. Charlie had not been hurt at all. He stood by impassively, holding basins of cool water, bringing coffee, guiding those who were staying over into the little guesthouse when Joe and Arla's house was full. Surprisingly, Edgar was the most hurt. His lip had been opened somehow in all the pushing and shoving—no one had noticed how that had been done and he did not seem to remember who had done it or when it had happened. Later he said his shoulders and elbows were sore, and as soon as he could be spared from the hunt for Jessie Longerich's shoe, Arla ordered him to bed. He was awfully pale, she said, pale and sick-looking.

In the morning they all ached. No one had slept well, the old folks prowling the house all night long, unable to commit themselves to sleep. They were embarrassed in each other's presence. They looked away from one another over the un-eaten breakfast. Edgar was grateful to escape to school even though Mike and Glover would be there and he would have to face them again. Perhaps the Praise had been a sudden, sick reaction, an explosion of fear and hate in which their awful tension about graduation and the scholarships had burst out into meaningless rage. No doubt they would be sorry today, ashamed. What was worse to think about was that there would be questions from everyone. A fight at Founder's Praise—Inge Longerich and Betty Ede were sure to have taken the story to school. In a place like this, every-thing is always known, everyone always seen, every thought always guessed. He shivered. Perhaps someone had seen Mike and Glover attacking him, Glover holding while Mike hit him. Would that be enough to start people guessing about lies and duplicity and a three-way scholarship? Maybe not. There had been too much shoving, too much confusion, and besides, everyone had been looking toward Charlie and the group on the other side of the circle. He picked up his books and left the silent house.

Early in the day he stood aside and watched the Truth being made. Mike and Glover hadn't come in yet and a boy from Willow Springs was telling it all to a group in the hall.

"Some old guy began to say crazy things about Founder—real crazy talk. It made everybody mad, a guy sayin' things like Founder hated his mother and hated people and that the Apostles were breakin' the law. A bunch of people started to rush him. Edgar must have known it would be a really bad fight, so he started yellin' for them to break it up. Then Mike and Glo grabbed him and held on to him to keep him from tryin' to bust it up, but by then everyone was pushin' and shovin' and I guess he got knocked down, and the crazy guy was fightin' everybody. He was just crazy; they're gonna take him up to Pueblo and put him in a straitjacket up there."

"Who was the crazy guy?" someone asked.

"Couple of people said it was a stranger. I heard someone say it was one of the hired men on the Kornarens place, some old guy up there." Then the group saw Edgar and they assessed his bruises quickly. Most moved away, not wanting to embarrass him with questions, but they looked covertly at him as they left. A few stayed. One of them was Ansel Case.

"Heard you had a fracas over at your place yesterday."

"Oh," Edgar said, "it wasn't as big as all that—old Charlie was a little drunk and said some things and there was some shoving."

"You look worse than that."

"I was. Grandpa was there in the middle of it and I started to go toward him and I had my head down and someone shoved Mike back—he was in front of me, and his elbow caught me on the lip. I was the worst hurt of anybody in the whole thing, which was over in two minutes. I felt stupid because it was my fault, really—I didn't look where I was going."

"I'll bet it hurt," Ansel said, a little carefully, Edgar thought.

"You know those stars you see—" and Edgar smiled as much as his lip would allow, "well, mine were blue and yellow." Ansel laughed. He was a self-protective boy, the sort of boy who makes sure first, and his envy of Edgar was circumspect and very carefully measured out. The story sounded good, even to Edgar. All he had to do was get to Mike and Glover before anyone else did and work up the details. Charlie's part could be played down. They wouldn't think to do that by themselves. Drunk. Drunk was the best way, and he could see to that.

Luckily for everyone, the graduation plans overwhelmed everything else. There was no private time together for Mike and Glover's embarrassment or apologies. In the arena of school they were all best friends full of quips and good feeling, easily nostalgic at Burkett's for the good times that would soon be over, interested and cooperative about the graduation plans. When mention of the trouble at Founder's came up they simply followed Edgar's lead with trained grace. Edgar didn't even have to lie about going to the parties and then on to Graduation Praise. The Praise was supposed to start at one or two in the morning and go on until dawn, when they would all see the sunrise together. Everyone assumed he would be there—he had only to smile.

He stayed late at school the last few days before graduation. It was easier than treading the dubious waters at home, his father silent, Charlie taciturn and grim, Anne more nervous and upset than ever, racked with headaches and neck cramps, Joe looking wounded and incredulous, even Arla shaking her head uncertainly and peering into her batters and butters as though she had never seen them before. Corella was the most maddening of all. She went on as though nothing whatever had happened. Once, when he accused her of smirking at him, she said only, "I'm smiling, just like you are. I'm Miss Teenage America."

Charlie's having been drunk was accepted by everyone. They fell gladly into the lie, grateful that they could pass Charlie back into his obscurity with only a bit of derision: "Queer bird, old Charlie—sour when he's sober, mean when he's drunk, that's what you call *dependable*." It saved them all from hate.

Graduation day was warm and mellow. There was a rehearsal up at the school in the morning, but the seniors' minds were on the parties and they hardly listened to anything else. The Graduation Praise was going to be at Tucker's field near Cemetery Hill. There was going to be a huge campfire. The Young Apostles had planned on having food and soft drinks and music, too, after the formal Praise. It was a new idea to have a Praise on graduation night, and it pleased many people who wanted a more religious note struck on so important an occasion. Arla had been baking all day.

Edgar knew he could not lie to Mike and Glover outright, but he did not want to deceive them at all anymore, not even by smiling and letting them assume he would be at the parties or the Praise. He did as little as he could. He had told Martha's parents that he would bring her home no later than one. He had told Martha that he was planning to take the bus to Denver the morning after graduation, catching it at the junction at ten-thirty. He could get it in town at seven forty-five, but he did not want anyone to see him. There would be too many questions, and if he didn't get into the university after all, excuses to make, too many people knowing. In the afternoon he went home to get ready for the ceremonies. He felt released and happy. The afternoon opened before him: a long, slow bath, dressing, going over his speech. Maybe he could think of a way to make Mike and Glo see how much their strength in friendship meant to him, how much it had freed him and given him the strength to transcend its narrowest limits. You're my friends, he said silently as he lay in his bath and convinced them from the warm water, we've run to the ends of so many fields—the bond won't break. He would tell them that after he had been up at the university, when he knew for sure that he was going, that the school was what he wanted. He would tell them when he came back, and there would be all summer for them to see him as a friend, and not someone who had deceived them and broken faith.

Arla had made a feast. In addition to a huge pot of chili and two cakes for the Praise, she and Anne had made a holiday meal with all of Edgar's favorite foods—hardly balanced, Anne laughed, with corn and sweet potatoes, and cinnamon rolls and chocolate layer cake for desert. The cake said CONGRATULATIONS EDGAR on it and had icing flowers which Corella had made with a special set. For once Corella seemed willing to fall in with the mood. She had gotten him a new wallet, a nice one, and she presented it graciously at dinner. He knew that Andy and Anne and Joe and Arla had gone in together on his gift, a new Corvair. They had told him a week ago because there had been some trouble with delivery and it wouldn't be ready for another week or two. Charlie had gotten him a pig. 'I'm gonna fatten it for you and sell it off next year. You'll be needin' the money by then up there at the college."

When it was time to go, they loaded up the truck with the things for the Praise. Joe, Charlie, and Andy went in the truck, and Edgar drove the car with Anne, Corella, and Arla. He would take the truck after the ceremony, leaving the car for them to come home in.

The graduation ceremony was out of the ordinary in several ways. The student with the highest scholastic honors was a girl, Ivy Dann. She made a nice speech and looked

301

lovely in her graduation dress. The principal's welcome made note of the fact that there were three young men of high attainment this year and that the honors of valedictory were to be shared by the three of them. Mr. White's commencement address also mentioned "three young men." He spoke of a reawakening of love of community in members of this year's graduating class. Such love was rare in these times when the lure of other places made young people wish to leave towns and farms. He understood that the young men planned lives as farmers and would bring their knowledge back with them to a county that need not be anxious for its future if the creative and intelligent young people returned after school. He wished them well, them and all of the graduates coming into so changed and challenging a world.

It was by then no surprise when the principal announced that, thanks to the donating family, the farsighted planning of the committee, and gifts of extra money from the county commissioners and the state historical society, the Mohlencamp Scholarship was going to be granted to three recipients for the first time in the history of the award. The winners were not only exceptional young men but exceptional friends and the school was proud to be able to honor their noble ideals.

They stood drowning in the ovation. Perhaps it was no more than any recipient had gotten, maybe no more than all of them back to 1920, but to Edgar it felt as though the applause would never end. It was too much, too long, too God-defying. It struck him suddenly that people forty years his senior in age and wisdom were applauding his awful ambition. He stood on the stage of the auditorium, his dark suit and white shirt creasing and wilting in the sweat of his embarrassment.

When it was all finally over and they were in the vestibule of the auditorium with their families, Glover came to where Edgar was standing with Andy and Anne, Corella and Charlie, and Arla and Joe. Charlie had gotten a new suit for the occasion and looked, he said, like an Episcopal corpse. Glover greeted Edgar's family politely and stood chatting for a while so charmingly that even Corella laughed and relaxed. Then, smiling, he turned to Edgar.

"Come on with me in my car. I'll take you back to the party and then the three of us can go to the Praise." There was no way to get around an out-and-out refusal.

"I can't, Glo, I promised I'd stop in at the party and then take Marty home. Her folks are having a little party for her, you know, a little cake and wine. I'll stop by the Praise on my way back home." He tried to sound innocent and easy, and was turning away to say something to Joe when he caught Glover's changed face out of the corner of his eye. Glover was very quick. Moving close, he spoke softly in a tone that was icy.

"It's important. It's important for you to be at that Praise."

"I will, Glo, I will!" Smiling uncomfortably, he turned away. When he turned back again, Glover was talking to Arla and then was gone.

"What a lovely boy," she said. "It's a shame his mother is so shy and never goes out. You know, Mr. Randall says Glover does all the family's shopping—"

Edgar knew it was time to break away. He had brought Martha over for the obligatory words and she had brought her parents to say hello. Glover had come and gone, and he could see the others slipping away from parents and friends to join the party starting in the gym. He and Martha would put in an appearance there and, as soon as possible, slip away to be blessedly alone together in the mellow night, alone and unseen, and for an hour or two, unexpected, unresponsible. The urge was so loud that he barely heard the voices giving him good wishes and good-nights.

The moon was high and it rode clear. The night was warm, but a cool, wheat-fragrant breeze wandered now northward, now eastward, to make susurrant waves on either side of the roads they traveled. They stopped three times, once simply to walk hand in hand down the deserted highway between the black fields. On such nights the sky is so vast that it overwhelms the earth, and the earth sinks away until it is only a line on which to walk. Then footing is lost and, looking up, the walkers fall into the sky. For only a short while, Edgar and Martha were bound to the line, but when they fell into the sky they did not walk but glided like swimmers riding the waves, and they did not hear the sounds their shoes made, nothing but the low murmuring sounds of their voices and the rainlike sound of the wheat. It seemed to Edgar then that though he was not Praising, he had never been more conscious of the Keeper of the Stars. Twice he and Martha lay down together on untended places, low, moon-bathed plains of sand. At these times she took off her white graduation dress so as not to wrinkle it and they lay together, body to body, full of warmth and pleasure. Her home was at the end of this highway, a thousand miles away. Once she lay down on the highway in her thin slip and cried out with pleasure at the warmth of it. He helped her up and then she laughed.

"We'd better get back. You have all this way to come tonight and a drive early in the morning."

"I've just had a brilliant idea," he said. "I was going to go up to the junction to catch the bus. Why don't I come up here early and pick you up and leave from the Springs?"

"I have a better idea. Why don't I call my parents and tell them I'm going to the Praise and that I'll be home in the morning? That will mean one less long drive for you."

"They're waiting up for you with cake and wine, and we'll be late as it is—" He had a picture of the two pinched people standing close together over their tiny cake and thimblefuls of wine, waiting with motionless resignation for their daughter, the single warm and glowing thing in the house. "It's okay, Marty, really. I want you to see me off. The bus gets to the Springs about when?"

"I think it's nine thirty-six."

"I'll pick you up at your house at nine o'clock and that will give us some time." She put her dress back on, looking prim and reserved again, a change that always made him feel great wonder. What a secret her sensuality was. They drove on, dividing all the miles of darkness with their headlights and all the miles of silence with their little sound. No one was awake in all those miles, there was no other outpost of light or human noise. Rapt and silent themselves, they sat close to each other and smiled in their darkness.

It was only when he was halfway home again that he began to feel the tiredness creeping upon him with its warm, gentle weight. His eyes began to feel gritty. He remembered his mother telling him when he was small about the sandman. It made him smile. He felt the car veering a little and he snapped awake. He had nearly gone off the road. He switched on the radio as loud as it would go and hunted for an all-night station. Soon the car was full of the melismatic wailing of cowboy music, the same kind that they played in Burkett's all day. Plains people liked to think of themselves as reserved, optimistic, independent, and happy, but their music was all loneliness and lost love. It confessed that plains reticence was really shyness, a tragic binding of the tongue; that plains independence was a pose, tricked up by lonely men dwarfed by the endless sky and the intractable, capricious land. It keened with loss—from death, desertion, failure, drink, lies, and silence. The only virtue was in enduring. Feeling the wheel slipping again, he forced himself to sing along with the radio. Beneath the song his mind went roaming on, half asleep.

To the southeast was the town and north of that, on the only hill for miles, the cemetery where the dead lay, freed from the tyranny of the sky.

Martha had been willing to lie for him. He had felt a quick pang at that, at how easily the words seemed to come from her, "Oh, I'll tell them I'm staying over for Praise." Was it right to have the power to make so vulnerable a person as Martha an instant, calculating liar? He shivered for a second, and his mind went to Charlie yelling at that last Praise, "Stop lyin'! Stop lyin' to the Lord—He ain't got no defense against the lie!" What did that mean? Did it mean that the Apostles should erect no defenses against the lie? What he and Mike and Glover had done seemed to be a kind of lying. Why was he thinking of it just now, and why in the context of Charlie's ravings?

As he came nearer town, he turned the radio off as though to go silently past the sleeping people. Most of the lights were out, but over to the north at the bottom of Cemetery Hill there was a glow, almost like the sun about to rise. It was the Praise campfire. Glover had told him to come—had almost demanded it. They were probably waiting for him, Glo and Mike, perhaps to apologize or forgive him or in some way come to terms with his change.

But he was tired, too tired, and now a little more than that; he felt the beginnings of the great letdown after the tension of all the days of waiting and work. Coming closer, he saw the fire and the shapes of people moving back and forth. It was almost a mile away on the dirt road. He had halfway decided to turn into the road but remembered his early day. He would have to leave the house before seven—five hours from now. It would be better to sleep.

He was startled awake. Outside, it was full light. Seven forty-five by the clock, and why hadn't it gone off! He saw a white slip of paper by the clock and read it groggily:

> You were in so late last night, I
> turned your clock off to let you
> sleep in a little. Love, Mother

Desperately, he tried to think of how he could save things. Luckily he had packed for the trip yesterday and the final things could be thrown in. If he left now, he could just make it. He couldn't shower or shave, but would just have to splash water on his face, dress, and go. As he ran past the amazed Anne, who had been waiting for him with a special breakfast, he cried to her to say good-bye to everyone for him. Yes, yes, he had money. Yes, yes, he was fine. Andy had had the forethought to have plenty of gas in the car. He was out on the highway before he had come fully awake.

The road was full of traffic. At every stop Edgar found himself riding the pedals nervously. Was everyone moving his tractor today? Was everyone's damn stock crossing the highway? He had a picture of Martha waiting angrily, her foot tapping on the sidewalk, and then getting disgusted and going back inside the house. If he didn't hurry he would miss the bus altogether.

At last he was on open highway and he sped along in a rage of speed. How could his mother have done it—that kindly, well-meaning, deadly interference of hers. If he missed the bus he would have to drive up, an all-day drive, and have the car to wrestle with in city traffic! Damn!

When he got to Willow Springs he went straight to Martha's house. She was waiting at the corner and he nearly passed her before he saw her and screeched to a stop.

"You just missed it!" she cried. "But we can catch it on the stretch before Forks! If you signal, he'll stop for us, and I'll get a ride back with anyone coming this way!" As she was speaking she jumped in beside him, pulling the door shut, and he headed back out of town.

As soon as they got beyond the houses and trees, they were able to see the long straightaway and in the distance the bus, moving with that slowness that distant objects have. Edgar floorboarded the car and it bounded ahead, bucking a little with the vibration of all that speed. He was past the town limit now, and the car was doing ninety or so. He saw the cow on the road ahead of him, began to brake, and then knew he could not brake in time. The cow was moving clumsily into the center of the road to stand staring at him. On the right, the road was deeply banked and then fell off; to the left there was a small sideroad, an opening. If he could go around the cow to the left— He swerved left but not fast enough. They hit the cow with the force of an explosion. The windows were suddenly covered with blood and viscera, and they crazed into a bloody sunburst through which he could not see. He had lost all control of the car. Then the car was hit again, picked up, and hurled somewhere, Edgar could not tell where or how. He could not tell anything more.

There was a time of roaring noise and terrible pain, lights and darkness again, nausea and men's voices, one speaking very close to his head, quietly, but with great clarity:

"Don't worry about the girl right now, let's get this one up." There was a feeling of falling, but he didn't know what position he was in, and when he reached for something, his hand was taken away and that was all.

He woke later, and later again. Each time, there was so much pain in his head, chest, and legs that he began consciously to try to find his way down again, away from the light and voices of people. There was noise whenever he woke, sometimes so loud it rang in his ears, and he was shocked when at last he realized that the noise was noise he was making, crying out when he came close enough to the surface for the pain to ride him down again.

At last there was a time when he awoke into what was only a grinding ache and silence. He looked about him, glad for the quiet. It was a simple, strange room, in a hospital. Beside him, as incongruous as only the characters of dreams can be, sat ugly, unkempt Charlie Dace. When Charlie saw him awake he got up.

"You lay still now—I'll go get 'em. You just lay there—" Edgar opened his mouth to say something. He tried to speak and a bolt of pain shot from behind his eyes and exploded light into his brain. He almost screamed. Charlie came back with a nurse, and then there was a doctor, and they poked and probed at him, waking pain as they went. Through it all, Charlie, who had been sent outside, shouted encouragement through the half-open door until the nurse sent him away. The doctor told Edgar nothing.

His father. He was sitting where Charlie had sat, dozing gently. He looked very old and lined and his breath whistled past his upper lip with a little fluttering. Edgar was afraid to speak, afraid that the sounds he made would hurt his head again. But he was more truly conscious this time of where he was, and afraid for how badly he had been hurt. He moved his head very slowly until he could see down the length of his body. The left leg was elevated slightly and was in a sort of sling contraption. He could feel the right leg to the thigh and assured himself of its soundness by moving it around a little and feeling the friction of the sheet against his heel. He was surprised to find that his left arm and shoulder were immobilized in some way and that moving the fingers of his left hand sent a series of sharp pains up the fingers and into every articulating bone of his wrist, outlining each in fire, and traveling up the bones of his arm until they ground into the marrow at his shoulder. He began to weep with the pain and his father woke up. It was only after Andy had wiped his eyes and helped him blow his nose (also a painful process) that the knowledge of his having been hurt became part of a memory of how he had been hurt.

"Dad—there was an accident. I had an accident. I hit a cow—"

"I know, son."

"But something else—something I couldn't see."

"I know. That was the truck. There was a truck coming out of the sideroad and he couldn't stop in time. The collision with the cow threw you into him and he hit you from the side and then the car went into the field."

"Martha—Dad, Martha Wyer was with me."

"Yes. She was on the side the truck hit. I have to tell you now, son, Martha is dead. She died right away."

Edgar lay absolutely still for a long time, barely breathing. He was trying to concentrate on the silence, waiting for it to obliterate the words. Then he remembered the dream he had had, or something he had heard once, a darkness and a man's voice saying, "Don't worry about the girl right now, let's get this one up." How long ago had that been?

"When did it all happen?"

"Three days ago, almost three days. It's been a pretty bad time."

"It wasn't fair," Edgar said, hating his voice, which came petulant and whiny as a child's. "Our whole lives, our whole lives."

Later he heard more. Andy, Charlie, Corella, Anne, and Arla had been taking turns sitting up with him. The hospital had let them come at all hours and stay with him constantly, because he had been so badly hurt that he was not expected to live. He had been under restraint for part of the time because his thrashings were further injuring him. He had spent many hours, half in coma, screaming, "Innocent! Innocent!" The family had assumed that this related to his part in the accident. After the accident he had been identified almost immediately, but for almost two days no one had known who Martha was. Her handbag had been found later, fifty yards from the wreck. Until then it was thought that she was a hitchhiker Edgar had picked up on the road. The Wyers had had to come from Willow Springs to identify the body, which they were able to do by her clothing and purse. The funeral had been yesterday, a day he had slept through for the first time without coma or delirium. Charlie had been with him all day, leaving the family free to attend the funeral. The Wyers had not come to the very scantily attended Funeral Praise held at Willow Springs. They had been quiet mourners at a small service overseen by Mr. Wyer's people who had places on the Methodist side of the Willow Springs cemetery. They had asked to see Edgar but had been told that he was too ill.

The thought of facing that worn, quiet couple tore away the last of his courage. It was Arla who told him about the Wyers. He did not answer her, but lay back and sobbed, his cries growing louder and louder until Arla was frightened and went to get a nurse. The nurse came back and then went away quickly and a doctor came and gave him a shot. His mother was the next one he saw, with Corella. He was quiet with them, and if he had to talk or answer them he did it desultorily, in a vague, hazy way. He was no longer in danger of dying, but his family was still allowed to come when they could and stay as long as they liked. The hospital was a small one, and its nurses and attendants were drawn from the farms nearby. People knew how hard it was for farm families to come great distances in the middle of working days to stay for an hour and then go home. The staff liked Edgar's family. Nurses told him so when they worked on him. They were neutral and impersonal in the face of his suffering, but when they spoke of his family their voices became lively and interested. As they worked on him, talking about his father's silent attentiveness or his mother's quiet charm and gifts of cookies and jam to the people on duty, Edgar realized that the nurses were seeing his family as American pictures— the Proud, Lean Farmer, the Patient Mother, the Fine Old Grandpa, the Old-Fashioned Grandma, who knitted while she waited. Even old Charlie Dace fitted at last into the Picture.

"That's your Uncle Charlie, isn't it?" the night attendant said. "He sure is a card. I'll bet he has everybody laughing down at home. The first night I brought this saline bottle in, he was sitting right there and he gave me one of those long looks of his, and you know what he said—"

American pictures—the Farmers. And now, what was his picture? Edgar wondered. Was he still winner of an important scholarship—bearer of the Difference? Could he make anyone in this impersonal pain-mill wear a pocket feather if he wished it?

25

They came in slowly, their faces fearful, Mike and Glover, trying to smile. They had been here before, they said, but he had been sleeping and they had not wanted to wake him. They seemed surprised that he should have so much pain. Once, when he tried to sit up a little and a cramp caught at his upper leg so that he winced and bit his lip against it, he saw them exchange a quick glance like conspirators caught in a lie. He found himself facing them across his bed like years, hungering for the old normal talk and easy laughter and not knowing how to start it anymore. In the handful of days since the accident and his almost-death, years had gone by. Had he been busy with his brokenness, his pain, his functionlessness forever? He almost blurted out:

"I had to have another enema this morning." Desperately, he cast back to time beyond time to remember something that might work.

"How were the parties—the graduation parties?" They looked at each other again. There was a silence and then Mike said:

"We didn't go to the parties—you know that—you know where we went—" Glover silenced him with a look.

"I thought everybody was going—I saw one of the fires on my way back. . . . Oh yes, the Praise. I forgot. There was a Praise, wasn't there?"

"Yes," said Mike, "there was a Praise." The talk lapsed. He could see them getting more uncomfortable in the silence.

At last Glover said, "Hey, we didn't tell Ed about old man Hemingway!" They laughed and Edgar said, "Tell me then," and they went gratefully into the story.

"You remember old man Hemingway—where we got that soddy? Well, Mike and I were in town the day after graduation. We didn't know about your accident then. Mike's dad had given him some errands to do, so we were in the hardware store and then we stopped by Burkett's for a Coke. I can't say how, but all that morning I had the idea that someone was following us and now and then when I looked back I saw this old, old Ford coming up the street. The windows were so dirty you couldn't really tell who was driving it, but it was following us for sure."

They told the story as they had trained themselves to do with all their stories, one after the other, sharing it carefully. "We decided to walk down toward the depot and see if the car would follow us. It did. When that happened we really started feeling strange. We walked up to Fifth and the car was following us, and then we turned quick and went up to it and Odel Hemingway stuck his head out of the passenger side and started to yell, 'We got the right! We got the right!'

"Mike was on the driver's side—Sam was driving, Odel was yelling at me, 'We got the right,' and I didn't know what to say to him. Finally he turned to the back seat and I saw Sam's wife back there and their kid and the three other little kids—Odel's other grandkids, I guess—and Odel says to them, 'You kids take a good look now and look hard at these here boys!' I asked him why they wanted to look at us and he said, 'We're taxpayers and we pay the county, state, and federal taxes, and seein' as it's our money we got a right to see the ones we're sendin' through college.' Then he said, 'Where's the other one?' I said we didn't know, and he gave us a hard look and said, 'You study hard now, you hear, and don't go runnin' around with no chippies!' Then he gave us a nod and drove away."

"Chippies!" Edgar said. The boys laughed.

"What we wonder now," Mike said, "is how many *other* winners Odel has, uh . . . *reviewed*. I mean do you get Odel right along with the scholarship?"

"And all the kids with their fingers in their mouths, peering at you through the dirty windows."

It still hurt to laugh, but Edgar laughed anyway. It felt so good to be with Mike and Glover again, to be part of a trio, two members of which had just come in from sunlit places where their bodies moved easily and without pain. For an instant he thought that at the time Odel had been trailing Mike and Glover in his ancient Ford, a voice had been saying close to his head, "Don't worry about the girl right now; let's get this one up." He thought of it and still laughed because the laughter hurt with the pain of living.

When he could, he said, "I remember about the Praise now. I know I should have gone, but I was so tired and I had to catch the bus. Martha—" His voice caught and he turned away. In a minute he said, "Martha's dead. Did you know that?"

"Yes," Glover said, "in the accident.'

"Yes." It was a struggle to bring his voice back again and to turn his face to them. He tried to think of their lives, not his. "Was it a good Praise? Arla made chili, I remember."

"Yes," Mike said. He spoke in a voice gone strange, full of intensity, almost of violence, "and it wasn't only us, it was everyone; everyone was in agreement in that Praise, and when you know about it you'll know that it was God's will, God's work, and the whole Praise knew it and felt it together. *Everyone!*"

"When I know what?" Edgar said, "when I know what?"

"We *told* you," Mike said, "we warned you—"

"What are you talking about?"

Mike's whole manner had changed. His face was contorted, his breathing rapid. Glover took Mike's arm as though he had done it before, as though by now he was used to doing it, calming him.

"We're talking about the Praise," Glover said, "about the Praise for you."

"For me? What Praise was there for me?"

314

"The Graduation Praise," Mike said, "it turned into a Praise for you—"

"Wait a minute, will you?" Edgar began to feel dizzy again. He had a momentary desire to fall back to unconsciousness and innocence. "There was a Praise for me? What for?"

"Well," Glover said, "it was the Graduation Praise but during it we asked the Spirit of the Lord about you and your running away. We asked the Spirit of the Lord if it was good and right for you to break your word to us and to the town and to the Apostles and leave like that to go to some city school. The Spirit of the Lord said no, that it was wrong —said it to all of us, all together."

Edgar felt his face go hot and his hands get cold. "What right did you have to put that kind of question?" he said. His voice sounded strange to him. Glover and Mike disappeared behind a wall of red dots that began to pour before his eyes. Behind the wheeling dots Mike's voice came blurred and distorted.

"We knew you were doing wrong. We asked the Spirit to keep you from what you were doing. We never thought it would be this way—I mean, you hurt like this and Martha dead. We never asked the Spirit of the Lord to kill . . . just to stop you . . . just to keep you from going against his will—"

"Edgar," Glover said in his old reasonable way, "you remember that we tried to stop you. We told you how wrong it was. You were so busy with Martha you didn't listen. Even after you had made up your mind I tried to get you to come to the Praise. If you had come you would have been stopped in a gentler way, you would have seen—"

"But we didn't want *this*," Mike cried, "not this pain and death—we didn't mean for this—"

Edgar began to shout Martha's name, first as though he was calling her, then louder, until a nurse came, and by that time he had begun to scream. The nurse looked in and then disappeared, coming back with two men who held Edgar for a long time until another man could come with an injection. His friends had been hurried away, as though the sight of his disgrace was too much for ordinary people to bear.

Between his screams he could hear the nurse placating them, calming them:

"Of course it wasn't you . . . still so ill . . . of course, his friends—his best friends . . . of course come back."

Arla. Something had opened up in him again, because there was a thick, sweetish aftertaste of blood in his mouth. She was sitting with her handwork—it was mending, this time. He ached so badly he could hardly talk. He asked for water and she gave him a little through a plastic straw. He remembered Mike and Glover and moaned.

"Pain?" she asked. "I can get a nurse."

"Grandma, have there been any Praise petitions for me at Founder's?"

She looked away. "I'm sure the Spirit of the Lord sees you here and knows what you've been through."

"That's not what I asked."

"I didn't go last Sunday. We've been taking turns here with you and I missed Sunday. I heard though that your father had spoken out for you."

"The Praise didn't take up his Witness, did it?"

"You must understand how upset everyone has been, Charlie drunk, and the fight, and then this, and Glover and Mike so upset and strange. It's caused a lot of confusion. But people love you. Give them time."

Two doctors. They were measuring something, pulling on his left arm and leg and causing the searing fire to flow up and down his limbs while they spoke to each other in soft, companionable tones. When he asked them about his injuries they looked perturbed and left. When his mother and Corella came that evening, he begged them to make the doctors tell him.

"But they don't know themselves," Anne said. "It depends on the way the bones heal. There was so much damage done that they think your left leg may be a little shorter than the right and your left arm might not be able to move as well as it did before."

"Then why didn't they tell me when I asked?"

"They're scared of you," Corella said, "scared of what you do."

"I don't understand—"

"Edgar," Anne flashed a frightened look at Corella, "you see, you were so badly in shock at first, you screamed when anyone touched you, and then when Mike and Glover came —your oldest and dearest friends—boys who'd come so far to see you and waited so patiently—you had to be held down and given a sedative. Perhaps the doctors think you're not ready to know—it's been so hard for you—Martha, and your own injuries—"

"I'm a bad patient, aren't I? I make scenes," he said bitterly. She looked down.

"We have to bear . . . we all have to try to bear . . . what we are given. . . ."

His father, smiling. "You're looking much better today, son. I see they took the bandages off—" and he motioned to the left side of Edgar's face where scabbed-over lacerations were beginning to itch maddeningly. "At first they told us they'd have to do plastic surgery there, but now they say there'll be hardly any scarring at all." He sat in the chair for a while but not so quietly as he had before. A nurse came in to give Edgar medicine. She looked approvingly at the wind-burned, sunburned father sitting stoically at his son's bedside. He wore a white shirt and a tie, but it was easy to look at his hands and face and see the relationship between the man and the seasons of his work. With no other clue than the placement of rough spots and calluses on those two battered hands, an experienced person would know that this was a farmer and the time was early summer. She gave him a warm smile and left.

"Nice girl," his father said. Edgar shrugged.

"They never tell you anything. Tubes, shots, pills, and they never say what they're doing or how long they're going to do it or why there's pain or how long it will last."

"Life doesn't either," Andy said.

"Dad?"

"Yes?"

"Are you still having those dreams?"

"I don't know if they've stopped, but I haven't had any since your accident."

"You probably haven't had much sleep."

"I don't think it's a question of sleep. Maybe the nightmare has gone into the daytime, into reality, now. I'm sorry —that sounded like self-pity."

"What was it like there in the camp? You never talked about it."

"I tried to put it out of my mind—to forget about it."

"And now it's come back—the hunger, or the sickness—"

"No, not those things. When you're full, you can't really remember hunger; when you're not drowning in your own sweat, you can't really imagine that wet heat where even your skin rots. What comes back are the old sins—the old disgraces."

"What disgraces?"

"Taking a blanket from a dying man. Pulling a gold tooth from a dead one."

"What did you do with the gold tooth?"

"We bribed a guard for mosquito netting. Four of us did it—Petrakis, Olesen, someone else, and me. I wish I remembered that fourth man. I lived four years with him in conditions as close as any family, and now I don't remember who he was."

"You never mentioned your dreams in the Praise."

"No."

"And yet we say we give everything—"

"Is there an everything to give? Do we know everything we are or are becoming?"

"Is it wrong to take a blanket from a dying man?"

"Yes, it's a sin, a necessary sin."

"But if it's necessary—why don't I understand? Why haven't these questions ever come up before? Dad—why do we cherish innocence?"

"Shouldn't we?"

"No," Edgar said.

They were quiet for a time.

"I have something to tell you." Andy said. "I wanted to ease your mind in case you've been worrying. There won't be any legal troubles about Martha's death. I've been to a lawyer and although you were speeding, it looks as though you weren't what they call 'willfully and wantonly negligent.' Martha was in the car of her own choice. The Wyers say they won't press any civil action for damages. The truck that hit you was slightly damaged and the driver was shaken up, but that's all, and that case is being adjusted by the insurance companies. Only Clyde Scott is going to go for damages, and there I think we're liable—he had signs posted and you were speeding. . . ."

"Clyde Scott?"

"For the cow. We're liable for the cow."

For a long time after his father left, Edgar laughed and then cried. Since his treatment in the morning they had taken his pillow and leveled his bed and he lay flat on his back, the tears running down his throat and soaking the sheet on either side of his head. Nurses came, administering pills and shots. They were embarrassed to see him weeping, and so they did not speak to him, but took his pulse, put the thermometer into his wet mouth and took it out again gingerly when it was time, and left him. The day passed into night. Lights went on. A nurse came with some liquid for him to drink. When he shook his head, she clicked her tongue and tried pressing him, holding the straw to his lips. He had been lying quietly for a while, but when she held the straw against his bottom lip and tried to push it through his teeth he turned away, saying, "Please, no," and started to weep again. She sighed disgustedly and went away. Later, two orderlies came and a nurse, and they gave him an IV bottle, tying his uninjured arm to a board as though he would break away. When they tied his arm he began to weep again. They did not speak to him.

26

Charlie. He sat as usual, stiff as a convict posing for the pictures: front view, side view, his cadaverous, chinless face in sharp relief against the pastel walls. Edgar sighed. How the nurses could make a kindly old uncle out of such unyielding material was beyond him. When he saw Edgar looking at him, Charlie's eyes lit up a little.

"How're you feelin', boy?"

Edgar remembered that he was no longer brave and special. "It hurts, Charlie. It hurts so much I hate waking up for more."

"You want a needle or somethin'? I can call a nurse."

"No, they've stopped them. They're scared I'll get addicted."

"I seen that Glover yesterday in town. He said to say he hoped you was feelin' better."

"He's lying. He and Mike think I deserved this. They think all this is a just punishment for my sins."

"I didn't think the Apostles knew what sin was."

"I still don't know. If it was a sin I don't even know where or how it began."

"Them boys can't be glad to see you hurtin' like you do, and the girl dead."

"Not glad, but righteous, justified. Oh, God, I'm sorry! Please don't look—" He began to weep again.

Charlie's voice came dryly through his tear-blindness. "I never cry. In all my life I never did, and you know how loved I am, and how much I'm thought of. But your dad cried. He cried at Martha's funeral, and here by your bed. I seen him. Before he got God-struck, Edgar never cried, but afterwards he cried a lot. It's true. The Founder hisself that was supposed to be some kind of a example of dancin' happiness, he cried for so many things I could hardly count 'em. Cried because of his own weakness, and because his God was far away. He cried because he couldn't answer people's questions and because he wasn't a better man, a better son, a better uncle, a better friend. You heard me, a better friend." Edgar tried to stop crying by breathing long and slow but only worked himself into hiccups. They sounded so ridiculous that soon he was laughing. "You're havin' quite a time for yourself," Charlie said. They waited until Edgar was quiet and then Charlie took out a foul cigar, looked at it, and put it back. "Smell of it'd probably make you sick."

Edgar lay easily in Charlie's silence. After a long time he turned his head.

"You can't be comfortable in that chair."

"You're right," and Charlie hitched the plain chair forward, then rode back on it until the front legs were off the floor and he was leaning against the wall, his feet hanging.

"Light up, Charlie."

"I couldn't. You'd heave."

"A cigarette, then." Charlie rolled himself a cigarette, using the coarse paper he had bought by the lot once and which had not been produced since 1943.

"Stuff's no good," he muttered, "burns before the tobacco does." They were still. The day went down slowly.

"Charlie?"

"Yeah."

"Did you ever—did it ever seem to you that I was different —special some way?"

"How come you're askin' that now?"

"Because it's all changed. Because I cry and the nurses don't like it. I have pain and nobody likes that, and because I'm going to walk funny all my life. Was I special once— really different, extraordinary?"

"Oh, yes, you were. Special, that's the word. Everybody always knew that."

"What was it, then? How was I special?"

"You don't know?"

"It still hurts some to talk—I wouldn't be asking if I knew."

"Hell, boy." He looked almost gleeful sitting back against the wall, his shadow overwhelming the delicate tracery of tubes of the fluid bottle hanging suspended near him. "Hell, you was *happy*. You was happy to see people, even me. You was happy with life, all over, all the time, simple, real, decent, out-and-out happy."

"That's all?"

"And you didn't know? Well, that's one for the books. You could have did about anything you wanted and been forgiven because of that happiness of yours. People need that, you know, they're drawn to it. It's what they saw in Edgar; not his religion, not really; it was that light of his, that happiness. You had it, too. Always did."

"Always? Did I always?"

"Seemed to me, that is until a year or two ago, and then it got a little nervous. It seemed like you was lookin' around all the time to see who was watchin' you be happy."

"Then why did people still look at me the same way? If the happiness I had, the specialness, started to go phony, why did people still accept it?"

"Habit, I guess. You ever seen how people will sit by a dead campfire out of habit and then feel warmer anyway, because there was a fire there once?"

"Do you know what we did, Mike and Glover and me?"

"Not really. You was runnin' around a lot, I knew that."

"We set out to make the county give us those scholarships. Three of them instead of one."

"Boy, you never had to work at that. They would have given you the county reservoir if you'd asked 'em."

"The three of us—"

"Them boys with you was part of you."

"As simple as that?"

"As simple"—chair legs to the floor—"as that." The chair

tipped back again. The IV bottle danced a little. "Maybe not so simple. I ain't a very happy person—maybe you noticed that. I get drawn to it, though. I once told your dad that I don't friend easy, but I friend long. Edgar, he had the joy, and I was his friend, and I was lookin' around the Praises for it, here and there, little glitters of the kind of joy that used to be in him. When you was a kid it was in you, that joy."

"Every kid is happy sometimes."

"That joy was more than just bein' happy or contented—it was you lovin' all the things and people around you. It was a good thing to see—to be near. A real good thing."

More tears. He did not know he had more tears. This time he didn't need to have his eyes wiped for him. He wiped them with the sleeve of his hospital gown.

"I'm so sorry—this is stupid—I should—I've got to control—"

"Don't stop on my account. I never held with that kind of courage. Costs too much."

"But damn it, I can't seem to quit."

"Maybe it's all the tears Apostles don't shed, pains Apostles ain't supposed to feel, comin' out all at once. Oh, hell, don't listen to me. I don't want to criticize the Apostles. They're good people tryin' to come along like everyone else, but they're tyrants with love and joy the way other people are tyrants with sin and death."

"Charlie, how could they do it, hold a Praise against me?"

"Ever confuse your own hunger with God's will?" Charlie said gently.

This time the tears were not quiet. Edgar lay back and sobbed. A nurse walked in with medicine. She came up to the bed shaking her head slowly back and forth with impatience and disapproval. Charlie gave her a slow, dazzling smile. His wrinkled face pulled itself up like a drawstring bag, his lips opened back to give full sight of the toppling, yellow teeth. His eyes sparkled. "Boy ain't snivelin' no more, y'notice? Boy's grievin' now, full-sized, like grievin's supposed to be done. Don't it do your heart good!" She put down the pill cup and fled. Charlie said quietly, "My friend,

Edgar Bisset, he was always strong on law. He used to say that the law was a whip God used on people, but that He used it on himself worse, and because of that, the pain of it was eased for him and us both. I ain't a believer like he was, and I didn't understand him when he talked like that. I never understood what he saw in the old laws, all the Thou Shalt Nots. I guess they was mostly to keep God from gettin' contaminated by man. God ain't like us, He's fragile. He don't know how to lie or be afraid or choose the evil just to get even. He's got to be kept safe, 'cause even if He is immortal, He ain't no match for us!"

His father. Edgar saw he was surprised, that the sudden turning of that corner toward recovery was something he hadn't been ready for. They were shy with each other, as they had not been in Edgar's sicker days, when he had been strung with tubes and pulleys.

"Your mother, she got upset and didn't think she looked good enough to see you. I wanted to come and talk to you before anyone else came—It's about Mike, your friend Mike."

"What is it?"

"Uh . . . I suppose you've been wondering why he and Glover haven't come to see you lately—"

"Not really, not since they told me about the Praise."

"Well, we did, the family. You've been so close, the three of you, for so long now, and then—nothing. Lately when we saw them in town, they'd cross the street. I tried calling Mike once or twice but he was never home, or never wanted to talk to me."

"What's this all about, Dad?"

"Yesterday afternoon, Mike—well, yesterday afternoon he took his own life."

They faced each other, Edgar feeling his face go cold in the overheated room. He said "Oh—" and was silent. "Yesterday?"

"Yes."

"How did he do it?"

"A strange way, not any of the usual ways—"

"Please tell me."

"This is upsetting. I don't know why you want to know."

"Please, I have to know *something*—I have to make sense of *something*."

"He took a plastic bag and poured some laundry bleach into it and then added ammonia and put his head into it. Somehow the chemicals reacted to one another."

"Chlorine gas," Edgar said.

Andy shook his head slowly back and forth. "I wish I understood—we Praise and love God and each other. Our children are raised in love instead of fear, and yet we have flogging and wildness and anger and now suicide."

"I love you, Dad."

His father looked at him, puzzled. "I know that, but—"

"Do you think it was in us, the flogging and wildness and suicide, or is our being Apostles part of it?"

"I don't know."

"You know we were forcing God, don't you, making Him bless us."

"That would be doing magic, you know, forcing God. That's a definition of magic."

"And what if the will isn't good and the ends aren't good? What happens if the thought or the wish is sick and jealous? Then the magic goes bad, doesn't it? Mike and Glover and all our friends in that Praise—they were doing black magic against us, Dad, against Martha and me. They were calling down a power against us, not with voodoo and demon books, but in an ordinary Praise with all the ordinary and well-meant words. For our own good, they said. All in our own best interests."

"Could it be—?" and Andy shook his head back and forth slowly. "Could I have forgotten *evil?* Good God, I survived the place where all the good people died, and I put it out of my mind because the land here is high and dry and flat and nothing like the jungle where I thought I had seen all the evil there was." He looked starkly at Edgar. "They were doing black magic, weren't they."

"Mike knew it when he saw me here, what they had done. It began to dawn on Mike then."

"If only we knew—could know what he thought or felt. Your best friend. Such an awful waste."

"I think I know what he felt."

"How?"

"Dad, what's the punishment for murder in this state, first-degree murder?"

"Death, you know that—"

"And the method of execution?"

"What are you getting at?"

"The method of execution here is death by gas, lethal gas."

Charlie again, smiling in his threadbare ugliness against the ordered, featureless, pleasant room. "I see they unhung you from them bottles and things."

"Most of them."

"Boy, what happened to your pa? He come home yesterday with a look on his face I ain't seen since the dust days when a man'd wake up in the mornin' and not see anything out his window that he recognized."

"We were talking about Mike, about his suicide."

"It was a shock, him doin' that. Now, of course, people are sayin' it was his pa bein' like he is, all them dreams and nothin' to show, nothin' real."

"Do you believe that?"

"Hell, no. I believe that people need to jump at the reasons that'll save 'em time or pain or shame or—"

"Or what?"

"God."

"How are the Antons taking it?"

"Any way they can. Nobody expected such a thing, and reasons be damned, it's eatin' the Praise alive."

"Did Mike say anything to anyone? Did he leave any messages?"

"No, unless the message was in the way he done it. He had his good clothes on, shoes shined. And he didn't just dump them chemicals together either; he measured them out before in little caps and had them by his bed. His room was clean, spotless, Addie Wilkins said. There was a Bible by his bed, the family Bible, and the bed was pushed against the wall. He faced the wall while he done it."

"It sounds so official—so formal. And no note—"

"No. The plannin' of it is what hurt his folks more than anything else, I'd say; it seemed to speak so hard against them."

"Charlie, I don't think his suicide had anything to do with them. How is Glover?"

"I don't know. Nobody has seen him and he ain't been to Founder's since the Praise the weekend you got hurt."

"Charlie—is God all-powerful?"

"He ain't powerful enough to make me a believer, though I prayed for it in my day."

"We made Him say yes to the scholarships, but you said it was only our happiness all the time. I wonder what a cripple's God is like. Maybe He's a God of less ecstasy and more hard edges. I won't ever dance in a Praise again or run out into a field until I force Him to yield up a vision. Charlie, did you ever dare God to kill you?"

"Hell, yes, as a kid I did, and a few times after Edgar died, just to see if He thought I was important enough to waste the lightnin' on. You see the results."

"Maybe He doesn't have that power, Charlie. Maybe He denies it to himself because that's magic and it's wrong. Maybe the cripple's God has laws that He obeys because I'll have to have laws that I obey, awful laws, laws against envy and greed. I'm going to envy the happy and the strong people so much—"

"Is there anything left for you, out of all them Praises?"

"Yes, the possibility of God."

"Oh."

"And then—"

"Then what?"

"The wonder."

Charlie tipped back his chair. He laughed a long, slow series of dry chuckles. 'Oh, whew!" he said when he was finished. "You put me so in mind of Edgar. He was always talkin' like that, askin' questions, turnin' things inside out. He did it believin' and sometimes half believin' and you do it half doubtin', but some way it's like I hear him now. Night'd come and the people'd be gone home and we'd set easy, him and me, easy and quiet together. I'd make him some cocoa maybe and then he'd start to talk about God. He never called him God, you know, he called him the Presence, and once I remember it was in March, back in forty or so . . ."